WALTER SUTHERLAND
SCOTTISH RUGBY LEGEND 1890-1918

WALTER SUTHERLAND

SCOTTISH RUGBY LEGEND 1890-1918

KENNETH R. BOGLE

TEMPUS

First published 2005

Tempus Publishing Limited
The Mill, Brimscombe Port,
Stroud, Gloucestershire, GL5 2QG
www.tempus-publishing.com

British Library Cataloguing in Publication Data.
A catalogue record for this book is available from the British Library.

ISBN 0 7524 3613 9

Typesetting and origination by Tempus Publishing Limited
Printed in Great Britain

CONTENTS

ACKNOWLEDGEMENTS

I kick off my list of acknowledgements by thanking my former history teacher and friend Ian Landles, who set the whole thing off by introducing me to Walter Sutherland and telling me his story. Ian's knowledge and enthusiasm for all things Hawick truly knows no bounds. I am grateful to Derek Robertson, one of Ian's disciples and a fellow Walter enthusiast, who made many useful suggestions and criticisms.

Bill McLaren, the famous voice of rugby and a distant relative of the Sutherland family, generously wrote the foreword for the book. Bill's sister, Mrs Kitty Oliver, was extremely supportive of my research and let me examine some precious relics and rare photographs as well as providing cups of tea. Michael Mee, the editor of the *Hawick News*, was very enthusiastic about the project. He kindly gave me access to his newspaper files and gave me permission to reproduce several images in this book. Thanks also to Mrs Myra Oliver, who shared her memories of the Sutherland family with me.

I wrote this book while working with the Department of Education of the City of Edinburgh Council. I would like to thank many work colleagues for their help and encouragement, and for covering my many absences, both official and furtive. I owe particular thanks to Ian Grahame, Graham Munn ('Mr Pipe'), John Sowerby, Joanne Burns and Len Grannum. David Walker helped me to master scanning technology and kindly drew the map of the Western Front and the family tree. I am grateful to my parents, Jim and Grace Bogle, and also to my family and friends for cheering me on from the touchlines, especially my cousin Robert Cranston.

Like all researchers, I am indebted to the staff of various libraries, museums and archive centres, who answered my enquiries with politeness and professional expertise. In particular, the staff of Wilton Lodge Park Museum, Hawick; Hawick Public Library; Scottish Borders Library Service; The National Library of Scotland; The City of Edinburgh Library Service; The National War Museum of Scotland; The Mitchell Library, Glasgow; The National Archives of Scotland; and The Imperial War Museum, London.

Fiona White, formerly librarian at the Scottish Rugby Union, gave me great help and allowed me to use photographs and other treasures from the SRU archives. Her colleague Louise Freedman was also very helpful. Further afield, Ross Hamilton and Jed Smith gave me access to the library of the Rugby Football Union at Twickenham and showed me, among other treasures, the scrapbooks of Ronnie Poulton and Adrian Stoop. Rod Mackenzie let me access the Regimental Museum of The Argyll and Sutherland Highlanders at Stirling Castle. Tom Tulloch-Marshall, a professional military researcher, did sterling work on my behalf in the National Archives in London.

Rugby Union has a wonderful camaraderie about it and I am grateful to many people in the game who expressed an interest in the book. Particular thanks to Adam Robson, the former Scottish internationalist and true Renaissance man, who gave me great encouragement. I am also indebted to many people in the Rugby Memorabilia Society, whose members might be described as 'the nicest kind of nutter', in particular Gary Alexander, Tim Auty, John Jenkins, Tony Lewis, Mike Stanton of Gardenia Press and Dave Richards of Rugby Relics. A special mention to my friends Dave Fox (Bristol and Wales) and Ray Ruddick (Pontypool and British Lions). Between the three of us we'd make a solid front row.

I am, of course, extremely grateful to Tempus Publishing, who agreed to tackle Walter Sutherland from faraway Stroud. Extra-special thanks are due to James Howarth and Holly Bennion, who guided me through the publishing process with proficiency and great skill.

This book is adorned with some marvellous illustrations, most of which have never appeared in book form before. I am grateful to the following people who kindly gave me permission to reproduce them in this book: Michael Mee and the staff of the *Hawick News*; Jake and Margory Coltman, Hawick; Teviotdale Harriers; Hawick Rugby Football Club; the Trustees of the National Library of Scotland; The Scottish Rugby Union; Zilla Oddy and David Hill of Wilton Lodge Park Museum; and Derek Lunn for his photographic expertise. Special thanks to Annie Docherty and Alan Russell of Scottish Screen Archive who kindly provided images from the short film *Border League Championship*. The author and publishers have made every effort to contact the holders of copyright material and we apologise in advance if we have inadvertently infringed copyright.

I owe an enormous debt to my wife and friend Alison. For the past few years she has lived in a bizarre *ménage à trois* between herself, her husband and Walter

Sutherland. Without her love and encouragement, this book would not have been written.

What follows is my own work, interpretations and, in some places, opinions. I need hardly add that any mistakes are mine and the good people mentioned here are entirely blameless. I apologise now for my own fallibility.

Finally, and I hope that this is not too sentimental, my biggest debt is to the man himself. Like, I imagine, all biographers, I sometimes felt that my subject was looking over my shoulder and, I trust, pointing me in the right direction. Walter Sutherland was a rugby player, an athlete and one of Kitchener's volunteers, but also a cherished son, a brother and a friend. This book is his.

Dr Kenneth R. Bogle
Edinburgh, 2005

FOREWORD

I feel deeply honoured to have been invited to provide a foreword to this fascinating narrative for it was always a matter of pride for me that I was related, even in only a distant perspective, to Walter Sutherland. My mother was Walter's full cousin and she was tremendously proud of him and of his fame as a Scottish international rugby player with special gifts.

I have vivid recall of the huge praise lavished upon Walter by the inimitable Andrew 'Jock' Wemyss, the doyen of Scottish rugby journalists. Andrew had covered international rugby for the *Express* newspapers for years and he rated Walter as one of the finest players he had ever seen, having played alongside him in the 1914 international against Wales. I remember Jock speaking highly in praise of Walter's powers of acceleration and of his command of pace-change that rendered him such an elusive target. Although of comparatively frail physique, Walter tackled like the crack of doom and also had the gift of shepherding opponents into the lanes he wanted them to run. His scalding pace was underlined by his successful participation in summer amateur sprint events.

This fascinating study of one of Scotland's greatest international rugby players revives memories of famous times in Border and Scottish rugby lore and of one of the most skilled and speedy practitioners in the modest artiste they called 'Suddy'.

Bill McLaren
Hawick, 2005

INTRODUCTION

A young man stands on the green turf, slightly apart from his team-mates, his closely cropped, silver hair glowing in the spring sunshine. He is wearing a navy blue shirt with a white collar, an embroidered thistle on the left breast. To keep his fingers warm in the snell March breeze, he puts his hands into the pockets of his shorts which stretch down to his knees, occasionally stooping to adjust his belt or his stockings or to check the laces on his brightly polished boots. He is a slight figure of medium height, pale almost to the point of anaemia, and hardly looks strong enough to withstand the hurly-burly of international football. But he has already proved his worth to his side. His tactical kicking has been astute and accurate, and in defence he has not shirked from bringing much heavier men to earth. And just watch him run when he is given space! A sprinter's speed, wings on his boots, elusive as an eel, always a threat to the white-shirted opposition. The second half has barely begun when his side moves into attack. Taking the brown leather ball after a slick passing movement, he flies down the touchline, miraculously eludes the defence and squeezes in at the corner with only inches to spare. The tightly packed spectators forget their customary reserve and clap and cheer him wildly, hats and walking sticks waving in the air. Their man has done it. The Auld Enemy will lose this day. Wattie Suddy has scored for Scotland.

Walter Sutherland was one of the best and most popular Scottish rugby players of his generation. Born in 1890 in the rugby hotbed of Hawick in the Scottish Borders, he first played for the famous Hawick 'Greens' as a callow seventeen-year-old in the autumn of 1908. Within sixteen months he was turning out for Scotland, going on to make thirteen international appearances between 1910 and 1914, and scoring four memorable tries in the process. Lack of money and time prevented him from taking his place on the British tour of South Africa in 1910, but later he captained his club and the South of Scotland district side. He was also an outstanding performer on the annual Borders seven-a-side circuit, winning eighteen first prizes, including six prestigious Melrose Sevens medals. Blessed with natural speed and athleticism, he was good enough to become a national sprint champion and to wear the Scottish athletics vest. Tragically, this magnificent footballer and athlete was destined to lose his life in the closing weeks of the First World War, aged only twenty-seven.

Walter's home in the Scottish Borders has always been a great place for nicknames. In the olden days, the Border Reivers were often better known by their nicknames rather than the real thing. Kinmont Willie, Sim the Laird, Fingerless Wull Nixon: dark men living on the edge of the law, their names used to scare children into good behaviour. The tradition endured, and endures. In the Scots Border tongue, few people used the formal 'Walter': in the streets and the factories, they preferred 'Wattie'. Likewise, the surname 'Sutherland' was too unwieldy and it was often shortened to 'Suddy' (or 'Suddie'). Everybody in the Borders knew Wattie Suddy, despite his natural modesty and unassuming nature. He was idolised in his hometown, a local hero, an icon in a tatty rugby shirt and baggy shorts. Poems were written in his honour. When James Y. Hunter wrote *A Laddie's Thoughts*, in which he imagined a young boy dreaming about his future and what he might become in life, he opened with the words:

> *I should like to be a High School Dux*
> *With medals and books galore;*
> *Or swerve like a Sutherland down the wing*
> *To a rattling Mansfield score;*
> *Or watch my ball from the Cricket Field*
> *Right into the Coble soar.*

Young boys naturally look up to great men, and so did many of Walter's friends and contemporaries. No-one who saw him play forgot the experience and the pleasure it gave them. In his first season for Hawick Walter played under the captaincy of Sandy Burns, a tough little quarter-back. In an interview given many years later, Burns remembered:

Wattie was the best player I've ever seen. He was very fast, he could swerve, in fact, he could do anything. He had great hands. He was just a real fitba' player.

Another local man, John 'Chap' Landles, a past president of the Hawick Rugby Club, said much the same when he looked back on a lifetime of watching the game:

[Sutherland was] one of the finest rugby players that I ever saw. There was no feature of the game that he wasn't adept at – goal-kicking, running, passing and tackling. There was no feature of the game that he wasn't top notch.

Most of the people who watched Walter Sutherland had few pretensions to high culture. They rarely went to art galleries, or to the opera, but they knew beauty when they saw it. Wattie Suddy was a player who was capable of great things, a man who aroused deep passions, who could express dreams through the accessible language of sport. There were hundreds of football players, some of them very good, but Walter Sutherland was special. Why? What made him stand out? Off the field and dressed in his civvies, he was an unremarkable person, apart from his striking fair hair, small and pale, just another young man on the high street. But once the game had started, that was a different matter. Who was ordinary or delicate then? Walter had all the essentials of a great wing three-quarter. His principal weapon was his explosive speed, his ability to scorch the ground. He was very fast and few players caught him once he had moved into top gear. In his six years of club rugby he averaged twelve tries a season, an excellent strike rate in an era of claustrophobic defence and monotonous forward play. But Walter was more than just a good finisher, a mere sprinter who ran fast with the ball. One of his friends and training partners in Hawick, Jimmy Grierson, later recalled that, 'Walter was one of the best that Scotland ever had. He could run, he was fast, but he could play rugby though.' Walter possessed a shrewd footballer's brain. He was clever, sharp and quick-thinking. He was a good kicker, both out of hand and from place kicks. One of his favourite attacking ploys was to cross-kick at speed, bringing the ball back into the middle of the field and causing panic among the defence. He had great powers of deception, which enabled him to escape from situations that looked hopeless. In attack he was an unpredictable target, possessing a subtle change of pace and carefully controlled body movements that could produce a bewildering series of side steps and swerves. He was a veritable weaver of spells who was capable of near-impossible escapes. Andrew 'Jock' Wemyss played in the same Scotland side as Walter and always kept a photograph of his old friend above his desk. One of rugby's great writers, Wemyss knew a thing or two about the game. In his time, he saw all of the great wing three-quarters, but he always maintained that Walter was one of the best, if not the best, comparing him with the Welsh maestro, Gerald Davies. Sixty years could not cloud his memory. In the early 1970s, he wrote:

Besides great pace, Suddie could beat an opponent with what I can only describe as a 'stutter' on his feet. I remember Walter Forrest, Scotland's full-back, saying that the only way to stop Suddie was to tackle him before he got into his stride.

Sometimes, wing three-quarters are unpopular members of a team. They can be prima donna figures, reluctant to get their hands dirty and flinching from the hard work, but happy to grab all the glory by taking the final pass and scoring a try. Nobody ever accused Walter Sutherland of being a shirker. He was a strong defensive player and few people got past him, despite his seemingly delicate and frail physique. Tireless and dogged, he was good on the floor, always willing to mop up loose balls and courageously falling at attackers' feet. There is no sense of irony that his greatest display in the cauldron of international rugby was in a defensive role, covering the role of an injured colleague as well as his own and thwarting wave after wave of opposition attacks.

Any assessment of Walter Sutherland's reputation must take into account his personality and character. By all accounts he was a pleasant and good-natured young man who was genuinely modest about his talents and achievements. It's unlikely that he would have been remembered so fondly if he had been a boastful, superficial or empty-headed person. At this time, rugby football was strictly an amateur sport and Walter made little or no material gain from his endless hours of practice, dedication and self-sacrifice. He played the game simply because he loved and enjoyed it. His reward was the honour of representing his town and his country, and the recognition that this brought him. He played in the right spirit, always giving his best and trying hard to win but quick to praise his opponents and accept defeat with good grace. In short, he represented all that was good about rugby football. Naturally, these qualities extended far beyond the field of play. At the outbreak of war in August 1914, Walter enlisted in the army within a matter of weeks, ready to do his duty and serve his country and, if necessary, to give his life for a cause that he thought was right.

I first became aware of Walter Sutherland in the mid-1980s when my former history teacher and friend Ian Landles showed me a photograph of him winning a race. I'd never heard of him until then, but I was intrigued, being passionate about rugby and also having studied the First World War. Walter was from the same town and background as me. Sport had shaped his life and war had destroyed it. He personified two opposites: the youthful exuberance and excitement of rugby football, and the futility and waste of the First World War. Life and death. Something lodged in the back of my mind and I wanted to know more. The result is this book.

There are very few historical biographies of rugby players, apart from the 'great player' type of book. In general they do little more than scratch the surface by recounting old matches and a few anecdotes, but rarely explore an individual's background and influences, what drove him forward or made him tick. My intention was to delve a little deeper and examine the life of Walter Sutherland, to write his story and record his achievements and to place him in an appropriate historical context. In so doing, I hope to illustrate the nature of rugby football and sport in general before the First World War. If this book leads to greater recognition of Walter Sutherland, then I will have achieved my purpose.

Fortunately I got off to a flying start with E.H.D. Sewell's *Rugby Football Internationals Roll of Honour*, which was published in 1919. Sewell was one of life's great characters. Descended from an old military family, he spent much of his life in India blasting the local wildlife, although he was also a county cricket player with Essex and coach of Surrey. Sewell was a prolific journalist and author. His books include the daringly titled *Rugger: The Man's Game* and his autobiography *An Outdoor Wallah*, which includes a photograph of him calmly reading a newspaper with a coal scuttle on his head during a German doodlebug raid. The *Rugby Football Internationals Roll of Honour* is an evocative and moving collection of biographical essays about each of the international rugby players who died in the First World War, eighty-nine in total, although the book did not include French players as France was then considered a second-class rugby nation. To compile his great work, Sewell contacted the families and friends of the deceased and asked them to supply details about an individual's upbringing, playing career and service in the war. In Walter Sutherland's case, Sewell acknowledged his debt to Walter Hume, a teacher in Hawick and a stalwart of the local football club who knew the Sutherland family. Consequently, Sewell's book contains information that would have taken me a long time to find in other sources or which is unrecorded elsewhere.

However, there are limits and I am the first to admit that my portrait of Walter Sutherland might appear a little thin in places, especially concerning his private life. Despite making an extensive search, including appeals for information in newspapers and magazines, I was unable to find any of Walter's personal papers, diaries or letters. Sewell's book mentions that after his death in 1918 a notebook was found among his belongings in which he had recorded his rugby exploits and achievements. Perhaps it's still lying in an attic or a drawer somewhere, unrecognised and forgotten, but most likely it was destroyed many years ago. Sewell also mentions that during the First World War Walter wrote letters home to his parents, but once again these have vanished. The same goes for the

Sutherland family photograph album. To fill in the gaps, I have used an array of books, newspapers, magazines and ephemeral items, such as match programmes. At the end of this book, I have given some suggestions for further reading for anybody who wants to explore things a little further.

I have written this book out of my love for rugby football and its history, something that the game has lost sight of in the modern professional era. I never saw Walter Sutherland play, but I wish that I had.

one

THE AULD GREY TOON

Strictly speaking, Walter Sutherland's roots were not in Hawick but in Wilton, the neighbouring parish across the River Teviot. Wilton has long been swallowed up by urban sprawl, but it was once a separate entity from its larger neighbour. The locals spoke with a different accent from that of their Hawick cousins, using their own words and phrases. As the parish minister wrote in 1834: 'The language generally spoken by the lower orders, throughout this district, contains many provincialisms, but these are becoming gradually obsolete.' Wilton had its own school and church, which was built in 1762, but there was no town centre or market place. Locals had to cross the river to conduct their business and when they did so they talked about 'going into Hawick' as if they were visiting another country. The natives of Wilton were fiercely proud of their origins and distinctiveness. The first rugby team in the Hawick area was originally called 'Hawick & Wilton' and there was a great furore a few years later when the 'Wilton' part was trimmed away from the name.

Only the bare bones are known about Walter Sutherland's ancestors. Their origins appear to have been relatively humble and they were not the types of people to leave behind boxes of family papers for posterity to mull over. Indeed, at least one of Walter's grandparents, his maternal grandmother Isabella Riddell, was unable to read or write. When Walter's half-brother James was born in 1878, she was only able to sign the registrar's logbook with a letter 'X'. Sutherland is not a traditional Border surname, being instead associated with the far north of Scotland, but around 1800 one branch of the family was living in Wilton or Langlands Dean, just to the west of Hawick. 'The Dean', as it is known locally, was then little more than a row of cottages built for workers on the Langlands estate, which had been named after a Norman family who had settled in the area sometime around 1290. The Langlands' main claim to fame was that they were allies of Sir William Wallace who, according to the legend, visited their home and tied his horse to a nearby tree, the site of which was still pointed out as the 'Wallace Thorn'. On 6 March 1814, a man called Alexander Sutherland, Walter's great-grandfather, married Mary Kerr and set up home in one of the Wilton Dean cottages. Among their children, Alexander and Mary had a son called James or 'Jimmy', who was born on 29 April 1821. When he grew up, Jimmy was renowned as a talented fiddle player and was in great demand to play at various events. As the *Hawick News* recalled in 1901: 'Many are still alive who vividly remember him officiating at local weddings.' Jimmy's own marriage took place in Hawick in 1845 when he wed Isabella Cairns, a farmer's daughter from a well-known family in the Wilton area. Living in Wilton Dean, the couple had five children, including a son called Alexander or 'Alex', Walter Sutherland's father, who was born in 1855. Four years later, in February 1859, tragedy struck the young family when thirty-five-year-old Isabella died, possibly because of difficulties during pregnancy. Her premature death left Jimmy with five children to raise on his own. Fortunately his mother, Mary Kerr, lived next door and she was able to lend a hand, especially with the three youngest children, Jessie, Alex and Helen.

In common with many people living in the Hawick area, several generations of the Sutherland family earned a living in the textile and knitting trades. Since the early 1800s, Hawick has been famous for the production of high-quality knitwear, woollens and tweeds, an industry that still survives despite many ups and downs. Commercial frame knitting is believed to have started in the town in 1771 when Bailie John Hardy, a wine and spirit merchant, began to manufacture linen and woollen stockings. Hardy gave up the trade soon afterwards, but other entrepreneurs were encouraged to set up similar schemes in the Hawick area. Initially the fledgling industry made slow progress but, from 1800, it rapidly expanded. In 1834, the minister of Wilton estimated that, in his parish alone, the industry consumed 11,500lbs of wool every week. Almost a third of his parishioners were employed in the manufacture of woollen yarn and hosiery, blankets, plaids, flannels, tartan shawls and 'other goods of a similar nature'. The textile trade was very much a family affair with jobs for everybody, young and old. By tradition, men worked the machines ('the teazing, scribbling and carding engines') and the knitting 'frames' where the basic goods were made. Framework knitting was a highly skilled job that took many years to master, often being passed from father to son. It was rigorous and physically demanding, and for good reason the knitting frame was known as the 'four posts of misery'. At the time of his marriage in 1814, Alexander Sutherland was employed as a woollen framework knitter, a profession that he handed down to his son Jimmy. In turn, young Alex Sutherland followed his grandfather and father into the trade, first as a wool dyer and then as framework knitter. Women also had an important role in the textile trade, especially in preparing the wool for the knitting process and in many of the finishing processes and finer work, such as sewing on buttons or delicate embroidery. In the 1840s, Mary Kerr, Walter Sutherland's great-grandmother, was working as a 'mounter of hosiery' and the other Sutherland women were involved in the trade in one way or another. Many local women had knitting in the blood and were born virtually holding a pair of knitting needles. In their book *Pictures from the Past of Old Hawick*, which was published in 1911, J.J. Vernon and J. McNairn wrote:

The girls were brought up from the earliest years to be industrious… Little things of four or five years of age learned to knit… Strangers passing through Hawick were struck at seeing of an afternoon so many females plying their knitting needles: tongues and fingers busy. No woman thought it decent to go about without her knitting.

Children were also employed in the knitting trade, often to do the awkward little jobs or to run errands. The various members of the Sutherland family might have worked from home, but it is likely that some of them were employed in a small spinning mill in Wilton Dean situated next to the estate workers' cottages, which was driven by water power from the fast-running Dean Burn.

Meanwhile, four doors away from the Sutherland home there lived another branch of the family. Way back in the 1820s, Mary Kerr had given birth to a daughter called Isabella. In December 1848 she married a man called Thomas Riddell who, like her father and brother, worked as a framework knitter. Isabella and Thomas had five children together. Their second daughter was called Isabella after her mother, but was better known as 'Bella'. By the tender age of fifteen, Bella Riddell was already out to work, employed as a weaver in one of the local textile mills. Living almost next door to one another in Wilton Dean, the Riddells and the Sutherlands would have been on fairly close terms, the grandparents, uncles, aunts and cousins all crowding together as one big family and providing mutual support. The links between the two families were reinforced on 3 December 1880 when twenty-five-year-old Alex Sutherland married his cousin Isabella Riddell, who was a few months his junior. Like many working-class marriages the ceremony did not take place in a church but at the bride's home, which was then at 1 Maxwell Street, Hawick. There might have been more behind the marriage than first appears because, two-and-a-half years earlier, Bella had given birth to an illegitimate son called James Sutherland Riddell, who was later known as Jimmy Sutherland. Whatever the truth of the matter, Alex and Bella were to remain together for forty-eight years. There seems little reason to doubt that theirs was nothing but a happy and successful union.

As well as young Jimmy, Alex and Bella (Walter Sutherland's parents) had six children, five of whom survived into adulthood. After James came two girls: another Isabella, who was born in 1881 and who was variously known as 'Bella' or 'Tib', and her younger sister Mary, sometimes 'May', who was born in 1883. When they grew up, Bella was the slightly taller of the two (although neither was very big), dark-haired in contrast to her fair-headed sister, who in looks and colouring would resemble her famous brother Walter. Then came two boys: Thomas, who was born in 1885, and Alexander, who was born in 1887 and who was known in the Scottish style as 'Sandy'. It must have been clear quite early on that there was something not quite right about little Sandy. When I talked to people in Hawick who could remember the Sutherland family, they recalled that, as an adult, Sandy was a small, rather misshapen man, possibly a hunchback, who was sometimes given to erratic behaviour. My impression is that he would now be described as a child with special needs. Two years after Sandy's birth, on 19 November 1890, Bella had another son who was named Walter Riddle Sutherland, the subject of this book. The maternal surname was 'Riddell' but, on this occasion, the registrar spelt it 'Riddle', which Walter used during his life. Finally, in December 1892, Alex and Bella had their fifth son, John Simpson Sutherland, but sadly he died of whooping cough at thirteen months old. Like any mother, Bella would have been deeply marked by the death of John and she might have sought compensation by lavishing special attention on her next youngest, Walter. Judging by his adult appearance, Walter would have been a pale and thin child whose survival was by no means assured, and he might have received a little extra encouragement from his doting parents.

Like most families at the time, the Sutherland children were all born at home in conditions that now seem hopelessly inadequate and unhygienic. Infant mortality of the kind that claimed the life of John Sutherland was a sure sign of poverty, overcrowding and unsanitary surroundings. The death rate in the Edwardian Borders was shockingly high. In May 1906, the *Southern Reporter* quoted health authority statistics that the rate of infant mortality in Roxburghshire was 80 per 1,000, but in Hawick it was 127 per 1,000. In other words, one in eight babies and infants did not survive to adulthood. Alex and Bella Sutherland had started their married life together at Bella's home at Maxwell Street, a tenement block consisting of eight flats and eight families. Shortly afterwards they moved to Wellington Street but, by the time of Sandy's birth in February 1887, the family were living at 10 Myreslaw Green, which was rented from the local Co-operative Society and was where Walter Sutherland was born. All of these were typical areas of workers' housing, mostly tenements and by modern standards appallingly cramped and mean. Perched above the store butcher and grocer's shops,

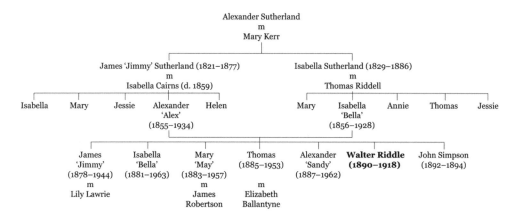

The Sutherland Family Tree
Showing main branches of Walter Sutherland's family

the flat at Myreslaw Green had only two rooms with windows, in which two
adults and seven young children lived, ate and slept. In such conditions, an illness
or a bad mood was likely to have affected all of them. Unsurprisingly, a great deal
of the time was spent outside in the streets. The Sutherland family, and hundreds
like them, lived in conditions that were in sharp contrast to those enjoyed in the
various manufacturers' villas and mansions that gazed paternally down from the
slopes above the town.

Sometime around late 1896 or early 1897, the fortunes of the Sutherland
family started to change. They moved to more commodious rented accommodation at 8 Beaconsfield Terrace, which gave the growing family more space
and freedom. However, this was only a temporary move. Two years later, in May
1900, the family severed most of its links with the woollen trade and began a
new life as the proprietors of the Imperial Hotel, a public house and hotel in
Hawick's Oliver Place. A publican, like a shopkeeper or a skilled tradesman,
occupied an esteemed position near the top of the working-class hierarchy, a
short step away from lower middle-class respectability and comfort. The trade
was risky and uncertain. In 1895, the owner of the Imperial Hotel, a man called
James Martin, was declared bankrupt with debts of over £11,000. However,
there was also prospect of great rewards. The new venture was very much a
family concern, Alex and Bella and the three eldest children pooling their
resources together to make it work. Standing in a prime site in the centre of
Hawick, the Imperial Hotel had been opened in 1875. The first proprietor was

a man called Andrew Paterson, who ran the business until his death in 1888. In the 1890s, which was a time of severe trade depression in the Borders, the Imperial passed through various hands until it was taken over by the Sutherland family. Alex Sutherland had insufficient savings to buy the business outright, but instead he took out several loans to finance the venture. One of these was with the Edinburgh brewing firm W. and J. Raeburn, who had business interests throughout the south of Scotland and who advanced credit to Alex on condition that he stocked their products. Before taking up the trade, Alex would have had to convince the local licensing board that he was a fit and proper person to be in charge of licensed premises.

In towns and cities all over Scotland, public houses had undergone a remarkable transformation in the second half of the nineteenth century. Taverns, inns and alehouses had been around since time immemorial. The traditional Scottish 'howff' was often little more than a private house with a collection of small rooms and a pantry where the drink was served. In the early 1800s, one of Hawick's most colourful characters, Robert Wilson, ran the Burns Inn, a rough-and-ready drinking den with dark corners and shady characters, a natural haunt of political radicals. The Imperial, by contrast, represented the latest in public house design. The ground floor of a substantial tenement building, it was light, open and attractive with punctilious bar staff, polished brass fittings, spacious meeting rooms and statutory hours of business. The name itself, the Imperial, celebrated the Empire and patriotic endeavour. (Hawick also had the Balmoral Bar, the Queen's Head and the Royal Bar, all in honour of Queen Victoria.) The Imperial building had living accommodation attached to it and also ample cellar space. The Imperial was principally a pub but, as the name suggests, it was also a hotel, catering for commercial travellers and others. The business seems to have been an immediate success. On 26 October 1900 the *National Guardian*, the organ of the licensed trade in Scotland, reported:

Mr Alex Sutherland, the new landlord of the Imperial Hotel, Hawick, is proving his worth as an ideal host and, since he took over the hotel in the early summer of the present year, he has been doing a very large and profitable business. Good liquor and a faultless service can always be relied upon at the Imperial.

During the early 1900s the Sutherland family did not feature much in the pages of the local press, probably because most of their energies were taken up running their new enterprise. At this time there were few labour-saving devices such as washing machines, vacuum cleaners or fridges, which meant that the work was often backbreaking, tedious and dirty. By the nature of their

The Imperial Hotel features on this page of Edgar's Hawick Guide and Directory 1903. *(Author's collection)*

trade, hoteliers and publicans worked very irregular hours, often late at night and early in the morning. There was always something to do and not much time for anybody to stand still. Just across the street from the Imperial was a variety theatre (affectionately known as the 'Wee Thee') which could accommodate 900 customers, many of whom flooded into the Imperial after the show, especially at the weekends. Fortunately, Alex Sutherland seems to have had a good head for business and put his heart and soul into his work, not only running the bar but also supplying drinks and refreshments to various functions and events, including some organised by the town council and sports clubs. He was none too shy about promoting his interests and exploiting his local connections, but he was also proud of his town and enjoyed being in the company of like-minded men. Alex was one of the earliest members of the Hawick Callants' Club, an exclusive organisation for local worthies which had been set up in 1904. The club was designed to promote the town, although it was also a vehicle for its members to network with each other. Alex was also a member of the local Conservative Club. In those days, publicans and brewers were Tories almost to a man.

There was always more to life than work, especially at the annual Trades holidays when the town closed down for the week. Like many Border people, the Sutherland family often took their holidays at the seaside village of Spittal, next to Berwick-upon-Tweed, a mere forty miles away from Hawick. Family ambitions in the pre-1914 era now appear to us as pathetically modest, in particular over the matter of holidays and travel. Spittal seems small and inadequate, hardly the sort of place to spend a week's holiday but, in the early 1900s, it was considered an attractive location, the height of sophistication. In Hawick, the names of holidaymakers were formally announced in the local newspapers, as if they were going on the aristocratic Grand Tour. In August 1901 the *Hawick Express* provided a list of 'Hawick Visitors to Spittal', which included 'Mr and Mrs Sutherland, Miss Sutherland, Mr Alexander Sutherland and Walter Sutherland'. Being in England, Spittal offered a different culture to the Borders, but its principal attraction was its beach, promenade and bracing ozone airs. A battered old fishing boat called the *Susan* offered pleasure trips to Berwick and up the River Tweed. With so many Hawick people around, Spittal was a comforting home-from-home. As the *Hawick News* observed in August 1909: 'At all hours of the day, and up till a late hour at night, the strains of well-known Hawick airs are heard in the streets or by the shore, sometimes sung, sometimes whistled, or sometimes hammered out of the pianos.'

Back home, the biggest event of the civic year was the Common Riding, which took place every year in early June. The Common Riding was derived from the ancient custom of a ceremonial procession on horseback around the town lands to inspect the boundaries and check any encroachment by neighbouring landowners. For a couple of days each year, the town was given over to the event and almost the entire population turned out to take part in the traditional customs and processions. The Common Riding was (and still is) more than a chance archaic survival. As the *Southern Reporter* explained in June 1906:

Of all the Border centres of industry, there is not one whose inhabitants are more clannish, or where the people take greater pride in each other's efforts and successes than in Hawick. Consequently, their Common Riding is not merely the performance of so many ceremonies. It is rather a continual round of brotherly enthusiastic rejoicing in which everyone takes part.

At the heart of the Common Riding was the Cornet, a young, unmarried man who was chosen to lead the festivities and carry the 'Banner Blue', a replica of a flag captured from the marauding English in 1514. In May 1901 Jimmy Sutherland, Walter's eldest brother, was chosen for the ultimate local honour. The family already had close connections with the Common Riding. In the 1870s, the young Alex had been a successful runner at the professional Common Riding games, winning several prizes. Later he became clerk of the course at the horseracing, a member of the games committee and, conveniently enough, had responsibility for organising the refreshment tents at the racecourse. The Cornet-elect, Jimmy Sutherland, had started his working life as an apprentice printer on the *Hawick Express* before moving to Hamilton, where the family had relations. Bella's sister, Jessie Riddell, was married to a man called Andy Gowans, who was a printer in the town and who took Jimmy under his wing. Uncle Andy also played football for Hamilton Accies (sport ran in the family). After a spell in London, Jimmy returned to Hawick to help his parents with the running of the hotel. Judging from photographs, Jimmy was a thin, slight man who looked rather like Walter, apart from his fine brush moustache. He seems to have had a great love for the Common Riding, following the Cornet on horseback for several years before his own selection. As the *Southern Reporter* commented, 'he is a young man thoroughly imbued with the true Hawick spirit'. The position of Cornet was very prestigious, although it also required considerable personal and financial commitment from young men and their families. In 1911, John Lockie Thorburn was left £28 out of pocket after the Common Riding, despite having sold his horse. Jimmy Sutherland's appointment suggests that his family was prosperous enough to meet the costs and that the Imperial Hotel had become a successful business venture. Heavy drinking and the Common Riding were closely linked and it was a good time for all those working in the drink trade to cash in. The Imperial Hotel was no exception. In June 1901, the *National Guardian* reported:

The hotel keepers and licence holders of Hawick did an exceptionally brisk business during the Common Riding holidays, and the scene at the Imperial Hotel, where Host Sutherland, the Cornet's father, is the life and soul of the establishment, was quite unprecedented.

Happily, the Common Riding of 1901 was an unqualified success. For once, the weather was on its best behaviour and the main event took place in brilliant sunshine. 'Umbrellas and waterproofs were conspicuous by their absence,' reported the *Hawick Express*. Large crowds turned out and the streets and houses were brightly decorated, especially the Cornet's home at the Imperial Hotel, which bore a large sign with the traditional slogan 'Safe Oot, Safe In'.

Much of the credit was down to twenty-three-year-old Jimmy. Accompanied by his 'Acting Father', the redoubtable 'JED' Murray, and his charming 'Lass' Lily Lawson, the daughter of a local town councillor, Jimmy proved an excellent choice of Cornet, eagerly throwing himself into the role. In the words of the *Hawick Express*, he deported 'himself with great dignity and honour'. 'Cornet Sutherland is accepted on all hands as a splendid Cornet,' reported the *Hawick Advertiser*. 'He is displaying keen enthusiasm in connection with the details of the festival, and no doubt he will perform his part admirably at the celebration… It was the proudest moment of his life to know that he had been honoured to hold aloft the glorious standard of 1514.'

Jimmy was fortunate enough to inherit his grandfather's musical talent, which came in useful during various Common Riding functions and singsongs. Like old Jimmy, he played the fiddle and was an accomplished tenor vocalist. Later in life, he was much in demand as an after-dinner singer and for amateur operatic productions. In March 1911 he gave a memorable performance as Ralph Rackraw in *HMS Pinafore*, having a voice 'of good range and power'. Cornets were required to be competent horsemen and it is likely that the Sutherland household had some experience with horses. Before the First World War there were few motorised lorries or vans. In the pub and hotel trade horses were indispensable for heavy work, such as transporting barrels of beer and crateloads of bottles. Around the back of the Imperial Hotel there was a block of stables which Alex Sutherland rented out to a man called William Andison, who ran a cab business. The Sutherland family might have owned at least one horse of their own. During the Common Riding, Jimmy rode his mount 1901, taking part in several of the races and winning a new horsewhip in one of them. However, it appears that his brother Tom was the real horse lover in the family. In 1901 he followed Jimmy on the appropriately named Imperial Lass, also winning one of the races. He took part in many later Common Ridings, for instance winning the Cornet's Silver Challenge Cup in 1905 on Forest Queen. It is not known if ten-year-old Walter also followed his brother Jimmy or if he was familiar and comfortable with horses. It might be relevant that, at the outbreak of the First World War, Walter (and five of his friends) chose to join the yeomanry rather than the local infantry regiment.

The Sutherland family continued to be great supporters of the Common Riding after 1901. Jimmy played his allotted role as Right-Hand Man to Cornet William Graham, a plumber, in 1902 and Left-Hand Man to Walter Scott, a farmer, in 1903. Three years later Mary Sutherland, Walter's sister, was Cornet's Lass to James Robertson, a young man of 'pleasant and affable disposition' who was well known to the family. James worked in the drink trade, helping his father to run the Mansfield Bar in Hawick. He was a keen amateur runner and cyclist as well as being a territorial member of the local yeomanry regiment. The big moment for the Cornet's Lass was 'bussing' the town flag by tying ribbons onto the head of the staff of the flag, and then presenting it to the Cornet under the watchful eyes of the town. This was said to imitate the ancient tradition of women decorating their menfolk as a sign of affection and good luck before they went away to war. Once again, the Common Riding was very successful. Mary and James made a fine couple and, in July 1912, they were married.

Very little is known about Walter Sutherland's childhood, but it seems likely that it was fairly conventional and happy. Hawick was certainly a good place for a boy to grow up. At this time children relied mainly on their own resources and imaginations to amuse themselves, most of them knowing nothing better than a few simple toys. They had fewer possessions than their modern counterparts, but they did have much greater freedom to run about and explore, spending much of their time out of doors, often barefooted, safe in the knowledge that they would come to no harm unless they broke a window or were caught pilfering. The greatest danger was from a runaway horse and cart; motorcars did not arrive until well into the 1900s. Echoing the Border wars of long ago, boys played at 'Scotch and English' or local curiosities such as 'Pape-a-Go', a kind of trading game played with cherrystones, or 'Sommers', the gutter version of what is now called Pooh Sticks. Few boys could afford the luxury of their own leather football, but some made do with a 'dirty blether' (a pig's bladder) from the local slaughterhouse, blown up with a 'pipe stapple' (a clay-pipe stem). When someone made a mess of a drop kick, the boys would shout: 'That's no' a drop, it's a flunk!'

In 1891 the population of Hawick was measured at 19,204 people, over 4,500 more than today, although the town occupied a much smaller area. This meant that it was very crowded, especially in the tenement areas, but, unlike the cities, the countryside was close at hand, only a few minutes' walk away from the town centre. Unless they had overly protective parents, children grew up familiar with nature and thought nothing about taking long walks in the surrounding country, scouring the roadsides for fruits and other windfalls. A typical boy spent a lot of his spare time hunting for rabbits or birds' nests, gathering chestnuts and 'scrogs', or playing in the rivers and streams. Hawick was principally a manufacturing centre, but town and country regularly overlapped. There were cattle byres within the town and several families kept cows, each morning taking them through the streets to nearby pastureland. It was also a common sight to see shepherds bringing flocks of sheep into the town to be sold at the local market, the sheep leaving behind their mess to mix with the ever-present horse manure.

Unlike today, Hawick had a railway link with the outside world, but transport was expensive and most things were made and provided locally, the town having an incredibly wide range of shops and services. In 1903, *Edgar's Hawick Guide and Directory* listed, among others, nine blacksmiths, fifteen milliners, sixteen bakers, eighteen boot and shoemakers, twenty-nine tailors and forty-two grocers as well as a range of more esoteric occupations, such as two manufacturers of aerated waters, two umbrella makers and eight conductors of orchestras. The average child would have been more interested in the products of local toy manufacturers and confectioners, although there was little money to buy things, apart from a Saturday 'hapny' for the lucky ones. Next door to the Imperial Hotel was a sweet shop owned by a man called Robert Welsh, which was the first shop in Hawick to sell ice cream and was well-known for its sticky toffees and sugary creations. It might not be a coincidence that, as a young man, Walter Sutherland had great trouble with his teeth, having all his uppers pulled out by his mid-twenties. (I always wondered why he never smiled in photographs. The answer was that he had very poor teeth. Most people at the time did not value their teeth very highly.) With its factory smoke, narrow streets and sooty railway line, Hawick had a reputation as the 'Auld Grey Toon', but occasionally there were some memorable splashes of colour. As well as the Common Riding, there were old-style hiring days and fairs when farmers and country people surged into the town although, by 1900, these events had lost much of their economic significance and piquancy. The Friendly Societies, the churches and the Freemasons held colourful parades and often there were visits from travelling entertainers and tradesmen, such as knife-sharpeners, barrel-organ or hurdy-gurdy players, men who brought dancing bears or monkeys, and German brass bands resplendent in their uniforms and peaked caps. In the early 1900s, the town also had a strong military presence and it was quite common to see groups of soldiers strolling around the streets. In 1901, the War Office had purchased Stobs estate a few miles down the road and established an army training camp, partly because the hills around Stobs were thought to resemble the kind of terrain encountered in the Boer War. The camp grew into an enormous enterprise, at one point housing over 20,000 men and earning the name 'The Aldershot of the North'. Soldiers visited Hawick during their time off and there were regular parades through the town, stirring the soul with brass or pipe bands, kilts and uniforms, cap badges and buttons brightly gleaming.

Little is also known about Walter Sutherland's education. From 1901, school attendance in Scotland was compulsory between the ages of five to fourteen, in theory at least. Walter would have attended one of Hawick's four 'elementary' schools where, as the name suggests, he was taught the three elements of writing, reading and arithmetic, the dreaded three Rs. The curriculum also included subjects like history, geography, languages and elementary science as well as some semi-vocational elements: woodwork for the boys, cookery and 'domestic economy' for the girls. The emphasis was on the formal and factual. All that is known for certain about Walter's education was that, from the age of about ten, he went to a school called Teviot Grove Academy, which was situated in North Bridge Street, just across the road from the Imperial Hotel. James Brand, who came from Fife, had established the Academy in 1869. Originally it had been a high-class private school, which set out to provide 'a thorough and systematic training for a mercantile or professional career'. In other words it was aimed at the aspiring middle classes and the upwardly mobile, the kind of people who were keen to give their offspring a head start in life. An energetic man, Brand seems to have been able to produce good academic results. One of his star pupils in the 1890s was Francis George Scott, the eminent composer who went to the school at the age of twelve, although he later dismissed the Academy as 'a kind of upper-class school, although that was the only thing about it'. In 1895 the Academy was taken over by the Burgh School Board on behalf of the town council, although James Brand remained as rector until two years before his death in 1908. Subsequently it became the secondary centre for older pupils, who transferred from other local schools to complete their education.

By Walter Sutherland's time, the Academy was divided into two sections: the junior school, for pupils aged between ten and twelve, and the senior school, for those aged twelve and upwards. Children had to sit an entrance exam and the most successful were excused the school fees. The Academy may have had some social pretensions, but school inspection reports make it clear that it was woefully under-funded and seemingly in a state of near collapse. The Academy was a mixed-sex school with over 100 pupils, but it had only four permanent members of staff. They were expected to teach all curricular areas apart from some specialist subjects, which were taken by visiting part-timers. In the early 1900s, the staff were described as 'most zealous and energetic', which was just as well, as they were working in almost impossible conditions. As the inspection reports put it, the school was 'seriously under-mastered'. Class sizes were often very large; sometimes over fifty pupils squeezed together in a single room. In fact, the school only seems to have survived because large groups of children were often left to work on their own without proper supervision or support. To make matters worse, the school building was hopelessly inadequate, consisting of four separate rooms divided by thin partitions with little effective soundproofing. 'The rooms are so crowded that the atmosphere within them is frequently most unhealthy,' commented the school inspectors in 1903. Art and science classes were taught in a separate building, the Buccleuch Memorial, which involved a five-minute walk for the pupils. 'At present the school is working under most unsatisfactory conditions,' reported the inspectors in 1902. 'It would clearly be unreasonable to expect a very high standard of attainment.' Two years later, the inspectors saw little evidence of improvement. 'Every teacher works hard and the results are about as good as it could be possible to secure under the depressing conditions.'

Did Walter and the other boys learn rugby at the Academy? The annual prospectus made no mention of the game but boasted that the school devoted time to 'Drill' and 'Callisthenics', which meant exercises to promote general fitness and improved muscle tone, a formal version of the modern aerobics. In schools like the Academy, physical education was treated as a peripheral subject, although attitudes were beginning to change after the shocking evidence of the Boer War medical examinations, which revealed a very low standard of physical efficiency among the working classes. Around 1900, the Academy employed a soldier called Sergeant Buchanan from the local drill hall to take the pupils for periods of physical instruction, usually for one hour a week. Buchanan seems to have been a typical Victorian army man, a fearsome character who stood no nonsense. According to the inspection report in 1899, he carried out his work 'with great firmness and precision... No slovenliness and no laxness being allowed to pass unnoticed.' The school lacked a properly equipped gymnasium so classes were held out of doors, whenever possible. 'The energetic instructor is hampered by inadequate accommodation,' commented the school inspectors. In general, classes consisted of physical drill and exercises, the kind of thing that many of the boys would later become familiar with when they joined the army after 1914.

Blessed with natural speed and athleticism, Walter Sutherland would have excelled at sports and games from a young age and this might have attracted special attention from his superiors. As E.H.D. Sewell commented:

As a boy, Walter Sutherland not only evinced a keen interest, but showed a rare aptitude in all games. At his School sports he was successful in all events for which he entered; and, in the School cricket and football teams, he was looked upon as the leader of his side.

Every year at the beginning of July, an Inter-Scholastic Sports Day was held for all school pupils in Hawick. In 1906, the fifteen-year-old Walter won the throwing the cricket ball event, but could only finish second in the 100 yards and the long and high jumps, in all cases behind a fellow Academy pupil called

J.J.S. Thomson, who must have been a very fast boy indeed. In November 1906, Walter was a member of the Academy rugby team that won a school sevens tournament at Mansfield Park and he also played for the Hawick Higher Grade School team against other Border sides. However, it seems unlikely that the boys had much in the way of formal instruction in the game. The school did not have the time or the money to invest in teaching staff or facilities for games. Most likely, the school team was thrown together without any practice or coaching. If they were lucky, the boys might have had an enthusiastic master to pass on some basic skills, but for the most part they were left to organise themselves.

Walter left Teviot Grove Academy in the summer of 1907 when he was sixteen years old, although his attendance may have been uneven during his final year, possibly due to him working as a student teacher. At this time, most people left their formal education at fourteen, under pressure from their families to go straight out to work and bring in some much-needed money. The fact that Walter stayed on for an extra two years suggests that his parents could afford to keep him in education, that they were ambitious for his future and willing to make the financial sacrifice to give him every chance of success. It also indicates that Walter had at least some academic abilities and was intelligent and thoughtful; a young man with great promise. He was taken on as an apprentice surveyor with the town council, working in the office of Mr Brown, the Hawick burgh surveyor. It was a good job with prospects, the first step on the professional ladder, although it meant that Walter had to study in his spare time. His family employed a private tutor to help him, which is another sign of their relative prosperity and social aspirations. Walter was described as a 'diligent student' and applied himself hard, but for the most part surveying was a dry subject. There would have been many times when the young student found his attention drifting away to the football field.

two

FITBA'

W hat was the nature of rugby before the First World War? What sort of game did Walter Sutherland play?

Some form of street football had taken place in Hawick for many centuries, but rugby as it is now known was first introduced into the town in 1873. The original players were from the local cricket club, who adopted 'fitba' as something to keep them fit and healthy during the long winter months. The new game was haphazard and would be barely recognisable today, but by the 1880s 'football mania' had taken a firm grip in Hawick. There were lots of local teams, some based around churches, workplaces, pubs or streets. In the Scottish Borders, rugby was a game for all classes, as it was in south Wales, although local factory owners often nurtured it. The Border towns were not big enough to support a professional soccer team, but the game also struck a chord with the Border character. In the immortal words of the *Hawick Express* in 1873, it was 'manlier and more congenial to the Border nature than the tamer Association game'.

In September 1888 the Hawick club moved to a new home at Mansfield Park, which was rented from the Duke of Buccleuch. The ground had a rickety wooden stand and a draughty changing pavilion with a cold stone bath, but no clubhouse or social area. Gradually, the Hawick fixture list expanded with various Border derbies and games against city teams, despite their reluctance to travel down to the uncouth Borders. In the 1890s Hawick began to make an impact at national level. Matthew Elliot, a quarter-back, became the club's first international player in 1895 and in season 1895/96 the club won the Scottish club championship for the first time.

By Walter Sutherland's day all this was in the past and rugby had developed much of its modern appearance. The season ran from late September to the end of March with the sevens tournaments bringing down the curtain in April. In the Borders, the principal focus was the Border League, which was established in 1901. Originally, the league was made up of five teams (Gala,

Hawick, Jed-Forest, Langholm and Melrose), who played each other home and away. The league was very successful and Selkirk joined in 1909, followed by Kelso in 1912. Spurred on by ancient local rivalries, the league encouraged a fiercely competitive spirit, but the Scottish Football Union (SFU), who ran the game from distant Edinburgh, treated it with some suspicion. League rugby was associated with professionalism and the English Northern Union clubs, which had split from the Rugby Football Union in 1895 over the payment of players and 'broken time'. The SFU was doggedly resistant to professionalism. It was also feared that league rugby encouraged a 'win-at-all-costs' attitude, that the imperative to win led to violence and would impose itself at the expense of other aspects of the game, such as fair play and the social side. It says much about the intensely conservative nature of Scottish rugby that an official league structure was not established until 1973. A national cup competition was not introduced until 1995.

As well as the Border League, Hawick had regular fixtures with teams from Edinburgh, such as Watsonians, Heriot's FP, Royal High School FP, Stewart's FP and Edinburgh Academicals (or 'Accies'). Student rugby was very strong at this time and one of the most important games of the season was against Edinburgh University, a side that could usually boast several international players. These matches were designated as 'friendly games' and the result was supposed not to count for anything. There was no official club championship in Scotland, but some newspapers published an unofficial table. One point was awarded for each game lost and the side with the least number of points at the end of the season was declared the winners. In theory, a side could draw all its games and not win any of them, but still top the table. The championship had other weaknesses. Not all of the sides played each other and games that were cancelled for bad weather or other reasons were rarely replayed. The number of sides in the table varied from year to year: twenty in 1908, twenty-three in 1913, depending how a team rated itself. The absence of a genuine league structure with promotion and relegation undoubtedly contributed to the low standard of club rugby in Scotland and in turn of the national team, although the other rugby-playing countries were in the same boat. Border clubs could focus on their own local league, but this might have encouraged them to believe that a national league was unnecessary.

Further afield, Glasgow had several senior sides, such as Glasgow Accies, Glasgow High School FP and Kelvinside Accies, but Hawick's only regular fixture in the west was against Clydesdale, who played at Titwood Park in the south of city, not very far away from Hampden Park. 'The Dale', as they were known, had close links with Dollar Academy, the exclusive fee-paying school. The club produced a handful of international players and won the Hawick Sevens in 1908, but was a casualty of the First World War. (The current Clydesdale club was founded in 1981.) Hawick did not play outside of the Borders or Edinburgh area very often because of the prohibitive costs of transport, which was a big strain on the club's finances. In addition, most people worked on a Saturday morning and there was limited time available for travelling. The trip to Glasgow was something of a tortuous journey, involving two changes of train, but it was well worth the effort. Hawick were always popular visitors, especially among the numerous Border exiles living in the city. Writing in the *Hawick News* in November 1908, 'J.G.G.' gave his impression of 'The Hawick "Greens" in Glasgow':

Saturday last saw a big turnout of Borderers, and it was heartsome to hear the shouts of welcome when the familiar green jerseys appeared on the field. The keenness with which the City-Borderers… watched the play, and the shouts of encouragement in the broad Border tongue, were worth going far to hear. The contrast between the genteel shout of 'Go on, the Clyde' piped in choicest Kelvinside English, and the vehement broad vowelled 'GO ON, HAWICK' was most marked, and even the remarks and instructions given to the players were very amusing and made the Hawick players rise to the occasion. 'Go on the Bottler,' 'Jump, Hawick,' 'Merk yer men,' 'Use yer feet,' must have somewhat mystified the Glasgow club supporters, while even the Border damsels present could not restrain their enthusiasm.

Unwittingly, J.G.G.'s article captured the social division that existed in the Scottish game. In the Borders, rugby attracted widespread popular support, but in Edinburgh and Glasgow it was almost entirely a middle-class game. The city clubs were mostly linked with exclusive independent schools and restricted their membership to former pupils. The international team was largely drawn from the FP and Academical clubs, the universities and the military. There were some 'open' sides, such as Edinburgh Wanderers and West of Scotland, but their membership came mainly from the professions. In other words, the social base of Scottish rugby was not very broad. Taking the Borders out of the picture, the Badminton Library volume *Football* summed up the Scottish game in 1899: 'Rugby is the game of the classes; the masses are devoted to Association.'

Rugby had important associations with manliness and the development of character, and therefore it had a strong moral sense about it. The game was thought to inspire the cardinal British virtues of decency, discipline and restraint. At all times, the players were expected to keep a tight lid on their feelings and to exercise self-control. When they scored or won a game, they were not supposed to throw their arms up in celebration (although sometimes they did) or to show passion outwardly by screaming, shouting or hugging their teammates. Winners did not gloat and losing teams were treated generously with the watchwords 'well tried' or 'hard luck'. Defeat was to be taken with stoicism and a stiff upper lip, and the victors heartily congratulated, even when it was not deserved. The referee's word was final and nobody was allowed to argue back. There was also a great sense that the game was to be enjoyed and that the result was less important than the pleasure of taking part. As E.H.D. Sewell wrote in 1911: 'The boy or man who cannot be on the losing side, in a 30 points to nil defeat, and enjoy himself, is a poor specimen of sportsmanship, who ought to give up the game forthwith.' Rugby taught important lessons about life and about working in a team, but it was also about friendship and having fun, about laughter, making jokes, singing together and, of course, drinking. The final score was soon forgotten or dismissed. The game was the thing.

However, it would be mistaken to be too idealistic about the nature of Edwardian rugby. Players stuck to the rules for most of the time, but on occasion they were tempted to bend or break them, especially if they thought that they could get away with it. In only his second senior game for Hawick, against Jed-Forest at Riverside Park in October 1908, the opposition took advantage of Walter's rawness by illegally playing him off the ball, repeatedly throwing him into touch when he did not have possession. Given the intense physical nature of rugby, it was inevitable that tempers sometimes boiled over. There was no lack of ferocity, punches were thrown and there could be some nasty rucking and footwork. In an article in the *Evening News* on 27 January 1912, 'A Borderer' complained about the state of Border rugby:

A disturbing element in the game at the present moment is the prevalence of rough play. This has been very flagrant in recent matches at Hawick and Selkirk. A fortnight ago a referee is said to have threatened to put the 'best forward' on each side off the field if the teams did not mend their manners… and only last Saturday there were 'hot' exchanges and unseemly 'asides' in a so-called 'friendly' match.

In December 1910, Hawick and Stewart's FP fought out a very rough match at Mansfield Park. Towards the end, one of the visiting forwards made 'an unwarranted attack' on the Hawick full-back Tom Wilson and was sent off the field. The Stewart's captain was appalled at the referee's decision and marched his team off in disgust, an action that cost him a suspension from playing the game.

Occasionally, there was also trouble when spectators let their emotions get the better of them. At the end of an important Border League match at

Mansfield Park in February 1910, which Hawick lost to their old rivals Gala (6-8), there was 'a noisy demonstration of feeling' against the referee, Mr John Gillespie of Edinburgh Academicals, who had made several baffling decisions in the visitors' favour. According to the *Hawick News*: 'Heated altercations were also proceeding between Hawick and Gala supporters, and three policemen who were in the centre of the throng looked like having a stormy time of it.' On leaving the ground, the unfortunate Mr Gillespie was subject to a 'hostile demonstration' with some 'nasty language' and divots thrown in his direction. The Scottish Football Union, never shy of making a mountain out of a few divots, was horrified at the incident and banned the Hawick club from playing at Mansfield Park for the remainder of the season.

Similar scenes took place during the match against Edinburgh Accies at Mansfield Park in February 1913. During a tense encounter, the ball was hacked over the Hawick line. A home player seemed to have touched it down but the referee, Mr Arthur Flett, who also happened to be the treasurer of the Scottish Football Union, awarded a try to the visitors. The Hawick supporters were furious. 'There was a chorus of booing and disapproval,' reported the *Hawick Express*. 'Where did it come from? Not from the yokels with cravats round their necks, hands in pockets, and shoulders awry. No, but from the "respectable" people in the grandstand!' At the final whistle, the referee and some of the visiting players were jostled on their way to the pavilion and were on the receiving end of some 'rude remarks'. As they were driving away from the ground, they faced a 'hostile demonstration from a lot of noisy boys, and there were one or two cases of divot throwing'. Letters of apology were hastily written and admission prices to the ground raised to 6d per head.

Problems of this kind around the football field reflected wider issues affecting Edwardian society. The era before the First World War is often presented as some kind of 'Golden Age', a time of innocence and stability, of straw boaters and long summer afternoons. This was undoubtedly true for some families, especially those at the top of the social hierarchy, but there were also great tensions and many uncertainties just below the surface. When Scotland played England at Inverleith in March 1912, it was feared that the attendance would be adversely affected by the national coal strike, which prevented people travelling to the match. Similarly, when Scotland played Wales in February 1913, there were rumours that the match would by disrupted by militant suffragettes running onto the field and chaining themselves to the goalposts. Women entering the ground had their pockets and handbags searched in case they were harbouring stones or offensive weapons.

If a modern spectator travelled back in time to watch a game around, say, 1910, what would he or she have seen? By then the days of gratuitous hacking, twenty-a-side and arguments over the rules were long gone. Rugby had passed out of its formative stage and assumed a shape and a set of laws that would hardly change until the 1960s. The game would be instantly recognisable today, although there were many technical differences. For instance, players were allowed to kick directly into touch outside the twenty-five-yard line so there was lots of lineout play. Lifting of a player in the lineout, which is standard practice today, was heavily penalised. Players could make a 'fair catch' anywhere on the field by catching the ball straight from a kick, knock-on or a forward pass and then mark the spot with the heel, similar to a modern 'mark'. From this, it was possible to drop a 'mark goal', which was worth three points. In his senior career, Walter did this once, against Clydesdale in October 1912. It was illegal to pick up the ball straight after a tackle, but instead it had to be brought back into play with the foot. Many games had very low scoring, often finishing only 3-0 or 6-3. It was very unusual for a team to score more than fifteen or twenty points in a single match. In season 1909/10, Hawick played 21 matches and scored only 198 points in total, less than ten per game. The scoring system was different from today. Three points were awarded for a try and four for a drop-goal. Penalty goals were worth three points, but were very scarce. In season 1908/09, Hawick kicked only two for the entire season. The reason was that the opposition could stand at the place of the infringement and were allowed to charge as soon as the ball was placed on the ground. Therefore, a kicker had to retire a long way to have enough time to try for goal.

At club and international level, Scottish rugby was famous for its robust and skilful forward play. Mark Morrison of Royal High School FP was a big, strong and fiery player who won 23 caps between 1896 and 1904. David Bedell-Sivright, an old Fettesian who played for both Cambridge and Edinburgh Universities, won 22 caps between 1900 and 1908 and captained the British Isles team that toured Australia and New Zealand in 1904. Raw-boned, vigorous and hard, the glory of Scottish forward play was the foot-rush, a carefully controlled dribble, either from a wheeled scrum or from broken play, with the ball passed among the feet of a rampaging pack. Honed by hours of careful practice, the foot-rush could only be stopped by a player diving at the forwards' feet and taking hold of the ball. Like tackling, this required courage and a defender was likely to come in for some abrasive treatment. 'There is no more terrible ordeal in football than saving from Scottish forwards when their blood is up,' wrote the England international John Raphael in his book *Modern Rugby Football*, which was published posthumously in 1918. Players were not allowed to lie on the ball and it was acceptable for an attacker to drag a loitering player out of the way by the heels so that the foot-rush might continue. This was also the era of 'first up, first down' among the forwards where the ability to shove hard was all-important. There were few specialists and forwards were expected to pack down, scrum and jump in any position.

A modern spectator would also be struck by the appearance of the players, especially in their style of dress. The Hawick club supplied the players with their green jerseys, which were made from wool in a local factory. Playing shirts did not have numbers on the back as these were considered to be a sign of professionalism. Advertising on playing jerseys was not even considered. Followers of Edwardian rugby would have been horrified that modern shirts, including those of Hawick and Scotland, are now routinely besmirched with advertising and manufacturer's logos. Players provided their own shorts, stockings and boots. In the 1890s, breeches or pantaloons had given way to football 'knickers', long baggy shorts that stretched down to the knees and which were held up by stout leather belts. Sandy Burns, the Hawick quarter-back and captain in 1908, remembered: 'They weren't strict about the colour of your shorts. As many wore navy blue as wore white because you didn't have to wash them so often. There were no laundries in those days.' Specialist football boots were available, but they were very expensive and some players made do with an old pair of working boots with wooden studs or bars hammered into the soles.

The players not only dressed differently, but they looked dissimilar from today. This was not just in the style of their haircuts, but also in their physical size. They were much smaller and lighter compared with the muscle-bound monsters of the modern game. Dare I say it, many of them would now appear decidedly thin and weedy. In October 1907, the *Hawick News* compared the weights of the Hawick and Jed-Forest teams before their meeting at Mansfield Park. Six of the Hawick team weighed under 11 stone per man, including two of the forwards, Willie Ogg and T. Simpson. In the backs, C. Davidson, the full-back, and John Haig, the right wing, came in at well under 10 stone each. The average weight of the Hawick forwards was around 11st 5lbs per man. By comparison, the average weight of a modern international pack is over 17 stone per man.

Like the population in general, players were also shorter on average than today. There were a few giants around, such as Alex Petrie, the great Royal High School forward of the 1870s who was 6ft 3ins tall, but most players stood well under 6ft. In 1913 two of Hawick's best forwards, John Corrie and David Fiddes, measured 5ft 11ins and 5ft 9ins respectively. Writing in 1911, E.H.D. Sewell reckoned that the ideal height for a forward was between 5ft 7ins and 5ft 10ins, preferably 'stockily built individuals'. Taller fellows were too awkward and gangly, easily out-manoeuvred in the lineout and 'all elbows' in the scrum. The best position for a very tall man, argued Sewell, was a touch-judge.

When Walter Sutherland first played for Hawick and Scotland, there were fears about his lack of stature and that he was not robust enough for the game. 'He was not built on generous lines,' said the *Evening Dispatch*, 'and was even fragile and delicate in appearance.' In December 1913, when he was twenty-three-years-old, Walter was 5ft 7½ins in height and weighed around 11st 7lb. By 1915, his weight had dropped to just over 10 stone. His army records show that he had a chest measurement of about 38 inches when fully expanded. He might have appeared rather frail and was certainly no Goliath, but by the standards of the time he was no mere slip of a lad either. And whatever he lacked in brawn, he made up for in quickness and determination.

A modern spectator would also notice that the speed of the game was much slower than today. Fitness levels were nowhere near as high, especially among the forwards, many of who were mere plodders, playing the game at little more than walking pace. Players were expected to attend weekly training sessions to build up their strength and stamina, and to develop a 'good wind'. This might include some sprinting sessions, a few laps around the ground plus a good workout with Indian clubs, skipping and medicine balls. They also spent time practising various skills, such as passing, kicking and dribbling, although some felt that tackling and scrum work was best left to the actual game. However, the prevailing logic was that excessive training was harmful to performance. It made players stale and took the edge off their game. Writing in his coaching manual *The Modern Rugby Game and How to Play It* (1908), Gwyn Nicholls, the great Welsh three-quarter of the early 1900s, commented:

It is important that one should be careful not to train 'too fine'. The rugby player is not training for a match, but for a season, and must commence with enough 'fire' and energy to last him right through it.

Regarding diet, Nicholls advised this was a matter for personal taste, admitting that he was neither a tee-totaller nor a non-smoker, 'and would not insist on any man being either'. In general, it was felt that players could get by with plenty of fresh air, exercise and 'regularity of habits'. A more practical problem for training was that there were no decent floodlights. In the depths of winter, most training had to take place in near total darkness. In 1912, the Hawick club invested in two oil lamps for evening training, but these were of limited value. 'There was nae licht at Mansfield,' recalled Sandy Burns, 'so we sometimes ran into each other in the dark. The only ball work was done in the pavilion.' Modern ideas about the effects of dehydration on performance were unknown, which made rugby slower and less dynamic. Players rarely took on fluid during a game, which was considered unmanly and not in the right spirit. At best, they were given slices of lemon or oranges at half-time. On occasion, players took the field slightly under the influence of alcohol. When Hawick played in Edinburgh, the team was given a shilling each to buy lunch, which generally consisted of a pint of beer and a meat pie. In the Borders, the trainer's bag always contained a bottle of port or brandy and it was common practice for players to be given a quick swig before they went on the field, just as soldiers were given a tot of rum before they went over the top. Jock Wemyss remembered: 'Strictly temperate beliefs were, of course, respected. But a gargle for the players immediately before taking the field – "only a gargyle mind; and spit it oot" – was regarded as nearly as essential as the ball. It was regarded as being good for the wind.'

Formal coaching was not encouraged as it was associated with professionalism, but most sides had a trainer who looked after the players and gave them help and advice. The Hawick club was fortunate to have the services of Peter Hope, who trained the players at Mansfield for over thirty-five years. A baker by trade and therefore known as 'Whitey', Hope's dedication knew no bounds. He was one of those slightly peculiar 'boy-men' who are the lifeblood of amateur sport, always hanging around the touchlines, a cheerful fanatic who never lost his youthful enthusiasm and asked for nothing more than to be involved. Hope was paid 5s a week by the club, but no doubt he would gladly have offered his services for free. He was the 'general fag' to the players, the rub-a-dub man who ran on with the magic sponge when they were injured and who spent hours after training and games massaging their muscles with coarse towels (the 'dry rub' was thought to prevent stiffness and colds, and also to harden the body). Honest and good-natured, he also looked after the ground and was out in all weathers preparing the field for play. 'His patience was inexhaustible,' said the club's fifty-year history book, 'though often sorely tried by the carelessness or absentmindedness of the youths under his charge.' Keeping a paternal eye on the young bucks, he admonished their inevitable high spirits with the words: 'Hey, behave yourself. I might be a bit deaf but I'm no' blind.'

Rugby was played at a slower pace than today, but changes in the style of the game had made it more attractive and open, especially after the introduction of the four three-quarter system in the 1890s and the move away from the old-fashioned forward-orientated game. By 1910, the chief job of the forwards was to win ball for the back division to run and exploit. These changes suited a fast man like Walter Sutherland, but they were not popular with everybody, in particular the mandarins who controlled the Scottish Football Union. In October

1912 William Walls, the SFU president and international forward of the 1880s, commented:

It would never do to have the game played in a way that only highly trained athletes and sprinters would excel in it, and it would be a great misfortune if it were allowed to degenerate into a circus show to attract spectators. They must not allow the game to become a mere monotonous exhibition of sprinting.

Two years later his successor, John Dallas of Watsonians, said 'that a great deal had been taken out of football by the appalling craze for pace'. These, however, were the views of a minority, showing that former players and officials were often sadly out of touch. Players and spectators were drawn to rugby because it had become a more exciting game to play and watch.

For many people, rugby was a temporary escape from the drudgery of everyday life, bringing light and colour into closely circumscribed lives. In the Borders the game was very popular, a kind of grass-roots patriotism, and attracted an enthusiastic following that was not limited to men and boys. Women also played their part, often as keen and knowledgeable as their menfolk. Reporting the match between Hawick and Edinburgh University in March 1914, which the students won with a last-minute drop-goal, 'A City Man' was impressed by 'Hawick's Sporting Maids' and their fervour for the game:

It was not the grimness of the fight in the field so much as the wild enthusiasm all around me that struck me most. I looked on and around with astonishment at it all! I knew the well-bred, 'well-played Accies,' of Raeburn Place and Anniesland, the long-drawn out 'Sonians' of Myreside, when J. Pearson and A. W. Angus are doing things; and at Inverleith I have watched the ladies working up an enthusiasm for 'Scotland,' but leaving the vocal trimmings to their brothers. But compared with the Border maidens, why, they don't know the least bit how to encourage a side. Hawick played gallantly because their women fought for them. They ran the whole gauntlet of the emotions from fear to hope and joyful exhalation. Every good bit of play got its due meed of reward; every slip drew forth a distressful 'Oh!' It was all so infectious, too. It was worth going far to hear that 'Oh! Beatson,' when the three-quarter looked to have scored, to listen to the praises of J. Corrie and Wilson, to watch the tenseness that gripped them when the subtle Fahmy began to open out the game, and to note the blank dismay when Thomas dropped his goal. In a wide experience I had thought that I had seen most and heard most that was striking in football... but that afternoon at Mansfield Park added another to a list of football memories. I lift my hat to the ladies of Hawick.

This, then, was the game that Walter Sutherland was familiar with, a world of passion and laughter, rivalry and friendship, tradition and eccentricity, aggression and art. The next chapter will look at Walter's career with Hawick and show how he excelled in club football.

three

THE GREEN JERSEY

Walter Sutherland is fondly remembered as one of the most exciting players who ever wore the famous green jersey of Hawick. At club level, he achieved everything that was possible for his time. In his six seasons of senior rugby, he was a member of the Hawick team that won a shared Scottish Championship in season 1908/09 and also five Border League titles between 1908 and 1914. He captained Hawick in season 1911/12 and played in many successful sevens teams, all before he was twenty-four years old. More importantly he was the darling of the Hawick supporters, the local hero who caused excitement whenever the ball came his way. This chapter looks at Walter's playing career with Hawick, highlighting his achievements in the club game and showing why he was so highly regarded and admired.

Walter Sutherland enjoyed what is usually termed a 'meteoric' rise up the rugby ladder. Leaving school in the summer of 1907 he joined the Hawick Football Club, turning out for the Second and Third XVs, which were also known as Hawick 'A' and 'B', during season 1907/08. At this time there were three 'junior' sides in Hawick: Hawick 'A', Hawick Linden Star and Hawick Waverley. These sides were made up of very young players, others who had reached the level of their abilities and also a few has-beens, although most men gave up the game when they got married. They played in the Border Junior League, which had ten sides from Hawick, Selkirk, Galashiels, Jedburgh and Melrose. Like its big brother, the Junior League was taken very seriously and matches were fiercely competitive. At a lower level, there were also a number of ad hoc sides, such as the Hawick Third XV, Hawick Rovers or the Tuesday Thistle, which were designed for the casual player who just wanted a kickabout and the chance to work up a good sweat.

Newspaper reports of junior rugby were very sketchy and individual players did not receive much notice. Occasionally, Walter Sutherland was singled out for special attention. Reporting a match between Hawick 'B' and Gala

Hearts 'A' in January 1908, the *Hawick News* noted: 'Sutherland was in great form for Hawick, running away from the Gala lads on several occasions.' By the end of the season Walter was beginning to turn heads, particularly for his displays in the sevens tournaments. His big break came on 25 April 1908 when he was the outstanding player at the Border Junior Sports, which were held at Wilton Lodge Park in Hawick. Walter put on a great show, scoring a splendid individual try in the semi-final and helping his side Hawick 'A' to win the competition, beating Newington of Edinburgh in the final. 'Sutherland gave a sparkling display,' reported the *Hawick News*, 'and seems a player with a brilliant future before him, provided he is not put in the forefront too early.' The rival *Hawick Express* was also very impressed:

The fine individual player was their full-back, W. Sutherland, who is quite a lad yet, but whose speed and handling of the ball is quite unique. Great things may be predicted for Sutherland, who only a short time ago was playing for a school team.

The following weekend, Walter had his first taste of senior rugby when he played for Hawick 'B' at the Langholm Sevens. His side reached the semi-finals and he 'dazzled' the crowd with his spellbinding running and firm defensive work. 'In the tie with Jed-Forest,' reported the *Hawick News*, 'his tackling of J.L. Huggan, the Edinburgh University Association player [and future internationalist], was a perfect treat.'

A good all-round sportsman, Walter spent the summer of 1908 playing cricket for the Hawick and Wilton Second XI, scoring a creditable half-century in one match and also taking 11 wickets over the course of the season. On 19 September 1908 Walter took part in the Hawick rugby trial at Mansfield Park, scoring two tries for the 'Probables XV' and firmly making his mark. 'The football career of this young lad has been almost meteoric,' observed the *Hawick Express*. 'Twelve months ago he was in a school team and latterly he played for Hawick 3rds, while he also played in a number of matches for the 2nd team... All over he is a brilliant player and, despite his youth and lack of weight, he would do credit in the first fifteen.' Walter played a couple more games for Hawick 'B' at the beginning of season 1908/09 before making his first senior appearance for Hawick against their old rivals Gala at Mansfield Park on 17 October 1908.

As usual for a local derby, the Gala match aroused 'extraordinary interest'. Both sides were unbeaten in the season and were brimming with confidence. There were doubts about Walter's selection for such an important game. It was felt that he was being introduced into senior rugby too early and that he needed more time to mature in the junior ranks. He was still a few weeks short of his eighteenth birthday and little more than a boy in physical appearance and stature. As the *Hawick Express* noted: 'There was some head-shaking and misgiving at this young junior being given a place as wing three-quarter for the senior team.' In the event, Walter made the doubters eat their words. He played with great confidence, 'a first-class game for the Greens', showing no signs of nerves in front of a large crowd and helping his side to a handsome 12-5 win. In the first half he put in a great run from under his own posts. His kicking was good and he came close to scoring a debut try, only losing the ball over the Gala line. As the *Hawick News* observed: 'Those who pulled a long face over the playing of young Sutherland at three-quarter got their prediction falsified by the brilliant display the youngster gave. Both in attack and defence his display was masterly.' The *Hawick Express* was also impressed: 'In every department of the game he excels, and for picking up the ball on the run, he has few superiors.' However, the *Express* had doubts about his size and lack of presence, suggesting that he might be found out on softer pitches and against bigger sides. 'If Sutherland was engaged in a gruelling sort of game against a heavy team, he might not fare so well, but in an open passing game, he is the style of player which is required.'

The following weekend in a 'hard tussle' with Jed-Forest at Riverside Park, who were the reigning Border champions, Walter scored his first try for Hawick, albeit a soft and unspectacular effort. The Jed-Forest scrum-half fluffed a kick and Walter, chasing hard, took the rolling ball, pirouetted round and crossed for the only score of the game. 'Young Sutherland deserves great credit for his smart work,' commented the *Hawick News*. One week later against a weak Langholm side at Mansfield Park, Walter had more opportunity to show the elusive, swerving running that would soon become his trademark, scoring two out of eight tries in Hawick's 30-0 win. 'Haig and Sutherland had a large share of the game,' observed the *Hawick News*, 'and one of the finest things in the match was the way in which the last-named scored his first try, having a long run and swerving past Bell in a most deceptive and masterly style.' Walter had taken to the senior game like a duck to water. He was clearly a player of outstanding talent and potential. 'As for Sutherland, he has come to stay as a senior, though still a "youngster",' said the *Hawick Express*. 'He seldom errs in judgement, and what he does is carried out with a cleverness and confidence which makes him a marvel.'

Walter was lucky enough to join the best Hawick team since the mid-1890s. It was a well-balanced side with a speedy back division and powerful forwards. At quarter-back, Sandy Burns had first played for Hawick in 1901 and was now in his second season as captain. At this time Hawick, like most Scottish clubs, still played the old system of two quarter-backs, essentially two scrum-halves who were inter-changeable and in theory not so easily marked.

Burns was partnered by Tom Neil, who was strong, tenacious and brimful of guile, especially from the base of the scrum. In the three-quarter line, Billy Burnet was a strong-running centre who would later form an effective partnership with Walter Sutherland at club and international level. On the wing, John Haig was fast, determined and difficult to put down.

Robert Lindsay-Watson was the glamour boy of the side. He was the son of a wealthy tweed manufacturer and his privileged background meant that he stood out, seemingly having more in common with players from the exclusive FP and university clubs. Lindsay-Watson had been privately educated at the prestigious Glenalmond School in Perthshire and at Trinity College, Cambridge. With his slicked-down hair and refined good looks, 'R.H.' was a great sporting all-rounder who was blessed with splendid natural athleticism and speed. However, his handling was suspect and sometimes he played indifferently, although he was still good enough to win a cap against Ireland in 1909.

Hawick also had some talented and hard-working forwards, including George Johnstone, George Laing and Willie Ogg, who possessed 'rare mettle' and was one of three brothers who played for Hawick before the First World War. At this time there were few specialist forwards, such as hookers or back-row men, and players were selected on their all-round ability. In William Elliot Kyle the club was lucky enough to have one of the best forwards of the Edwardian era. Bill Kyle played his first game for Hawick as a gangly teenager in the late 1890s. He was a great footballer who was clever with his feet, a strong runner, fast at following up and solid in the scrum and lineout. He won his first cap against Wales in 1902 and became an automatic choice for Scotland for the rest of the decade, only missing out in 1907 because of injury. He made 21 appearances for his country, which was an astonishing number for the time. Standing around 6ft in height and weighing just over 13 stone at his peak, his mobility and athleticism meant that he was also a great exponent of sevens rugby. A staunch Freemason, Conservative and churchgoer, Kyle was Cornet of Hawick in 1905, following in the footsteps of his father Alexander, who ran a tobacconist's shop, and also of Walter's brother Jimmy. Kyle's enthusiasm knew no bounds. His work as a joiner meant that he often worked in the country, but he thought nothing of running miles over the hills after a morning's shift just to turn out for Hawick.

Another important but lesser-known player was Tom Wilson, who joined the club in season 1906/07 having previously played for Clydesdale and Carlisle. Described as 'an exceptionally fast and clever forward,' Wilson was the son of a schoolteacher and a civil engineer by trade, but also it appears something of an outsider. He had a similar build and approach to Bill Kyle and was good enough to win representative honours. He played county rugby for Cumberland and was sounded out about his availability for the Anglo-Welsh tour of New Zealand in 1908. Unfortunately the Scottish Football Union was still in the huff about the payment of expenses to the New Zealand tourists in 1905 and forbade any Scottish involvement in the tour. By indicating his willingness to take part, Wilson almost certainly ruined his chances of winning a cap.

Hawick had another Tom Wilson, who was the heart and soul of the side and one of rugby's great characters. A small man with a big personality and a permanent cheeky grin, he was better known as 'The Bottler', although nobody knew why. One suggestion was that he once promised to 'bottle up' the opposition, although a 'bottler' was slang for a boy who collected the money at a show and perhaps he got the name when he was young. 'Bottler' Wilson had natural footballing flair and could turn his hand to any position on the field. As the *Hawick Express* observed:

As a rugby football player he had a distinctiveness peculiarly of his own... When at full-back he could field the ball, find touch or tackle with anyone; as a forward he played many a great game, and what can be said of his magnificent play in the three-quarter line, or his brilliancy as a stand-off half? A more versatile player the Borders have not produced, and he was a veritable handyman for the 'Greens,' and required an immense amount of watching, as his opponents knew, wherever he played.

His played his first game for Hawick in October 1902, typically scoring a try on his debut. He was a great stalwart of the club, engaging and cheerful, and a favourite of the crowd.

With such talent available to the side, Hawick were unbeaten until Christmas 1908 and were in the hunt for the unofficial Scottish championship. Unfortunately the wheels came off in the New Year's Day match against Heriot's FP at Mansfield Park. In front of a large holiday crowd, Hawick were leading 9-5, three tries to one goal. With only minutes remaining, Heriot's scored far out. The captain J.W. Drever kicked the conversion from an awkward angle to give his side an unexpected 10-9 victory and blow open the championship race. There was some compensation the following weekend when Hawick defeated Melrose 13-0 at The Greenyards to clinch their first Border League title for seven years.

The defeat by Heriot's FP meant that Hawick were now equal in the championship table with Watsonians, both sides having suffered one defeat. As luck would have it, Hawick's next game was against Watsonians at Myreside. Between 1908 and 1914, Watsonians were the strongest side in Scottish club rugby, winning or sharing five titles. The side had a strong set of forwards

Hawick's good form in the Scottish club championship in season 1908/09 caught the attention of the Glasgow-based Scottish Referee. *(Author's collection)*

and a brilliant back division, six of whom won international caps. There was huge interest in the match at old Myreside (which was situated across the road from the present ground). The crowd was estimated at around 4,000 people, 'a tribute to the visionary championship,' said the *Evening News*, happy to ruffle the feathers of the Scottish Football Union, which was opposed to league rugby. 'Hawick sent a big contingent of enthusiasts who wasted no time in awakening the echoes of Myreside,' reported the same newspaper. 'The home supporters responded with all their vocal might, and many an international has had a quieter opening.'

The Hawick supporters might have made less noise if they had known that their team travelled to Edinburgh with sixteen players and the side was only finalised shortly before the game. Because of his age and lack of experience, Walter Sutherland was asked to stand down for the veteran winger John Haig, a decision that might have cost Hawick the game. Led in rousing fashion by Bill Kyle, the Hawick forwards were 'wound up for a big performance', going about their job 'with great grimness' and giving their opponents 'a peppery time'. There was no score at half-time, although the visitors had dominated the match. In the second half, playing with the wind, Watsonians gained a little more possession and were rewarded when Jimmy Pearson, the talented centre, crossed for the opening try. 'You might have heard the yell in Princes Street!'

noted the *Evening News* with enthusiasm. Hawick hit back and, after a desperate struggle on the line, Tom Fiddes plunged over for the equalising score. 'The joy of Hawick's supporters knew no bounds,' reported the *Hawick News*. Both sides came close to scoring in the dying minutes, but the match ended in a 3-3 draw. Over sixty years later, when he was interviewed for the club's centenary history book, Sandy Burns, the Hawick captain, was adamant that his side would have won if Walter had been playing. The youngster's pace was badly missed against much faster opponents and he might have been elusive enough to penetrate their tight defence.

With Walter restored to the side, the other big test for Hawick was against the reigning Scottish Champions Edinburgh University at Craiglockhart on 13 March 1909. Now languishing in the nether regions of the club game, the University was once one of Scotland's leading sides, having won or shared the unofficial title five times between 1900 and 1910. In a 'fierce struggle' against Hawick, the University took a 10-0 lead early in the second half and the visitors' championship hopes seemed dead and buried. But gradually the Hawick forwards began to get on top and supply more ball for the talented three-quarters to exploit. Walter Sutherland scored two splendid tries in quick succession, the first from a skilful back move across the field, the second after a great run by Tom Neil, who slung out a long pass to Walter, allowing him just enough time and space to squeeze in at the corner flag. With two minutes remaining, the veteran internationalist Walter Forrest broke the defence and sent John Haig, the left wing, in for the clinching try, which Walter converted. At this time, players were not supposed to show their feelings, but some of the Hawick team could not hide their elation at the winning score. 'The players made no effort to conceal their delight,' observed the *Evening News*, 'and Haig was heartily congratulated.' Likewise, around the ropes, the travelling Hawick support, which was estimated at around 700 people, 'had passed through all the gradations of emotion between black despair and delirious delight.' Hawick held on for the remaining seconds to win 13-10. Lacking some of their key men and playing tough opponents away from home, it had been a great fight against the odds. As *The Scotsman* concluded: 'It was one of the most exciting matches seen in the district for years.'

Two weeks later, Hawick brought the curtain down on the season with a convincing 27-0 victory in a friendly game against Melrose at Mansfield Park. Playing at centre, Walter 'was the hero of the afternoon', scoring three tries and kicking a conversion. One of his tries was a classic, as the *Hawick News* reported: 'Almost tackled near the touchline, Sutherland doubled back and, with the whole Melrose team in front of him, he eluded the grasp of man after man and safely grounded the ball over the line – a really magnificent effort.' Hawick ended the season with only one defeat, which meant that the Scottish Championship was shared with Watsonians, who had also lost only once. This was a great achievement for the Hawick club, only the second time in almost fifty years that they had won the big prize. Walter Sutherland's contribution was recognised at the annual club dinner in May 1909. The club president, Alex Jardine, said that in Robert Lindsay-Watson and Walter Sutherland Hawick had the best two three-quarters in the country. 'The one had got his cap and the other was getting his shortly,' claimed Mr Jardine amid rousing cheers. Walter was only eighteen years old, but he 'was an old head on young shoulders… [with] a great future ahead of him on the football field'.

The next two seasons, 1909/10 and 1910/11, were less successful for Hawick. The championship-winning team started to break up and several key players were lost, either through retirement, emigration or the lure of professional rugby. For many working men the chance of earning a decent salary doing something that they enjoyed and were good at was very hard to resist. In late 1909 Tom Helm, a hard-working forward, left to play for Oldham, and Tom Neil, the talented quarter-back, went to Hull Kingston Rovers. Neil's departure seems to have been partly influenced by his lack of recognition from the higher authorities. He had played in several Scottish trial matches and was clearly a very good player, but his final call never came and he lost patience, believing that his lowly social status counted against him. 'There is a small chance of a working man to obtain his international cap,' he later complained in a newspaper. Around this time several professional clubs, including Barrow-in-Furness, approached Walter Sutherland and tried to attract his services. However, he refused to sign, knowing that he had a big future in the amateur game and also that he had secure employment and good prospects.

Hawick were unbeaten in the first half of season 1909/10, but their play was unconvincing, hardly the stuff of reigning champions. After an uninspiring draw with Langholm in October, the *Hawick News* observed: 'The Teries will have to improve if they are to maintain their position.' History repeated itself at the New Year's Day game when Heriot's FP once again smashed Hawick's unbeaten record. In front of an enormous crowd of holiday revellers, the Hawick selectors tried a modern half-back formation rather than the old-fashioned quarter-backs, but the experiment was not very successful. The visitors ran out easy winners 12-0 while the Hawick back division dithered around in confusion. 'Their great three-quarter line was under a cloud,' reported the *Hawick News*, 'and the cloud was pretty dense on one or two of them.' A fortnight later a weakened Hawick team, playing without Sutherland and Kyle, fell to a six-try hammering against Royal High School FP at Corstorphine, a defeat that ruled Hawick out of the championship race.

Meanwhile the Border League had still to be decided. In February, Hawick lost at home to Gala, which in turn opened the door for Jed-Forest, who would draw level if they beat Hawick at Riverside Park in early March. The *Evening News* commented:

Hawick have fallen from their high estate. Their back division has never been the same since Neil and Burns dropped out. Young Sutherland has maintained his high reputation as a scoring three-quarter. Without him in some matches the 'Greens' would have been in a sorry plight.

On the night, Walter could not prevent his side going down to a four-try defeat against a rampant Jed-Forest. Walter did his best to turn the tide, 'tackling, running and kicking in grand style', but the home side enjoyed a 'complete triumph'. Both sides were now joint-first in the League table, but no play-off game was arranged so the title was shared between them. Points difference was not then taken into account.

By the beginning of season 1910/11 Walter was firmly established as one of Hawick's leading players, adored by the Mansfield supporters. At twenty years old, he was a Scottish internationalist and capable of sensational play. 'Sutherland's remarkable powers are proving Hawick's greatest asset,' said the *Hawick News* in October 1910. 'Given the least shadow of a chance, Sutherland can bring victory to his side in marvellous fashion, and the glamour of one remarkable score succeeds another, Saturday after Saturday.' As Walter progressed through the ranks, his father Alex became more involved in the Hawick rugby club. Like many proud and ambitious fathers, he would have been anxious to push his son's case and provide him with as much support as possible. Alex became an honorary vice-president of the club, which involved paying a special membership fee, and he served on the committee for two seasons before the First World War. In the 1910s, the monthly meeting of the club committee was held in one of the back rooms of the Imperial Hotel.

In the opening match of season 1910/11 against Heriot's FP at Goldenacre, Walter was described as being in 'mid-season form'. He opened the scoring with a penalty goal, then caught a loose ball and sprinted clear to score. Straight from the restart, he was away again, swerving past several players for his second try. By the end of October 1910, Walter had already scored 9 tries. One of the best was scored against Gala at Mansfield Park, as this report indicates:

Sutherland scored the best try witnessed at Mansfield for many seasons. Gala were press-ing when 'Suddie' picked up and made off. He dodged opponent after opponent and, after running nearly the length of the field, planted the ball behind the posts amid great cheering.

Despite Walter's presence, season 1910/11 turned out to be a disappointing one for his side. 'Hawick looked a stronger lot on paper than they proved on the field,' said the *Hawick News*. After a good start, the team fell away and was too incon-sistent to challenge for the Scottish Championship. The highlight of the season was the win over Edinburgh Accies (13-3) at Mansfield Park on 11 February 1911. Walter was in fine fettle, collecting a kick across the field and romping past two men to score. However, he was faulted for his over-eagerness, which often took him in front of the passer before he had received the ball. In the Border League Hawick suffered two defeats, to Melrose (3-10) and Gala (3-8). Unlike the previous season, the title was decided with a special play-off match against Melrose at Riverside Park on Wednesday 29 March. In front of a huge crowd, the Melrose forwards 'dribbled and rushed in fine style' and starved the Hawick back division for a fine 10-0 victory.

The summer of 1911 was a productive one for Walter. He kept himself in shape by playing some cricket, but most of his energies were devoted to sprint-ing. In July, he won a Scottish athletics cap to go along with his rugby honours while in September he was appointed as the captain of Hawick for season 1911/12. The start of a new season is always a time of promise and anticipa-tion, the chance for a fresh start. There was plenty for the Hawick players and supporters to look forward to, especially in the Border League. As the budding poet 'G.H.' put it in the *Hawick News* in October 1911:

> *The Melrose champions – doughty lads –*
> *And Gala strive their ain to haud,*
> *And 'Jethart's Here' tak' up the fray*
> *Aye eager, ready come what may;*
> *We welcome them wi' a their means*
> *To tackle oor great lads, 'The Greens.'*
> *The fleet lads frae the muckle toon*
> *Tho' often routed, never froon,*
> *And Souter lads frae Ettrick vale*
> *Intent to mak' the auld clubs quail;*
> *But nane will show their heels sae clean*
> *As oor brave callants wi' the green.*

Then forwards, halfs, the way is clear
Be worthy o' the name ye bear,
Yer captain's guid advice tak' heed,
He and his 'threes' are there at need,
And prood we'll a' be then I ween
When victory crowns the far-famed green.

Hawick began the new season in cracking style, winning a nine-try romp against Heriot's FP at Goldenacre (37-0). Fit and raring to go after his summer on the track, Walter 'ran with unchallengeable speed', combining well with his centre partner Carl Ogilvy and helping himself to three tries and three conversions. 'Messrs Ogilvy and Sutherland were always ready for a scamper and will drill holes in a few defences this season,' warned the *Evening News*. As the season progressed, it was clear that the Hawick three-quarter line of Sutherland, Ogilvy, Burnet and Lindsay-Watson was one the best and quickest in the country. Walter Sutherland was faster than ever and thanks to his summer work he seemed to have added several yards to his pace. Playing against Gala in mid-October, Sutherland and Lindsay-Watson 'ran rings around the opposition', Walter scoring three tries in the 20-3 win. Hawick kept up their form as the winter drew in and the pitches got heavier, proving that they were more than a fair-weather side. In November, 1,200 supporters travelled by train to The Greenyards to see Hawick take on the reigning Border Champions Melrose. In a fierce battle, Walter was in 'sparkling form', always ready with the dangerous cross kick and helping his side to a narrow 3-0 win. By December, Hawick were still unbeaten and Walter had scored 12 tries. Unfortunately, the forwards could not match the quality of the men outside them. The week before Christmas, Hawick went down to a surprise defeat against Stewart's FP at Inverleith (8-18).

The second half of Walter's season as captain began well, but gradually it tailed off. On 30 December 1911 he was in great form in a friendly match against Jed-Forest at Mansfield Park, as the *Hawick News* reported:

It was Sutherland's game all over and the internationalist but served to again demonstrate how great an asset he is to the team he captains. His equalising try may be described as a marvel… our opinion is that no other player in Scotland could have beaten the Jed team in the manner Sutherland did, with as little room to work on.

On New Year's Day 1912, Hawick finally halted Heriot's FP's run of success in the festive fixture, John Haig scoring the only try after a 'strenuous effort' by the Hawick forwards. Two weeks later, Hawick achieved their second win over the reigning Border Champions Melrose (13-3). Walter led by example, running half of the length of the field and rounding the Melrose full-back to score a great try. The Edinburgh bogey struck again in early February when Hawick lost to Edinburgh Accies at Newfield (11-21). Hampered by injury, the great three-quarter line played below form, although the Accies were 'not a bit scrupulous' about their methods. 'Plenty of points, a great deal of feeling, and not much football pretty aptly sums up the game,' concluded the *Hawick News* gloomily. Now out of the championship race, Hawick were left to concentrate on the Border League. The following weekend there was a big win against Gala at Mansfield Park (30-8). Walter, who had been left out of the Scotland team to play Ireland, had a point to prove to the selectors. As the *Evening News* put it, he was, 'in rattling good form, had no fewer than fourteen points. He was simply great, scoring two tries, dropping a goal, and converting two tries.' The Border League was won at Riverside Park, when Hawick narrowly beat Jed-Forest (9-8). The season had been reasonably successful, but it was felt that the team had never quite lived up to its potential. The *Evening News* summed up the campaign: 'Hawick, this season, have developed a habit of raising expectation, which, at the crucial moment, they have been unable to fulfil.'

By season 1912/13 Hawick had unearthed some talented young players, particularly among the forwards, which seemed to bode well for the future. James Morgan, who was popularly known as 'Teddy', was powerful in the scrums and good at controlled dribbling. A native of Cockermouth who came to Hawick through the textile trade, Morgan won a cap for England in 1920. Willie Anderson was described as 'a thorough "Teri" and a typical West-Ender', full of 'impetuosity and dash, with a fearless disregard of the hard knocks sometimes going'. Andy Robson was a 'dashing young forward' and another who cultivated 'the art of close dribbling', never content just to hoof the ball aimlessly away. David Fiddes followed his brother Tom into the team and was 'a smart young forward'. Finally, there was John Corrie, a native of Langholm and a strapping six-footer who liked to read romantic poetry in his quieter moments. Under the expert eye of Bill Kyle, Corrie was developing into a player of great promise who seemed destined for the highest level.

Captained by Robert Lindsay-Watson, the performances of the team in season 1912/13 were described as being of 'a somewhat vacillating description'. Hawick kept their place as the leading team in the Borders and retained the Border League with only one defeat, but against city opposition the side was less successful, winning only three out of nine games. On a brighter note, the season brought some welcome innovations. In late September, Hawick were invited to open Gala's new ground at Netherdale, the club having moved away from their old hilltop home at breezy Mossilee. Always anxious to see something new, the match attracted great interest and it was estimated that over 5,000 people crammed into the ground, including three trainloads from Hawick. The prediction of one home supporter that it would be 'nae bloomin' picnic for Hawick' turned out to be fairly accurate, especially in the first half when the big Gala pack put the visitors onto the defensive. Walter Sutherland was caught napping at one point, failing to deal with a bouncing ball on his own line and allowing the Gala winger W.L. Hunter to score the first try on the new ground. 'Something of a gift,' fumed the *Hawick News*. Walter made amends by scoring two tries to spoil the Gala party (6-5), his genius tipping the scales in an evenly balanced match. The decisive try came from a good passing movement by the three-quarters, allowing Walter just enough space to beat two men and score at the corner. 'For rounding-off movements he is still unexcelled, his second try being a grand one,' said the *Hawick News*, forgiving him for his earlier mistake. The following weekend against Clydesdale at Mansfield Park, Walter ran in four tries, the third a beauty, as the *Hawick News* reported:

Getting the ball past midfield, Sutherland created a sensation by shaking off man after man in marvellous fashion, quite half-a-dozen players having their hands on him to no avail, and the Hawick right winger finished off by scoring the finest try of the afternoon.

Another new feature of the season was that Kelso moved up to senior club status and joined the Border League, expanding the competition to seven teams. Previously the Kelso club had lived out a rather precarious existence among the juniors. Several players had been forced to move away to other clubs to further their game. Walter Forrest, Carl Ogilvy and Speirs Black were talented three-quarters from Kelso who played for Hawick, the first two winning international caps while playing for the Greens. In October 1912 all three turned out for their hometown against their former colleagues. Wound up for the big occasion, Kelso created a sensation by winning the match 11-3. 'The Kelso team was a revelation to everyone,' commented *The Scotsman*, 'and they won grandly and deservedly.' The Hawick forwards were well beaten and it was only the vigilance of Billy Burnet and Walter Sutherland that prevented a much higher score. The news of Hawick's demise was quickly telegraphed to the Yetholm Shepherd's Show. When Sir George Douglas, a local bigwig, announced the final score, it was received 'amid enthusiastic cheering', although back in Hawick it was greeted with 'great consternation'. The return match two weeks later at Mansfield Park created great interest. Fancying their chances of an historic double, Kelso brought a small army of supporters, including their mascot Jethart Wull, an eccentric character who paraded the field with a black-and-white umbrella. In a very tight game, Walter was closely marked by his former colleagues, but in a moment of inspiration in the second half he managed to escape and score the winning try. 'The crowd were immensely delighted by the marvellous manner in which Sutherland beat the redoubtable Ogilvy,' glowed the *Hawick News*. Two weeks later Walter was at it again, scoring a great try against Melrose:

[He] raced round in his own bewildering fashion, swerved past Adkins and Brink beautifully, only to find himself grasped by the arm by the winger, Austin. This last brought Sutherland to a full stop but, by a supreme effort, he threw off his tackler and was again off like a shot to score a marvellous try... his score sent everyone home talking of his marvellous skill in leaving opponents in the lurch and scoring tries under circumstances which most players would find it difficult if not impossible to overcome.

Later in the season there was another new challenge for Walter when he was moved from the right wing to the centre, a position he would occupy for his thirteenth and final cap the following year. The intention was to bring Walter more into the game and also to make space for a talented new winger called Frank Beatson, a former soccer player and professional sprinter and a man with great potential. Walter's first appearance in his new position was against Gala on 15 February 1913 when he partnered Billy Burnet in the centre and Robert Lindsay-Watson on the left wing. The experiment was a great success, Hawick winning 10-0 and Walter scoring in customary fashion:

This versatile three-quarter gave a brilliant exhibition in his new position. In the first period, when Gala were in the ascendant, Sutherland tackled like a Trojan; and his try in the second period will not soon be forgotten. A number of Gala players were fairly mystified by the way in which Sutherland zig-zagged round about them, finishing a magnificent dodging run with a try.

Walter stayed at centre for the rest of the season, but returned to his old position on the right wing the following year.

The final season before the outbreak of the First World War was again relatively successful for Hawick. Under the captaincy of internationalist Billy Burnet, the Border League was retained and the club did well in the Scottish Championship, although injuries to several players disrupted the end of the season, none more so than Walter Sutherland, who managed to make only 11 appearances for the Greens. He was still a very young man, only in his early twenties, but perhaps all of those endless hours standing around in the damp and cold, the constant hard knocks and the incessant soakings were beginning to catch up with him.

As usual the season kicked-off in late September against Heriot's FP at Goldenacre. This had become the traditional opener to the Scottish rugby season, attracting a large crowd, including 'many notabilities in the rugby world' and day-trippers from the Borders. Heriot's scored the only try of the match thanks to some fast following-up after a sliced drop at goal, giving them a well-deserved victory (3-0). With Bill Kyle now retired, the Hawick forwards were outplayed and lacked direction and leadership. Starved of ball, the Hawick backs had little opportunity to show their pace. 'It was lamentable to see a man of W.R. Sutherland's scoring power so completely neglected,' grumbled the *Evening News*. Walter had one great effort to save the game, but was beaten by the bounce of the ball. Making his first appearance in the three-quarter line was William Ker, a promising young player from a well-known local family who had attended Teviot Grove Academy and was one of Walter's best friends.

Matters quickly improved and Hawick went on to chalk up some good results. Walter was in fine fettle in the drawn match against Clydesdale at Mansfield Park, scoring yet another sensational try. As the *Hawick News* reported: 'Sutherland picked up in a loose bit of play and, taking a wide sweep, the internationalist passed man after man up the touchline to finish with a brilliant if unexpected try.' Walter missed the Kelso game in late October through an ankle injury, but was back for the important league match against Melrose at The Greenyards on 8 November. He scored two great tries in Hawick's 16-0 win, the first a brilliant solo effort from his own half, as the *Hawick News* recorded:

Getting the ball from Burnet in his own '25', he never stopped until he had planted the ball between the posts. Opponents had him hemmed close to the touchline, and it seemed almost impossible for him to get past the Melrose full-back. Sutherland dashed up towards him, suddenly halted, had Hunter completely at sea, and all in the twinkling of an eye had dodged past his opponent.

Fortune however can change very quickly on the rugby field. At the end of the game, Walter was chasing back to cover a loose ball when disaster struck:

In almost the last minute of the game, when Hawick were defending, Sutherland, in running to touch the ball down, had the misfortune to twist his ankle and it gave way. He was carried from the field and subsequently conveyed home by motor. The news of the accident to the popular Hawick three-quarter was received with universal regret. This is the second time this season that Sutherland's ankle has given way, and there seems nothing for it but that he must give it a rest. Sutherland paid a visit on Sunday to Mr Crosbie, bonesetter, at Dumfries, who found a small bone out of position and, after putting it right, recommended a cessation of football for several weeks.

Despite Walter's absence, Hawick continued to grind out victories and were still unbeaten when he returned to the fray on 20 December for a friendly match against Edinburgh Institution (a side which later became known as Melville College FP). He was back to his old self, full of running and scoring two tries to help his side to a convincing 23-5 win. On New Year's Day 1914 he scored another fine try and did some 'brilliant stopping' to gain revenge over Heriot's FP (6-3). He missed the next match against Royal High School FP and also the final Scottish trial at Inverleith because of a slight strain in his right leg. Walter was Hawick's icon, a priceless asset to his side and a constant menace to the opposition. Being forced to concentrate on Hawick's danger man meant that there were gaps for other players to exploit. As the *Hawick Express* recognised in January 1914:

Sutherland inspires confidence. He can accomplish feats no one else can, and it is safe to say that the opposition side cannot afford to take risks when they know he is on the carpet.

There was great relief when Walter was announced fit enough to take part in the season's crunch match against Watsonians at Myreside on 17 January 1914. By this stage both sides had lost one game and the winner would be best placed to take the championship. There were also a number of international places up for grabs. Like their great encounter in 1909, the match attracted huge interest. Two special trains were run from the Borders, crammed with excited supporters, all eager to see the big game and cheer their heroes on. 'The utmost hilarity prevailed en route,' noted the *Hawick Express*. 'In passing through Galashiels the colour of the "Greens" was very conspicuously displayed.' It was estimated that over 6,000 people packed into Myreside, said to have been the largest crowd that had ever watched a club match in Scotland up to that time. 'Never before did so many Borderers travel with a club,' said the *Evening News*. 'Never before did the slope in front of the Watsonians pavilion appear such a solid mass of humanity.'

   Unfortunately, it turned out to be a rather one-sided affair, 'an extremely hard and fast if not especially brilliant game'. It was also a rough match, 'at times a bit too strenuous,' commented *Scottish Referee*. Straight from the kick-off, the Watsonians forwards took a tight grip on the game that they never relinquished, forcing some defence 'of true Border grit'. The visitors suffered a major blow in the first half when 'Bottler' Wilson sustained a shoulder injury. Pluckily he stayed on as long as he could, but eventually was forced to retire; later finding out that he had broken his collarbone. Watsonians opened the scoring with a soft try after a defensive fumble by the Hawick full-back Andy Turnbull, who dithered over a cross kick on his own line. They went further ahead when 'Gus' Angus, the international centre, made a blind-side dash from a scrum, feeding his winger Hyslop who touched down near the posts for a converted try. At half-time Watsonians led 8-0 and Hawick were clearly up against it. Despite the loss of Wilson, the visitors bravely fought back in the second half. Bill Burnet moved to stand-off, Fiddes came out of the pack and Walter Sutherland moved into the centre. Hawick came close when Frank Beatson kicked ahead and would have scored with a kinder bounce. Later, Walter broke away on a typical mazy run but lost his footing with only the full-back to beat. Gradually superior numbers began to tell and, towards the end, Watsonians ran in two further tries for a convincing 16-0 win. Hawick had been unlucky to lose one of their key men, but they could have few complaints at the final outcome. As *The Scotsman* saw it, the Watsonians forwards 'absolutely controlled the game and, as a consequence, their backs did practically all the attacking.' The Hawick forwards had done well in the open but their play was too often reckless and poorly directed. The final score would have been much higher if had not been for the outstanding defensive work of the Hawick team, who 'stuck to their work in a most praiseworthy manner'. Despite his recent injuries Walter Sutherland came through this stiff test, although he was groggy at the end because of all his hard work. 'The speed of Sutherland and his safe tackling had much to do with the keeping-down of the Watsonians score,' reported the *Evening Dispatch*. 'He was here, there and everywhere.' Similarly, the *Evening News* commented:

Burnet and Sutherland never lost heart, and Sutherland was as often on one wing as the other. The international put in a tremendous amount of chasing after Watsonians and the fact that he stood the strain seemed to indicate his recovery is all right... he had no opportunity of showing offensive powers.

But these were small crumbs of comfort. After so much expectation, the match had been a big disappointment, especially for the visitors. As the *Hawick Express* put it, the news of the defeat 'was received in the town like the intelligence of a great disaster'.

Walter was destined to make his final appearance for his beloved Greens two weeks later on 31 January 1914. On a foul day, a mere handful of hardy spectators huddled together in the Mansfield grandstand to see the 6–3 win over St Andrews University. The following weekend, playing against Wales in Cardiff, he badly injured his ankle and had to miss out the rest of the season, although he was back for some of the sevens in April. Meanwhile, several other players such as Teddy Morgan, Tom Wilson and Billy Burnet were also on the injured list and, as a result, Hawick fell away, winning only three out of seven of the remaining games. The season ended on an optimistic note. The club had invested in a sparkling new pavilion, which was 'handsome and replete with every modern convenience' and would be ready for season 1914/15. At the annual dinner in May, there seemed every reason to feel confident about the future. However, other events were about to intervene. The pavilion would be largely unused for the next five years as young men turned their attention to a greater game.

four

THE THISTLE

Walter Sutherland made thirteen appearances for Scotland between 1910 and 1914, eight on the right wing, four on the left and one, his last, at centre. Since rugby went professional in 1995, international matches have become very common. A modern player could easily win thirteen or more caps in a single season. However, internationals were much rarer before the First World War and caps were much harder to win. Normally, Scotland played only three or four times a year with only an occasional visit from a touring side. Walter Sutherland's record is impressive by the standards of his day and made him one of the most experienced Scottish players of the Edwardian era. Up until the 1970s, the name 'W.R. Sutherland (Hawick) – 13' still appeared on lists of leading Scottish cap winners. Moreover, the First World War cut short Walter's international career and it is likely that he would have won more caps if the war had not intervened.

This chapter looks at Walter Sutherland's early games for Scotland, but before doing so it's worth examining the nature of international rugby at this time. In Scotland, the international game was controlled by the Scottish Football Union (SFU), which was founded in 1873 and was based in Edinburgh. The Scottish team was selected by an eleven-man committee of the SFU, which included one representative from the south of Scotland. In retrospect, the work of the selection committee seems to have been erratic and much given to passing whims and fancies. There was little concept of a squad of players who regularly trained together, gradually getting to know each other's characters, strengths and weaknesses, and style of play. Instead the Scotland team was thrown together with a minimum of preparation and the players barely knew one another before they took the field. To make matters worse the selection committee was constantly chopping and changing the side, especially after a defeat. Players were given little chance to prove themselves and, as often as not, they were dropped if they had a poor game or put in a low-key performance.

Walter Sutherland's experience of the unpredictable nature of the selection committee was fairly typical. Over the course of his career, he was dropped from the side three times and he played with a total of sixty-five different players, an average of five new faces per match. This included six different centre partners, nine different stand-offs and the leadership of six different captains.

Before 1914, Walter Sutherland's club Hawick was one of the less fashionable sides in Scottish rugby. The international team was drawn mainly from a small and exclusive circle of Former Pupil clubs, the universities, the professions, the armed forces and from around the Empire. The historian Derek Birley has described this system as 'the royal road to international selection'; a world where the old school tie attracted influence and where having the right family, school or business connections brought favours and privileges. International rugby was first played in 1871 when Scotland beat England at Raeburn Place in Edinburgh, but it took thirty years before the social base of the Scottish team started to expand, and then only very slowly. In 1890, Adam Dalgleish, a factory worker from Galashiels, became the first player from the Borders to win an international cap (although some players with Border connections had played before then). In the Borders, where the game attracted a broad social following, it was felt that the SFU was biased against local players and often ignored them in favour of lesser men. As the *Hawick News* commented in January 1909: 'When it comes to a vote between a Borderer and a city player... the city player goes in every time.' The most notorious case was in the mid-1890s when the SFU ignored the claims of the Hawick half-back pairing of Matthew Elliot and David Patterson, who were said to be the best in the country. Both players were capped, but never together. It was widely held that the SFU hierarchy could not bear the thought of two men from working-class backgrounds playing a pivotal role in the Scottish team. A handful of working-class players did make it, but they had some additional hazards to face, having to adapt quickly to middle-class norms and behaviours. After each international match, a dinner was held in honour of the two teams and officials. Guests were expected to have their own evening suits, to know how to use the correct cutlery and how to select fine wines and foods: not the kind of things that working-class people had the luxury of worrying about. According to one story, Matthew Elliot, the Hawick quarter-back of the 1890s and a dour Border stonemason, was posted missing at an after-match function. He was eventually found in the hotel kitchens, happier to mix with the folk from his own class rather than the people upstairs. It was the same story in England. At an after-match dinner in 1891, John 'Buff' Berry, a builder's labourer from Lancashire, had never seen table jelly before.

He shouted to a waiter: 'Heh chap, pass us sum uv that doddering stuff.' It was not to his liking and he shoved it into his jacket pocket. Goodness knows what the RFU made of him.

In fairness, the elitist nature of Scottish international rugby probably owed more to accident than design, the product of ignorance and a lack of imagination rather than deliberate bias. The Scottish Borders were slightly removed from the centre of decision making, and the existence of a vibrant club scene and the Border League might have encouraged the Border clubs to live in a world of their own. Whatever the truth of the matter, a few bald statistics give an insight into the make-up of the Scottish team in Walter Sutherland's era. Seventy-nine players played for Scotland between 1910 and 1914, almost half of whom were university students or graduates. At this time, most people left school at fourteen and a university education was reserved mainly for the privileged few. When Scotland played France in January 1911, six different universities were represented in the Scottish team (Oxford, Cambridge, Edinburgh, Glasgow, St Andrews and Durham). Over a third of the players in Walter Sutherland's era came from either a medical or a military background, playing for such clubs as the London Hospitals or the United Services. The Scottish team also drew heavily on players from outside of Scotland, almost half playing for clubs south of the border, in particular London Scottish or Oxford and Cambridge Universities. By contrast, only six players from Border clubs were capped between 1910 and 1914. When Scotland played Wales at Inverleith in 1913, ten of the Scottish team played their club rugby in England, including the captain Fred Turner from Liverpool.

Another rich source of talent for Scotland was the Empire, and in particular colonial students at British universities. The Scottish selectors have recently been criticised for choosing players who are unknown to the rugby public and whose connections with Scotland are very tenuous. Home-grown players have been ignored in place of outsiders from England or the Southern Hemisphere. Surprisingly, there is nothing new about this. Before the First World War, the selection committee was unabashed about bringing in players from around the globe, often at the expense of local boys, including Walter Sutherland. Several players from overseas were parachuted into the Scottish team without having worked their way through the system, which led to many disparaging comments in newspapers and from rugby supporters. The rules of eligibility for Scotland were something of a running joke. As one music hall comedian put it: 'The qualification for Scotland is very strict. I knew a man that got his place owing to the fact that his grandfather, who was a South Sea cannibal, once lunched off a Scotch missionary.'

If the system was weighted against players from the Borders, it should not obscure the fact that many of those who did play for Scotland were very talented and able. So who were the outstanding Scottish players of the time? The domination of Watsonians in the club scene was reflected in the international team. When Scotland played France at Inverleith in January 1910, the entire three-quarter line came from Myreside. In Walter Sutherland's first international, against Wales in February 1910, there were six Watsonians players in the side, including four in the back division. Watsonians had two brilliant three-quarters in Angus 'Gus' Angus and Jimmy Pearson. It was rare for a Scottish side of this era not to feature one or both of them. Gus Angus made eighteen appearances for Scotland over eleven years and also won international honours at cricket. A strong, resolute runner and a good passer of the ball, he was very alert and quick to seize anything that came his way. Angus had a powerful personality and, as the club historian remarked, was 'somewhat aloof [and] a very intense person'. In contrast, his colleague Jimmy Pearson was disarming and engaging with a great sense of humour and a love of fun. Known as 'Jimmy P' or 'the darling of Myreside', he was a fast and subtle player with a great body-swerve and a natural ability for all sorts of games. Pearson was a very slight man who weighed just over nine stone, but despite this he managed to win twelve international caps between 1909 and 1913. Another notable player from Watsonians was Eric Milroy, who won his first cap against Wales in 1910 alongside Walter Sutherland. A modest and deeply intelligent man, 'Puss' Milroy was an ideal link player and one of the first specialist scrum-halves in the Scottish game.

There were also some great forwards around at this time. John MacCallum, another Watsonian, won an astonishing 21 caps between 1905 and 1912. He was the son of a Highland minister and a naturally unassuming man with 'a rather casual appearance', but on the field he was a polished and clever player. Small and light for an international forward, MacCallum was very fast, a first-class dribbler of the ball and a reliable goal kicker. He was also a very good captain, despite being a man of few words. The most that he ever said to his charges on the field was: 'Harder boys, harder!' John 'Jock' Scott was a gifted player from Edinburgh Accies who won the last of his 26 caps in 1912. Scott was a versatile and mobile forward, a proverbial workhorse who knew the game inside out. Fred Turner was another highly regarded forward, who played in almost every Scotland team between 1911 and 1914. A product of Sedbergh School and Oxford University, Turner was famous for his hard work and inventiveness.

Despite its rather exclusive nature, Scottish international rugby was enjoying growing popularity in the Edwardian era, partly because the game had become more open and attractive to watch. In March 1910, the *Evening News* commented: 'As the seasons pass, the interest in internationals increases amazingly.' The *Glasgow Herald* observed that rugby was 'booming' at the highest level. In its early days international rugby had attracted only a few hundred spectators, standing together around the ropes of an open field. Originally Scottish rugby had no permanent home, but instead rented the Edinburgh Academy cricket field at Raeburn Place. By 1895 the old ground had become inadequate for the size of the crowds, despite the erection of temporary grandstands. Subsequent internationals were played at Old Hampden Park in Glasgow and the Powderhall Stadium in Edinburgh. In February 1899 a new purpose-built ground was opened at Inverleith in the north of Edinburgh. Apart from club matches Inverleith now stands empty and rather forlorn, but it was once a marvel of its age. Along the western side of the pitch there was a handsome grandstand, which could accommodate 2,500 spectators. There were more seats in the enclosure, but the majority of spectators, around 20,000 at maximum, stood on the 'bob terracing' that encircled the rest of the field. In modern terms, an international at Inverleith was similar to The Greenyards during the final of Melrose Sevens: the prosperous in the grandstand and the enclosure, the rest of the crowd standing on grassy bankings around the field. Spectators entered the ground either from Ferry Road or Kinnear Road in the south. Inverleith had only very basic facilities for the players and instead they changed into their playing kit at their hotel and carried their boots to the game. At this time international teams were based at the Caledonian hotel at the west end of Princes Street, about a mile away from Inverleith, and they were taken to the ground in horse-drawn charabancs. The players made their final preparations in a separate pavilion situated behind the Inverleith grandstand, which often formed the backdrop to the traditional team photograph before the match. The pavilion had only six wash-hand basins with cold water and, at the end of the game, the players had to climb back into their transport for the long pull up to their hotel and eventually a hot bath.

By 1910 international days in Edinburgh had become something of a minor cult, a foretaste of the great days at Murrayfield. By today's standards, the attendance at Inverleith was quite small, usually around 25,000 people at most. It is worth remembering that, as David Parry-Jones has pointed out, spectator sport of this kind was still a relatively new phenomenon, having only begun within the previous forty years. Special trains were run from Glasgow and the Borders, and there were a handful of supporters of the visiting teams. However, the majority of the crowd came from Edinburgh and the Lothians. Reporting the English match in March 1910, the *Glasgow Herald* captured the slow build-up to the game in the streets of the capital:

Edinburgh, under the hypnotic influence of a championship rugby encounter, begins to gather at the four utmost corners in tiny streams, which converge on Princes Street, and the volume of traffic selecting Hanover Street as the easiest route of access to Inverleith pours down its inclined ride by motor, cab, car and on foot.

There were suggestions that some people went to Inverleith only for the occasion, just to see and be seen, and were not really interested in watching the game. Spectators could pay for admission at the gate, but tickets for the grandstand and the enclosure were in short supply and were often sold out weeks beforehand. Inevitably this led to criticisms that the interlopers were using their influence to grab the best seats for themselves and squeeze the genuine supporters out of the game. In 1910, the *Evening News* observed: 'Anxiety to watch leads to criticism in the way in which the tickets are vended.' Shortly after the First World War, Inverleith would be condemned as too small and Scottish rugby would move to a much larger stadium, Murrayfield, in the west of the city.

Across from the grandstand, one of the features of Inverleith was a commodious box for newspaper reporters, which had its own telegraph facilities, ready to rush the news to an insatiable reading public. As rugby became more popular, newspaper editors began to give increasing amounts of space to reporting matches and the latest rugby news. Anybody who studies rugby from the Edwardian era cannot help but be struck by the factual nature of these reports, which provided blow-by-blow accounts of the action, often in the kind of detail that can now seem excessive and downright boring. The difference was that the Edwardian rugby enthusiast had no other way of following a game. There were no radios, televisions or computers, and moving films were still in their infancy. Some short films of rugby matches were made, but these flickering images were merely impressionistic and not intended as reportage. Modern spectators take it for granted being able to watch live coverage of games, often from the other side of world, beamed straight into their living rooms, but the original experience of rugby was either by playing it or by going to a game. Once the action had taken place, it was gone forever and only existed in their memories and in newsprint.

Like the club game, international rugby had a strong moral sense about it. It would be insulting to say that the players did not try their hardest to win, but they were expected to perform like gentlemen, never to break the rules or to argue with the referee, to be humble in victory and gracious in defeat. What counted was the experience of taking part, of giving one's best for one's country. They would not have understood the attitude of modern players or coaches who routinely say that winning is the only thing that matters.

This low-key approach was reflected in the pre-match rituals. In modern rugby, players take the field having been psyched-up in the dressing room, eyes flashing and nostrils flaring, adrenaline on over-drive, ready to do battle. In contrast, before Scotland played England at Twickenham in March 1911, the two sides met together for a spot of lunch. When Scotland played South Africa in November 1912, the two teams had their photograph taken together, arms draped around each other's shoulders, rivals and comrades together. This kind of behaviour was also extended onto the field. When a Scottish player broke clean away against England in 1913, he had his shorts ripped off in the move. Instead of running on to score, he threw away a wild pass and stopped to protect his modesty. Likewise, swearing on the field was frowned upon. When Scotland played England in 1914 the leader of the English forwards, Harold 'Dreadnought' Harrison, exhorted his troops: 'Like hell, England; like hell!' By the standards of the time, this was strong stuff, pushing the limits of acceptability. Few players dared to swear openly, which would have earned them a good ticking off from the referee. However, it would be wrong to be too naïve about international rugby. It was a passionate and physical affair, men going against men. National pride was at stake and tempers sometimes boiled over. Some games were very rough and ill-tempered affairs, such as Walter's final international against Wales in February 1914, where there were 'no drawing-room tactics' and the Scottish captain David Bain had to have six stitches inserted into a head wound. But, in general, international rugby was much less intense than it is now and there was less pressure on the players to win at all costs.

At the heart of Scottish rugby was the formidable James Aikman Smith, the SFU secretary, who was known as 'Napoleon' for a lot more than his diminutive stature. Smith was a reasonable and decent man who got on well with the players, but his word was law and it took a very brave person to disagree with him. The greatest heresy in rugby was professionalism and the idea that players might be paid for their efforts. Anything that hinted at professionalism was ruthlessly suppressed and a player found guilty of taking money was ostracised from the rugby community with little hope of return. Writing in the *Rugby Football Annual 1913/14*, E.R. Ward, the rugby correspondent of the *Morning Post*, commented:

In the fight for sport pure and simple, there are a good many of us who are charged with ultra-amateurism, but it will be a bad day for rugby when the 'ultra-amateurs' withdraw from their vigil.

The different attitudes between the Edwardian game and today are shown over the matter of playing equipment. Modern players are cosseted with armfuls of free playing kit, training gear and all sorts of leisure clothes, some of which suppliers pay them to wear. Originally the Scottish rugby authorities were notoriously reluctant to give the players anything for nothing. The Scottish international outfit consisted of a navy blue shirt with a white embroidered thistle on the left breast. Players had to pay for their shirts, which meant that they often wore the same one for more than one season, even when it had lost some of its colour in the wash. When Jock Wemyss was selected for Scotland in 1914 he received a parcel from the official outfitters containing his shirt. He was delighted until he noticed that it also contained an account for 7s 6d. At this time, Scottish players did not wear numbered shirts. Numbers were thought to encourage individualism, for players to think of themselves rather than the team. Spectators and newspaper reporters might have benefited from numbers, but that was beside the point. In 1912 the SFU was aghast when the touring South Africans proposed to play the international match wearing numbered shirts. They were told in no uncertain terms to remove them. The exchange of shirts with opponents at the end of matches was not encouraged, although some players did so secretly. In the 1920s Jock Wemyss brought thistle badges from the suppliers, sewed them onto blue jerseys and sent them to his opponents. Players also had to provide their own shorts and a pair of dark stockings. Scotland might have worn red stockings at this time rather than the familiar navy blue, but in either case the players sported a motley collection of leg-wear. The only item that the players received for free was their international honours cap. Caps were based on the headgear worn by the boys at public schools, where the codified rugby game had originated. Scottish caps were made of light-blue velvet embroidered with silver braid and piping. The players received only one cap irrespective of how many times they played, which was embroidered with a silver thistle and the year of their first international appearance (in Walter Sutherland's case '1910'). Some clubs. such as Watsonians, also awarded caps and it was common for players to wear these when they went to a game.

That year, 1910, marked an important turning point in international rugby. Between 1900 and 1910 Wales had been the premier side, winning six championships and five Triple Crowns, largely due to the Welsh mastery of the passing game. England, traditionally the strongest country, had been weakened by the 'Great Schism' of 1895, which had ripped the game apart between the traditional amateurs and the Northern professionals. By 1910 a new generation of English players had emerged, principally from the Harlequins club, who dragged England out of the doldrums. In January 1910, England beat Wales for the first time in twelve years, going on to win the championship and begin a long era of English domination. For Scotland, the new century had started successfully. The Scots had won three Triple Crowns between 1901 and 1907, but by 1910 the memory of those great years was starting to fade into history. Walter Sutherland's era, immediately before the First World War, was rather an undistinguished one for Scotland. The Scots won only six out of twenty matches, including three wins against newcomers France, who were still finding their feet at international level. In fact, the only really significant victory of this period was against England at Inverleith in March 1912.

To win a Scottish cap, the talented or ambitious player had to climb a short representative ladder of district and trial games, which were held in December and January. Pre-eminent among these was the annual Inter-city match between Edinburgh and Glasgow, which had claims to be the oldest representative fixture in the world and which city people regarded as the most important fixture in the domestic calendar. Meanwhile, the leading players from the Border clubs came together as the South of Scotland, who played an annual match against their counterparts in the North of Scotland and other occasional matches against county sides. A full inter-district championship, with the South also playing against Edinburgh and Glasgow, was not introduced until the 1950s. Following the Inter-city and the South v. North games, there were two further trial matches at Inverleith that also involved the 'Anglo' players from outside Scotland.

Walter Sutherland's first taste of senior representative rugby came on 27 November 1909 when he played on the wing for the South of Scotland in a one-off match against a London Scottish and District XV at Richmond. Seizing his chance with both hands, Walter put on a good display, creating both South tries with his strong, elusive runs from deep. *Sporting Life*, for one, was impressed with the young Hawick winger:

In W.R. Sutherland, the South have a wing three-quarter of very great promise. Sutherland is a speedy and resolute runner, while the way he passed after he had paved the way for each of the two South tries by a strong run shows that Sutherland is a 'heady' player.

Two weeks later, playing for the South against the North on a sodden pitch at Gala, Walter caught the eye again, this time showing his adaptability in difficult conditions. 'Sutherland of Hawick attracted most attention,' reported the *Evening News.* 'Although to the small side, and light, he played a hard game and, appreciating the needs of the moment, he dribbled like an Association player.'

On Christmas Day 1909, Walter joined his Hawick colleague Carl Ogilvy in the Provinces XV against the Anglos in a trial match at Inverleith. His smart running and sound defence attracted some rave reviews. 'The outstanding figure in the Provinces team was Sutherland... an interesting player to watch,' observed the *Evening News. Scottish Referee* went further: 'Sutherland is the best wing three-quarter in Scotland at the present time.' In January 1910, Walter took part in the second trial at Inverleith, this time playing for the Rest XV against the Cities. He had 'several gallant attempts to score' and impressed with his kicking, but he didn't see much of the ball and some onlookers had doubts about his lack of experience and stature. His time would come, but he was too raw for the team to play France.

As it turned out, Walter's first cap was by the back door. He was not selected for the game against France at Inverleith in January 1910, which led to 'some pardonable grumbling' in Hawick 'at the blindness of the committee of the SFU'. The man in possession was the uncapped James Dobson, a solid winger from Glasgow Accies, who was chosen for both the France and Wales games, but a recurring ankle injury meant that he had to drop out each time. Dobson's loss was Walter's gain. In early February it was announced that he would take Dobson's place in the side to play Wales. The news was received in Hawick with great enthusiasm and a sense of civic pride that a local boy had reached the highest level. As the *Hawick Express* commented: 'No selection has ever given greater satisfaction on the Borders.' In the city, the *Evening News* was generous in its praise of the young Hawick player:

He is one of the youngest and most promising players ever capped... If he is slight of build, he makes up for any deficiency in weight by his speed and resource... On all the Border fields, as well as in the city, his attractive play has been favourably commented on, and there will be many outside the followers of the Hawick club who will rejoice at the promotion of so versatile a player.

The *Evening Dispatch* commented:

Sutherland made a very excellent impression in the only match (South of Scotland v. London Scots) in which we have seen him in the south. He showed great pace, cleverness and resolution in leading up to the South's winning try and, if he has the right tempera-ment for big matches, may be a great success.

Further afield, the Glasgow-based *Scottish Referee* was also pleased at Walter's selection:

In club football, Sutherland has been a huge success and, in the final trial, he did not belie his reputation. He is a young player, but one of the right kind, possessed of grit, speed and general ability… He is accustomed to play much the same game as has been practised in Wales, and is the very man for the place.

Wining his first cap was a great achievement for Walter. He was just past his nineteenth birthday and he had been playing junior football less than fourteen months earlier. He had overcome the doubts about his lack of size and physical presence by determination, enthusiasm and natural ability. As the *Hawick Express* put it, Walter's selection, 'was a clear illustration of the supremacy of skill and science over dash and weight'.

In 1910 there were few cars or buses and passenger aircraft were unknown, so rugby teams had to rely on the railway network to travel about the country. This could result in lengthy, even torturous journeys, especially for large, bulky men squashed together in cramped railway carriages. For the Welsh match in 1910, most of the Scottish team and officials left the Caledonian Station in Edinburgh on the Thursday afternoon, travelling by the 2 p.m. West Coast Express to London via the Midland route. The Glasgow and Border players, including Walter and his Hawick club mate Bill Kyle, were picked up in Carlisle. Unfortunately a derailment further up the line delayed the train by over two hours and it was not until the small hours that a weary Scottish party arrived at their hotel in London. The following morning, having collected the players from London Scottish, the team made its way to Cardiff via Paddington and the Severn tunnel. Having set up camp in their hotel in the centre of the city, some of the players took part in a practice 'kick about' in the Sophia Gardens Park, which was the closest thing that the team had to a training session together.

On the morning of the match the players had little to do except watch the crowds slowly gathering in the streets. By 1910, international rugby was attracting a large and passionate following, especially in Wales. Recalling the internationals of his boyhood in the early 1900s, the former Cardiff stand-off Danny Davies wrote:

Westgate Street was thronged. There was little or no horse-drawn traffic to hinder the crowds. The motorcar had not 'arrived' and police, some of them on horseback, ushered the fans towards the entrances to Cardiff Arms Park. Vendors were at large selling hot chestnuts and potatoes from smouldering coke fires, their stands magnets for urchins in winter. Others sold sweets, peppermints, bull's-eyes, brandy snaps and pasties from their baskets and even pepsin chewing gum. Their cries were well known in and around the field.

Spectator facilities at the Arms Park were very basic and mostly consisted of unreserved standing areas. The early birds queued for hours before the gates opened, some of them overnight, ready to rush in and claim the best places. Most of the crowd was solidly behind Wales, but the Scots had their own contingent of travelling supporters. For the first time, a special train for 'football enthusiasts' had run from Edinburgh and Glasgow. Looking on from the Cardiff press box, a roving reporter from the *Hawick Express* noted:

Half an hour before play was to be started the first good hearty cheer was raised when the national flag of Scotland was displayed by a 'Teri' in the crowd... The 'bagpipes' were much in evidence, and they too showed they were possessed of lusty lungs.

A train was also run from London and other specials brought crowds of supporters from the rugby hotbeds in the Valleys. Rugby was different in Wales. It attracted the kind of support that had more in common with Scottish football rather than the rarefied worlds of Inverleith or Twickenham. One Scottish reporter who attended the match was the pseudonymous 'Mickey Doolan', who contributed regular articles to the *Evening Dispatch* in the curious style of an Irish music hall comedian. Whatever his true identity, Doolan captured something of the spirit of early international rugby. Reporting from Cardiff in 1910, Doolan wrote:

Wilsh futball isn't like anny av the futball av the other countries. Dublin can turn out a show av sthrapin' bhoys and high stheppin' gurls that can run Inverleith to a dead heat; and London when it comes to a parade can about bate the wurrld. We hadn't anny fancy trimmins' at Cardiff. There was no young prayppossin' faymales prancin' about in high-heeled shoes. There was nuthin' av a frivilous natchure. We all stood up to the top of our boots in a sea av mud like a herd av cattle... Bands av desprit lookin' men came from the Rhondda Valley.

Many of the spectators whiled away the time by singing along with the brass band. At one point the band played *Stop Yer Ticklin' Jock*, the latest music hall hit from Harry Lauder. 'The crowd,' it was reported 'took up the refrain with something approaching gusto.' The only item of what we now describe as rugby memorabilia that was available to spectators was the official programme. In Wales, this was a flimsy eight-page effort costing 1*d*. It contained the team line-ups, but was mostly advertising, which in turn shows us the kinds of things that Edwardian rugby followers were concerned about. Templar Malins Dentistry was recommended for false teeth, which were 'unsurpassed for natural appearance

The official programme lists the teams for Walter's first international, Wales v. Scotland in February 1910. Spot the mistake. (Scottish Rugby Union)

and durability'. A drink called Kizla (non-alcoholic) was 'The Great Life-giving Tonic', especially good for footballers, but spectators might have preferred the products of Hancock's Brewery or Percy E. Cadle's tobacconist's shop with its Sweet Malt and Virtulat mixtures. Opposite the ground, the Palace Theatre had twice-nightly shows, conveniently situated for spectators straight after the game. By contrast, the Scottish rugby programmes of this era had no advertising, apart from a single line about Messrs Mackenzie and Sons of Lothian Road, who made the match ball, and the up-market Forsyth's Department Store on Princes Street, the official 'outfitters'.

At this time few rugby grounds had hot baths or showers. The players at Cardiff changed into their playing kit in their hotel, then walked around the Glamorgan cricket field to the ornate twin-turreted pavilion in the west corner of the ground, dressed in their overcoats and carrying their boots. Final preparations were made in the visitors' dressing room, which was said to have a strange atmosphere that affected the performance of visiting teams. Certainly very few of them won at Cardiff at this time, including the mighty New Zealanders who lost 0-3 to Wales in 1905. Shortly before kick-off, the Scottish team lined up for the traditional pre-match photograph. In the back row the fresh-faced Walter Sutherland looks on nervously, his fair-hair closely shaven and his long football knickers held up with a stout leather belt.

In their preview articles the Scottish newspapers tried to find some straws to cling to. The team was an experienced one and most of the players had already played against Wales. The intimacy of the Watsonians three-quarter line was an advantage while Walter Sutherland, the new cap, 'has good style and, though slightly built, is plucky'. However, there were doubts over Douglas Schulze, the London Scottish full-back, who had been picked on reputation rather than current form. Likewise Jim Tennent, the West of Scotland quarter-back, had merits 'entirely of an individualistic kind'. The Scots had a poor record in Wales, where they had not won since 1892. Speaking bluntly, the *Evening News* said: 'To predict a win for Scotland would be merely to betray blind, unreasoning optimism.'

But the Welsh also had some problems. The previous month, on their first-ever visit to Twickenham, they had gone down 6-11, their first loss to England for fourteen years. Rugby-loving Wales was shocked. The selectors made five changes to the team to play Scotland, including dropping the legendary Swansea half-back Dickie Owen. There was a recall for the erratic genius Percy Bush, veteran of the 1905 win against New Zealand, and a first cap for his Cardiff partner Willie Morgan. In the centres there was also a first cap for Billy Spiller, the crash-tackling Cardiff policeman, who would be partnered by the multi-talented Billy Trew from Swansea, a gifted and graceful runner who captained the side. At full-back, Jack Bancroft was 'hotter than ever'. 'Every man in the pack is a worker,' said the *Evening News* 'and the majority are distinguished by dash in the open.'

At this time, Cardiff was the coal-exporting capital of the country, a front-runner for the title 'Coalopolis'. It was a grey and grimy kind of place that suffered from an appalling climate. The weather at the beginning of 1910 had been particularly severe, with gales and storms raging across much of Europe. Even at the best of times Cardiff Arms Park was notorious for its mud bath of a pitch. Typically, the match was played on a miserable day under a grey, leaden sky and in incessant drizzle. As one reporter wrote: 'The rain was coming down as if it wanted to wash everything into the Bristol Channel.' Within minutes of the start, the pitch churned-up and play was reduced to 'a steaming mass of forwards wallowing in the mud'. In his inimitable style, Mickey Doolan wrote that by half-time 'the teams were like a squad av stokers that had been pulled through a mud-dredge, and a committee av inquiry was forrumed to scrape the players and find which was the referee.' Despite the pre-match predictions, the

Welsh forwards took control, playing the Scots at their own game, keeping it tight and denying the speedy Scottish backs any chance to pass or run. In the quagmire, the Welsh footwork was irresistible and laid the foundation for the four Welsh tries, two in each half. The Scots were almost entirely on the defensive, although the forwards managed a few rushes before the end. As the *Evening News* reported: 'The Scottish back division, chosen for combination in attack, spent the afternoon in throwing themselves among big feet at a "slithery" and elusive ball.' Their cause was not helped just after half-time when Jim Tennent, one of the quarter-backs and a key man in the side, was carried off with a badly gashed thigh. Old-fashioned pointed studs had caused the injury, which led to improved regulations being introduced the following season. By the end of 'a poor affair', Wales had run out easy winners 14-0. Scotland had put up a brave defensive display, especially the previously lamented Schulze at full-back. According to *The Scotsman*: 'There was at no time any disposition to show the white feather.' The Welsh had adapted much better to the conditions while the Scots seemed 'clogged and hampered' and had lacked zest and 'ginger'.

On a day not suited to open, running rugby, Walter Sutherland's name does not appear very much in the match reports. Our old friend Mickey Doolan was impressed by his courage in defence and his bravery at the feet of the Welsh forwards. 'The slim youth from the Borders was wurrkin' overtime fur all he was wurrth,' wrote Doolan, 'grippin' arrumfuls av mud on the off chance av sometimes findin' the ball.' The fullest review of Sutherland's play was given in the *Evening Dispatch* and shows that despite the conditions he managed to give a good account of himself:

W.R. Sutherland was another who was exceedingly useful in defence. His saving was of a most daring character, and no more is likely to be said about his lack of robustness. He was continuously cropping up when Scotland was in a tight corner. But we cannot recall that he got a single pass during the whole game.

Scottish Referee was more critical of Walter's performance:

Sutherland was not a brilliant success, but he played well at times... Had different conditions prevailed the Hawick representative would have done better. On one occasion he just missed scoring by the skin of his teeth... Had the footing been better a score would have resulted.

Walter's inexperience had been exposed in the build-up to the third Welsh try. One of the Welsh forwards cleverly kicked diagonally along the ground and over the Scottish line, catching Walter flat-footed, and allowing Baker, his opposite number, 'who knew what was coming, to dash past Sutherland to score'.

Stung by their defeat, the Scottish selectors changed tactics for the next international against Ireland at Belfast by selecting a more defensively-minded team. Among seven changes, Walter lost his place to a new cap called Donald Macpherson, a colonial from Otago who had played for New Zealand against Australia in 1905 but who was now a student in London and eligible for Scotland through his family connections. On the other wing James Dobson, whom Walter had replaced against Wales, finally won his first (and only) cap. Scotland had a good 14-0 victory in Belfast, including a try for Dobson, who was subsequently selected for the final match against England at Inverleith. But once again fate intervened. Two days before the England game, Dobson had to drop out through injury and Walter was recalled to the side, this time on the left wing.

For most followers of the game the annual match between Scotland and England was the highlight of the rugby calendar. Stretching back to 1871, the match was the oldest fixture in the world, 'the senior international' or 'the event of the rugby year'. Many members of the Scottish team had strong English connections, having been educated south of the border, living and playing in England and sharing the same attitudes and opinions, barely distinguishable from their English cousins apart from their accents. Nevertheless, the annual encounter had a certain spice about it, a reflection of the ancient rivalry between the two countries. As the *Glasgow Herald* put it: 'The stern relations which once existed between the two countries are now replaced by chivalrous rivalry in manly exercises, but something of the old spirit remains, and a Scottish triumph over the old enemy brings great joy.'

The England match in 1910 aroused greater interest than ever. Tickets for the Inverleith grandstand, which were priced at a hefty 5s, had sold out several months before the game. Special trains ran from Glasgow and 'for the Border enthusiasts', straight to the station at Granton, leaving spectators with a short walk along Ferry Road. Walter Sutherland would be 'assured of plenty of vocal support'. The crowd was estimated at around 25,000 people, one of the largest that had ever attended a rugby match in Scotland. As *The Scotsman* observed: 'It was the same well-dressed crowd that found its way by rail, taxi and other cab/cable car, and hansom to the field, which, lit up by brilliant sunshine, was in splendid condition.' The crowd was entertained for two hours before kick-off with a selection of cheery and stirring melodies from the boys of Dr Guthrie's Brass and Pipe Bands, who ended with 'appropriate airs' as the teams came out onto the pitch.

England presented a formidable challenge to the Scots. At stand-off they had one of rugby's most innovative tactical thinkers in Adrian Dura Stoop, who played for Harlequins. Stoop was a new style of rugby player who is credited with the development of specialist half-back and midfield play. He had studied the recent successes of the other countries and had adopted many of their ideas. Stoop realised the importance of good handling and that a pass delivered at the right moment could draw out the defence. Previously, back play had been about individual skills, based on one-to-one confrontations and trying to beat opponents either by bursting through, swerves or 'dodging'. Stoop recognised that with practice, quick thinking and teamwork, players could create space for each other. He was one of the first men to recognise the value of different lines of running and how subtle adjustments in the angles in midfield could produce openings for the fast men to exploit. It is also believed that Stoop was first British player to introduce code numbers for different moves among the backs.

Adrian Stoop's influence was written all over the 1910 game with Scotland. The match began brightly for the home team, who came close to scoring on several occasions and might have scored an early try if Gus Angus, the centre, had held an awkward pass. Gradually the English backs began to show their paces, cutting holes in the Scottish defence, only to be stopped by last-ditch tackling. 'Unless something extraordinary happened,' noted *The Scotsman*, 'the Scottish team was in for a drubbing.' And then, for a few moments, it did, largely thanks to Walter Sutherland. The Hawick wing stole away round a scrum and went off 'in a capital run', making ground before punting ahead. Jimmy Pearson retrieved the ball and beat several opponents before passing back to Walter, who was forced into touch deep in the English half. From the lineout, the Scottish forwards won possession and, after sustained pressure, Donald Macpherson, the right wing, scored from 'a short but sharp wriggling run', planting the ball at the foot of the post. John MacCallum converted to put Scotland 5-0 in front. Shortly afterwards Macpherson came close again, but then England hit back with a try straight off the Harlequins training field. Getting possession in midfield, Adrian Stoop set off on a great run, passing to his brother Freddie, who drew the defence to send his fellow Harlequins centre John Birkett on a clear run to the posts, 'amid rousing English cheers'. The try was converted to leave the scores level at the interval (5-5).

The Scots began the second half encouragingly with Tennent, Pearson and Sutherland 'showing to advantage', but soon there was only one team in it. As *The Scotsman* lamented: 'To those with a knowledge of the game it was evident that the speedy and bustling English halves and three-quarters only required to get their noses in front and the game would be all over.' The visiting forwards took control, providing a steady stream of possession for their backs to run the Scots off their feet. The Stoop brothers and Birkett were in fine fettle and England scored three more tries. After the final try, *The Scotsman* observed: 'Though fully ten minutes remained for play thousands of the spectators were leaving the ground.' Those who left early missed one of the tit-bits of the afternoon. A move started by the Scottish centres fed the ball to Sutherland, who ran brilliantly from the halfway to within a yard of the English line, only to be bundled into touch by a despairing tackle. 'Towards the end the Scottish revived,' said one report. 'Sutherland, making a big sprint, which F.M. Stoop half-checked, and Birkett, running up, smothered by a tackle that fairly grassed Sutherland.' Some writers claimed that Walter would have scored 'with a little more weight at his disposal'. At the end of a lively but slightly disappointing match, England ran out winners 14-5. The final score had flattered the Scots as some careless passing had denied the visitors further tries.

The win gave England the championship title for the first time since 1892. 'With one accord Scotsmen are ready to recognise that the Englishmen were their masters in practically every department of the game,' said *The Scotsman* with honest realism. The Scottish forwards had started well, but had faded away in the second half. Both Scottish quarter-backs had played poorly, especially Jim Tennent, whose passing had been laboured and whose fitness was suspect. 'Some of Tennent's passes out from the scrum would have excited comment if executed by a novice in a club match,' noted the *Evening News*. In the centres, Angus and Pearson had been guilty of dithering and delay. Up against bigger and faster men, some of the Scottish tackling had been 'rank bad... and must have made some of the old players present squirm'. The formation of the three-quarter line had also been faulty and allowed the visitors too much space to exploit. By contrast, the Scottish wings had been well policed and easily forced into touch.

Despite having to put up with poor service from his centres, Walter Sutherland was one of the few Scottish players to emerge from the match with credit. The pitch had been dry and firm, allowing him more opportunity to show his paces than his previous international in Wales. Reviewing the match, the *Evening News* favourably commented:

The only member of the line who attracted attention was Sutherland. Once or twice his inexperience was apparent, but he alone of the Scots approached the alert and lively style which characterised the English three-quarters. Once in the second half, he came very near a score and, if his tremendous effort had succeeded, many apart from Borderers would have been glad for the young Teri's sake.

Similarly, Walter's commitment and tenacity impressed the *Evening Dispatch*:

Alone of the four, Sutherland came out of the game with an enhanced reputation. He tried hard to turn the tide… There was a determination about his work which was in striking contrast to the down-hearted appearance of some of his confreres, and both in defence and attack he was the one shinning light in the Scottish back division… Apparently the young 'Teri' had made up his mind to show that J.D. Dobson was not to be so badly missed after all. What a pity it was, after getting so near, that he did not score… It would have been a fitting conclusion on a most meritorious display on the part of the Borderer.

Under the heading 'A Few Bright Spots', *Scottish Referee* commented:

If there were many conspicuous failures on the Scottish side, there were some who not only struggled hard to avert disaster, but who added to their reputations. Of the backs, none did better than Sutherland, who showed such clever play at times as to make it certain if all goes well with him he will be the recipient of further international honours… It was a pity that he didn't get more to do. The sympathies of the crowd were with him when he missed that try in the second half by inches only.

Walter had also attracted the attention of the international selectors. Following the meeting of the International Rugby Board in early April 1910, it was announced that Walter and four other Scots had been chosen to join the British team to tour South Africa in the summer, the forerunner of the British Lions. This was a great honour for Walter, considering he was only nineteen years old and in his second season of senior rugby. The British tour involved twenty-four matches, including three Tests, which meant being away from home for many months. The tourists did not, of course, receive any payment so they had to rely on private means or charity donations. Apart from privileged university students, few people had the option of taking several months away from work just to play football. Faced with these problems, Walter had little choice but to turn the invitation down.

If 1910 had been disappointing for Scotland, then 1911 was catastrophic. For the first time, Scotland lost all four international matches in a single season, including a humiliating defeat against France, who had just arrived on the scene, and also an eight-try drubbing against Wales at Inverleith. Over the four matches thirty-six different players were used, including sixteen new caps, a sure sign of panic among the selectors. Only two players, both forwards, Fred Turner of Oxford University and Rowland Fraser of Cambridge University, played in all four games. It was truly a black year for Scotland. As *Rowan's Rugby Guide* gloomily concluded at the end of the season: 'Never since Scotland began playing international rugby has she had a season of such bitterness as that of 1910/11.'

Walter Sutherland's representative season began in mid-November 1910 when
he played for the South of Scotland against a Monmouthshire County XV at
Mansfield Park. The visiting team included three Welsh caps and two players from
the British team that had toured South Africa in the summer, but they could not
stop the South recording a good win 17-3. In front of his home crowd, Walter
scored 'a clever try after eluding two or three opponents'. The following month,
the annual South v. North trial match was held in Aberdeen. In part, this was a
'missionary effort' on the part of the SFU to spread the gospel of rugby among
the heathen north but, according to *The Scotsman*, 'it cannot be said that success
crowned their enterprise'. Only a few dozen people turned up at Pittodrie football stadium where the South, perhaps affected by the general air of lethargy, went
down to an unexpected 9-8 defeat. *The Scotsman* rebuked the indifferent natives:
'Had the local football public, who are so keen on the Association game just now,
turned out, even as a matter of curiosity, they would have had the pleasure of seeing the men of the North gain a well-earned victory.'

Scotland's first match in 1911 was against France in Paris. Since the 1950s,
France has been one of the superpowers of world rugby, but before the First
World War they were considered to be a second-class rugby nation, something
like the Italians at the beginning of the twenty-first century. In 1911 France had
played international rugby for only five years. They had gone down to some very
heavy defeats and had not won a game at international level. The first Scottish
contact with France had taken place in April 1898 when an Edinburgh XV,
which included four Scottish caps (and one Irish), had travelled to France to play
a Paris XV. Two years later, a French XV made a return visit to Scotland, playing
a game at Myreside in Edinburgh and also at Hamilton Crescent in Glasgow.
However, it was only in January 1910 that the first full international fixture
between the two countries took place. The SFU was rather dismissive about the
French, partly because French rugby had a strong air of professionalism about
it. Indeed, it was only from 1947 that caps were awarded against France. Before
1914 the French match was considered to be little more than a trial game for the
sterner tests to come, an opportunity for the selectors to try out some promising players and tactical experiments. In 1911, there were six newcomers in the
Scotland side and several players who were selected outside their normal club
positions. Winning his first (and only) cap, the Gala player Borth Tod was chosen
at full-back, although he normally played at stand-off for his club. Jimmy Pearson,
the Watsonians centre, was selected on the left wing, a position in which he had
very limited experience.

However, the team also had a sprinkling of seasoned veterans, notably
at stand-off where Pat Munro from London Scottish returned to make his

eleventh international appearance. Munro was a fine all-rounder who had a very accurate punt and uncanny powers of anticipation. Several writers regarded him as one the best half-backs of his generation, but his sporting career shows how rugby, even at the highest level, was regarded as a mere distraction from the serious business of life. Munro was first capped against Wales in 1905 while a student at Oxford University. He had an outstanding match against South Africa in 1906, supplying the punt for Ken Macleod's famous try, but in 1907 he was posted to the Sudan with the civil service and rugby had to take a back seat for four years. In 1910, Munro returned to Britain on leave of absence and at once got back into the Scottish team. He made three appearances in 1911, captaining the side each time, but straight after the Irish game he headed back to the Sudan.

For the French game, the bulk of the Scottish team left Edinburgh on Thursday 29 December 1910, spending the night in London before taking the train to the coast and then the ferry and another train to Paris. Staying in the Hôtel Moderne, the team had two full days in Paris before the match, plenty of time to take in the sights and celebrate the New Year. The mood in the camp was optimistic, although there was an awareness that the French were improving and would be more than mere pushovers. As *Rowan's Rugby Guide* advised at the beginning of the season: 'The Frenchmen are learning and, it is quite possible, may do a great deal better in this season's match against the Scots, at Paris.' Nevertheless, it was felt that the greater experience of the Scots would see them through. As the *Glasgow Herald* said: 'If Scotland do not treat the match too lightly, they should win comfortably, and little anxiety as to the result need be felt.' The Scots would have been heartened if they had known of the chaotic preparations of their opponents. On his way to the match, Charles Vareilles, one of the French centres, had stepped off the train to grab something to eat only to see the train move away at once, leaving him stranded on the platform. The French reserve, André Francquenelle, also missed his train, leaving the selectors to hurry around looking for a replacement. At the last second, the hapless Francquenelle turned up, breathless and dripping in sweat. He quickly stripped into his playing kit and ran onto the field a couple of minutes after the game had started.

The match took place on a wet, greasy pitch at Colombes Stadium, home of the Racing Club de France, just north-west of Paris, in front of a passionate crowd of around 10,000 people. John MacCallum opened the scoring for Scotland with an unconverted try, but then to everyone's surprise France hit back with three tries in quick succession, the second by right wing Pierre Failliot, a big, long-striding winger who was nicknamed 'La Locomotive' for his devastating runs. In an exciting game with lots of movement, Pat Munro dummied through for a converted try to leave Scotland trailing 8–11 at the interval. In the second half the Scots kept up the pressure, but stout French defence prevented further scoring until Jimmy Pearson on the left wing dropped a goal from an acute angle. Soon afterwards Pearson turned from hero to villain when he kicked the ball straight into the arms of Failliot, who found himself in acres of space, using his pace and power to shake off Walter Sutherland and beat Borth Tod to score the decisive try. The Scots fought back in a desperate attempt to save the game. Abercrombie scored an unconverted try so that France led by a single point. The closing stages were played at a frantic pace. As the *Evening News* reported: 'As the minutes passed… Scotland just failed to score by frequent forward rushes, independent efforts, or pressing advances, the possibility of a French win began to dawn… a possibility always referred to in more or less jocular terms.' Right at the death Thomas Young, one of the Scottish centres, knocked-on a simple pass right on the French line, which would have given his side victory. But it was not to be and, at the final whistle, the French crowd went wild with delight, celebrating their country's first-ever victory in international rugby. Maintaining a stiff upper lip, *The Scotsman* observed: 'When "no side" was sounded and the victory was won, the enthusiastic demonstrations which followed was too characteristically French for description.' It was a result that shook the rugby world.

Scotland's failure in France was similar to their surprise defeat to Italy in February 2000. They had been expected to win, but had fallen to the up-and-coming side, who were determined to make their mark. What had gone wrong? Why had the Scots lost a match that they should have won? Carelessly they had underestimated the French, who had played better than anyone could have guessed. In fairness, some erratic refereeing from Mr Jones of England had not helped the Scottish cause. At this time it was very unusual to criticise a referee but, for once, the Scottish press did not hold back. The *Evening News* claimed that the referee had given the French an 'extraordinary latitude' in lying offside and obstructing men off the ball. Similarly, the *Evening Dispatch* noted the 'doubtful methods' of the French defence and that the referee 'conducted the match in terms of the tradition that France must be allowed a latitude in certain respects denied to other sides'. *The Scotsman* grumbled about the 'generous treatment' of the referee towards the French irregularities, claiming:

[It] was the direct cause of Scotland failing to win the match in the concluding stages. Time after time the Scottish forwards swept through the French backs, only to lose tries either by the speedy French backs securing the touch or by a man being held back by a French back when dribbling… The Frenchmen were never penalised for these very palpable breaches.

In fact, the Scots had contributed greatly to their own downfall. The forwards had been good, especially in the loose, but the three-quarters had played poorly, failing to combine effectively and being guilty of some laboured passing and throwing away several clear chances. Close to the French line, Thomas Young had given a careless pass, which was intercepted and led to the first French try. The French had also capitalised on the lack of physical presence among the Scottish backs and the folly of playing small men against much bigger opponents. Out of position on the left wing, little Jimmy Pearson had to mark the ground-rumbling Pierre Failliot who, at fourteen stone and six feet tall, had run straight through him. Walter Sutherland had also had a disappointing game, often being indecisive and caught in two minds. Like Pearson, he had been exposed when trying to stop much bigger, heavier opponents, especially in the build-up to the fourth French try. Walter had managed to get his hands on Failliot, but he been easily shaken off and the Frenchman escaped. *Et voilà!*

Scotland's humiliating defeat meant that heads rolled, Walter Sutherland's among them. The selectors made seven changes for the next game against Wales at Inverleith, including three changes among the three-quarters. In the 'queer and often harsh ways of the Scottish selectors', Walter was left out of the final trial on 21 January. His place in the team to play Wales went to a virtual unknown called D.M. Grant, who was still a schoolboy at Elstow School in Bedfordshire. In the event, things went from bad to worse. Despite home advantage and a good first-half showing, Scotland slumped to a 32-10 defeat against a rampant Wales, their heaviest defeat in history. Another six changes were made for the next match against Ireland at Inverleith. Walter was again left out in the cold, but there was some joy for Hawick with the selection of Carl Ogilvy. A strong individual player with sound defence and great kicking powers, Ogilvy was a Kelso player who had joined Hawick from Melrose in 1910. At this time Kelso was still rated as a junior club and Ogilvy, like several other players, had been forced to look elsewhere to further his chances. His best position was reckoned to be at full-back, but in their wisdom the selectors had chosen him to partner Gus Angus in the centre. Scotland had an improved performance against Ireland and Ogilvy had some determined runs, but they could not prevent a 16-10 win for the visitors, the Scottish defence letting in four tries.

In the wake of Scotland's third defeat in a row, the selectors drew up the barricades. The announcement of the team to play England at Twickenham was twice delayed, which led to some angry finger pointing in the press. The *Evening Dispatch* commented: 'It looks like as if the Scottish selectors had got into a state of "blue funk" over the selection or non-selection of the side to play England.' Similarly, the *Hawick Express* said that the selectors were in 'pitiable straits'. Local opinion in the Borders was that Scotland's problems came from the failure to pick the best Border players. Bizarrely, the selectors went to great lengths to get players from outside the country, but ignored an abundance of talent right under their noses. 'It has been a common sneer,' said the *Hawick Express*, 'that one of the first qualifications for the Scottish team is that of being an "Outlander"… is there any need for going abroad for talent?' The Scottish back division had been poor and lacking in combination. The solution then was to pick the Hawick three-quarter line en masse: Sutherland, Ogilvy, Burnet and Lindsay-Watson, arguably the best line in the country. The forwards had also struggled. It was time to add some Border steel by recalling Bill Kyle and giving a first cap to Tom Wilson, the Hawick forward. 'It is from pure "cussedness" that they have kept him [Kyle] out,' claimed the *Hawick Express*. Another complaint was that Walter Sutherland, the local favourite, had lost his place to an unknown English schoolboy. Even the Edinburgh newspapers agreed that Walter was clever and resourceful, and one of the most talented backs in the country. It was inexplicable to leave him out of the side.

In Hawick, there was an eager sense of anticipation at the announcement of the team, which was finally revealed just a few days before the match. A large crowd gathered at the Imperial Hotel, hungry for news and hoping to be among the first to congratulate their host and his pride and joy. When the team was posted on the notice board at around 9 p.m., there was great satisfaction that Walter Sutherland had been recalled on the right wing and that Carl Ogilvy had kept his place, but been moved to full-back. As usual, the selectors had sprung a few surprises and there was also some shaking of heads. 'The work of the committee will not give very general satisfaction,' said the *Evening News*. The three-quarter line contained 'a big element of risk' about it. Walter would play outside George Cunningham of Oxford University, who was normally a half-back. Controversially, Stephen 'Beak' Steyn, a South African student at Oxford University, was selected for his first cap on the left wing. A humorous and likeable fellow, Steyn had a Scottish mother and was renowned for his ability to throw bread rolls across his college quad into any window opposite. But jolly student japes did not endear him to the Scottish rugby public, who were suspicious of his tenuous links with Scotland. 'He might almost be called an interloper,' commented the *Evening Dispatch*, reflecting the popular feeling that Steyn and players like him were keeping true Scots out of the side. As the *Evening Dispatch* observed:

Why however should he, a South African and of Dutch extraction, find it so simple a matter to secure a Scottish cap, while others born in Scotland, who have played all their football in Scotland, find it impossible to do so?

The side to play England had three new caps among the forwards, including David Bain from Oxford University, who would go on to win 11 caps. However, there was no place for the veteran Hawick forward Bill Kyle, who had been tipped to captain the side. On the plus side, the selection committee had finally seen the light and chosen the Watsonians half-back pairing of Henderson and Milroy. The experienced John MacCallum, 'the doyen of the side', was recalled as captain.

In their preview articles, most writers agreed that Scotland's only hope was their great record in England. Scotland had not lost on English soil since the 12-3 defeat at Manchester in 1897, a run of fourteen years without a loss, a statistic that now seems barely credible. This was Scotland's first visit to the new English ground at Twickenham, which had been opened in late 1909 at a cost of £20,000. Twickenham subsequently became one of the great cathedrals of rugby, but in its early years it was something of an experiment on the part of its owners, the Rugby Football Union. Twickenham was then little more than a village in the country, yet to be swallowed up by suburban sprawl. The ground was a long way out of the centre of London and it was by no means certain that the general public would make the long trek just to get there. Few people at this time had access to private cars or their own transport. Indeed, the ground originally had parking spaces for only 200 'motors'. Special trains ran to the nearby Twickenham station and the London United Tramway Company laid on a 'frequent service of cars' from central London. Nevertheless, some members of the Scottish press contingent, who were based in the heart of the metropolis, grumbled about having to make such a long journey. Having finally made it, the press found that there was no telegraph line and they had to depend on a relay of small boys to take their reports to the local post office. The Scottish players were also confused by their new surroundings. Some of them could not find the entrance to the ground and had to walk over local allotments to get in. Once inside, they could admire the two single-decker stands along the touchlines, which accommodated 6,000 seated spectators. Another 24,000 people could be squeezed into the enclosures and on the terraces at both ends of the field. Unfortunately there was only one outlet for refreshments, run by Stansfield & Co. of Fulham, which must have caused an unsightly scrum after the final whistle.

Possibly discouraged by the awkward situation or the unsettled weather, a smaller crowd than expected turned out although, as the *Evening News* remarked:

The official programme for England v. Scotland in March 1911, Scotland's first visit to Twickenham. (Scottish Rugby Union)

'The Scottish element was conspicuous in the crowd… Scottish favours were in great demand, and some perfervid Scots waved miniature flags.' A few hardy souls had made the long journey from Hawick to support their local heroes. As 'Borderer's Account' in the *Hawick News* observed: '"Go on, Hawick!" was often heard from the stand, and also "Go on, Suddie!" showing even 300 miles away the Border spirit prevailed.' Playing into the wind, Scotland kicked off at 3.35 p.m. and within seven minutes they were a score to the good. This was a thrilling moment for Walter Sutherland, his first international try. *The Scotsman* takes up the story:

In a scramble for possession the ball came to the hands of Milroy, who parted with it to Sutherland. The Hawick player got the ball while he was on the run and, espying an opening, he made straight for it with three Englishmen at his heels. Williams [the English full-back] crossed over to intercept the Scot but failed to get up in time and, amid a rousing Scottish cheer, Sutherland threw himself over the line. It was a piece of sterling play.

Cameras were too primitive to capture close-ups so readers often had to make do with sketches. Walter scores against England in 1911, as depicted in The Illustrated Sporting & Dramatic News. *(Trustees of the National Library of Scotland)*

Walter had scored at the corner flag and the conversion was too difficult for Fred Turner. Stung by this early reverse, England roared back and, after some fine passing, one of the forwards, Norman Woodehouse, crossed at the posts with Carl Ogilvy clinging to his heels. The try was converted to put England 5-3 in front, but play swung again and Walter had another great run, as *The Scotsman* reported:

Again it was the Hawick player Sutherland who took the leading part in the attack, thanks to his accepting a timely pass by Henderson. On this occasion, however, the Borderer was hampered by the touchline and, after showing a clean pair of heels to the English 'threes', he ran full tilt against Williams, whose tackling was sure as it was effective.

Soon afterwards, good passing by the English backs led to a fine try out wide by the Leicester wing Percy Lawrie. At the end of an exciting and open half, England led 8-3, but the Scots were in the game and Walter had been very prominent. According to 'Borderer' in the *Hawick News*: 'When half-time came, the spectators all wondered who Sutherland was and where he had came from. Undoubtedly, he stood out on the Scottish side.'

Unfortunately, Scotland's efforts were disrupted in the second half because of an injury to 'J.Y.' Henderson, the Watsonians half-back, which led to some positional switches in the team, Henderson moving to full-back, Ogilvy to the centre and Cunningham to half. England cleverly exploited the Scottish weakness. Adrian Stoop broke away and fed his Harlequins partner John Birkett, who had no trouble rounding the injured Henderson to score under the posts. The English were now getting on top, which called for stout defence from the

International matches were followed by a formal dinner for both sides and the officials. This autographed menu is from the England v. Scotland match in 1911. Walter's signature is fourth from the top left. (Scottish Rugby Union)

Scottish backs, but then the visitors had a piece of good fortune. A loose pass from Stoop to Birkett fell into the hands of Ronald Simson, the Scottish centre, who raced away, kicked over the head of the full-back and won a scramble at the post for a converted try. Scotland now trailed by five points and a draw was still possible, but England held out for a well-deserved victory 13-8.

There had been plenty of mistakes but the match had been a great encounter, full of movement and not a dull moment from start to finish. Both sides had been fully committed to the task. 'To put it mildly,' said the *Evening Dispatch*, 'there was nothing namby-pamby about the play.' Despite the defeat, the Scots could take heart from their best display of the season. They had done much better than anyone had expected, playing with spirit and fight, tackling firmly and keeping up a furious pace. Both sets of forwards had been evenly matched, but England had held a definite advantage in the backs. Their heavier and faster three-quarters had been quicker to the ball and 'neater to the combination', and it was only strong Scottish defence that had prevented further scores. Playing in his fourth inter-national, Walter Sutherland had made his mark. The *Evening News*, for one, was impressed and described him as 'the brightest of the three-quarter line… a credit to the Borders'. He had scored a great try, beating three defenders with his speed and guile, and came desperately close on other occasions. Walter had combined reasonably well with Cunningham and he had gone looking for work, a reflection of his growing confidence and experience, although there were still doubts about his ability to take on bigger men. As *The Scotsman* noted: 'Sutherland was eager and effective in attack, if a trifle slack in defence.' Unfortunately the Scots had tended to feed the left wing rather than the right, which meant that Walter 'suffered from neglect'. Describing the Scottish three-quarter line, *Scottish Referee* stated:

Sutherland was the best of the lot... His try was a great effort, for he had only a yard or two to work upon, and squeezed through with difficulty. But this was not his only effort, for he played well from start to finish, and was equally good in defence.

At full-back, Walter's club-mate Carl Ogilvy had also played well, although his display had not been without its faults. According to the *Evening News*, he had showed 'real Border grit. He kicked a good length to touch, fielded reliably, and tackled like a Trojan.' One memorable tackle on A.D. Roberts, the English left wing, had prevented a certain score: 'It alone was worth going to London to see.' Perhaps the players from the Borders were worth a shout after all. As the *Hawick News* put it: 'The union are always reserved in coming to the Borders for their men, but had they selected more Borderers for Scotland's game they would have been winners.'

five

THE LAD WITH THE SILVER HAIR

A t the beginning of 1912, having just celebrated his twenty-first birthday, Walter was entitled to feel optimistic about his rugby career. Earlier in the season he had been made captain of Hawick, a popular choice and a great honour for one so young. His side was playing well and was still in the hunt for the Scottish Championship and the Border League, having had only one defeat in the first half of the season. Walter had already made four international appearances and had every prospect of making more. In December 1911 he had shone in the trial matches, both for the South of Scotland against the North and also for The Rest against the Anglo-Scots. He had missed the final trial in early January because of a slight injury. The *Evening News* still claimed: 'His equal as a wing three-quarter is not to be found in Scotland in these days.'

1912 turned out to be a much better season for the Scotland rugby team than the previous year. The Scots won two matches out of four and recovered some pride and credibility. The selection committee continued to make some baffling choices but, in general, the team was settled and players were given more than one chance to prove themselves. The Scots had a score to settle in the opening match of the season against France at Inverleith on 20 January 1912. The previous year, Scotland had been humiliated in Paris, the first-ever victory for France in international rugby. Now it was time for Scotland to take revenge. Despite that defeat, the French match was still regarded as little more than a trial game and the selection committee introduced eight new faces. On the left wing came George Will, a student at Cambridge University who had played at half-back in the Varsity match in 1911. A doctor's son, Will came from a different social background from Walter Sutherland but, as rugby players, the two had much in common. A natural athlete, Will was a fast and determined runner with 'ideal football pace', but he was a small and slender man who did not seem strong enough for international rugby. 'He looks a delicate slip of a youth,' said the *Evening Dispatch*, reporting the Scottish trial in January 1912. 'His face is pale, his body is slight, and his legs must surely have been the thinnest on the field.' Will was to prove his doubters wrong by scoring a try in each of his first three internationals. Also in the side to play France were two newcomers from Royal High School FP, Alexander 'Sandy' Gunn and John 'Jenny' Hume, who were the first players to play for Scotland as a specialist stand-off and scrum-half rather than a quarter-back pairing. John Hume was described as 'a gritty little fellow' and had played for Hawick in season 1909/10, although for some reason he is not usually included in the list of the club's international players.

In early January 1912 the French had come close to beating Ireland in Paris, losing only 6-11. It was clear that French rugby was making rapid improvements, although for most British observers the French game retained an air of mystery about it. Staying in the Caledonian Station hotel at the end of Princes Street, the French brought a fast and experienced team, including some 'heavily built and muscular fellows'. However the French did not travel well, in both senses. It had taken them twenty-three hours to reach Edinburgh by boat and train and, understandably, some of them were feeling 'a little fagged'. The Scottish newspapers believed that the French were weak in the forwards, especially in the scrum, 'a feature of the game in which the Frenchmen are said to be somewhat deficient'. Like the French, Scotland had a speedy back division, and a fast and open game was anticipated. 'A Scottish victory is doubtless the most probable thing to happen,' said *The Scotsman*, crossing its fingers, 'but the Scots will certainly not take their opponents cheaply on this occasion.'

On a dull, dreary and misty afternoon, the crowd of around 15,000 gave both sides a warm welcome as they took the field. France appeared five minutes early, which caused palpitations for Dr Guthrie and his brass and pipe bands, still getting ready to play *La Marseillaise*. Scotland played in their change strip of white jerseys and navy blue shorts while France, 'showing the tricolour in the arrangement of their dress' turned out in pale blue jerseys, white shorts and red stockings. Unusually the opening score was a penalty goal, kicked by Jimmy Pearson. Then, from a scrum near the French line, Sandy Gunn took a pass from his club partner Hume and cut through the defence to score a debut try at the posts. Turner brought out the full points to put Scotland 8-0 in the lead. There were further good passing movements among the Scottish backs, which were only thwarted by the speed and defence of the visitors. Taking time to settle, the French hit back with a try by Marcel Communeau, a forward who had no problems breaking through the Scottish defence. 'The try was skilfully and neatly obtained,' reported *The Scotsman*, 'and merited the cheering which followed.' The first twenty minutes of the match had been a fairly even contest, but slowly the French forwards began to fade while their backs were guilty of some wayward kicking. Both sets of three-quarters were eager to play an open game and the ball swung backwards and forwards across the field. France were denied a certain try because of a forward pass while on the Scottish left wing George Will also came close. Clever inter-play between the Watsonians pair Angus and Pearson saw the latter throwing himself over in the corner for the second Scottish try. Turner converted with a fine kick to put Scotland 13-3 ahead at the interval.

In the second half the Scots began to assert their superiority and were rewarded with tries from Will, who slipped neatly past the full-back, and also from Fred Turner. Until the closing minutes, Walter Sutherland had been largely anonymous, seeing little of the ball and having few chances to run. 'Sutherland had had little opportunity of doing anything for his country,' reported *The Scotsman*, 'and his Border friends were despairing of the ball ever coming near him.' *Scottish Referee* observed: 'Angus and Pearson did not attend to their wings as they should have done. Sutherland was particularly neglected and, for the greater part of the game, was a spectator.' Writing in his inimitable style in the *Evening Dispatch*, 'Mickey Doolan' expressed the general sense of frustration about the failure to get Walter more involved:

On Sathurday, the Borderer had a grievance. He had come up to see Hawick knock sphots out av France, and fur sixty minutes Hawick was takin' a back sayte compared wid thriflin' places like Kirkcaldy and Edinburgh. Howiver, the last fifteen minutes putt matthers right, and a rivolution was stared off.

Fortunately, matters changed towards the end when Walter made three strong dashes to the line, two of which brought tries. Walter's first came from a clever interception and a sprint to the right-hand corner, when he showed the speedy French back division a clean pair of heels. In the closing minute of the game, he romped over again after a great Scottish passing movement. Turner converted both of Walter's tries to leave Scotland comfortable winners 31-3. The final score had flattered the Scots and it was clear that the French had 'improved immeasurably'. They had prevented a much higher score thanks to their speed in defence and, to their credit, they had never stopped trying, even when the scores were piling up. However, they had been let down by some careless handling at crucial moments and their kicking and overall cohesion had been poor. For the home crowd, the big question was how would the Scots perform in the sterner tests to come? It was hard to tell against weak opposition but the Scottish team were 'hard workers and keen' and the forwards a 'good active lot'. The back division had great attacking potential, but undeniably it was lacking in physical presence. As *The Scotsman* concluded:

It may be that the lack of weight will tell against Scotland in the big engagements that lie before them but, in Angus, Pearson and Sutherland, the Scottish Union have men who are full of football, and Will completes a line in which there are great scoring possibilities.

Scotland's next match was away to Wales, which presented a much tougher challenge than the French had been. The selectors made three changes to the team, including a recall for Watsonians' Eric Milroy at scrum half. Milroy was a little more experienced than Hume and he was going to need all his craft and know-how. He was up against the legendary Swansea half-back Dickie Owen, who would be winning his thirty-fifth cap. This was an astonishing number for a man who weighed around nine stone, earning him the nickname 'Diminutive Dickie'. Wales were further strengthened by the return of the great Billy Trew at stand-off and the Swansea forward Ivor Morgan. Despite their defeat to England at Twickenham, the Welsh were confident about the Scottish match. 'There will be keen disappointment among the "Taffies" should Scotland gain her first victory in Wales since 1892,' reported *The Scotsman*, 'though there is not the same spirit of optimism as has prevailed in the past.' Until the 1950s, international matches in Wales were staged alternately between Cardiff and Swansea. In 1912, it was Scotland's turn to visit the distant St Helen's ground. The Scots arrived in Swansea from London early on the Friday afternoon, where representatives of the Welsh Rugby Union greeted them off the train. There was also a crowd of curious onlookers, 'who evidently were anxious to see what manner of men the opponents of Wales were.' The visitors were faced with a wintry scene. Snow was lying and there was some doubt if the match would go ahead. Overnight there was a sharp frost and a heavy snowfall, but the pitch had been protected by straw. The snow was cleared in the morning, but the ground was very hard in places, especially behind the goalposts, which led to several injuries. After the game David Bain, the Scottish forward, collapsed due to the delayed effects of a hard knock and had to be left overnight in Swansea instead of returning with the rest of the team to London.

After a cagey opening, play began to open out and there were good runs from both sides. In the second quarter, Dickie Owen broke away from a scrum on the twenty-five-yard line and flicked a pass back inside to George Hirst, the Newport wing winning his first cap, who just beat Walter Sutherland to score at the corner flag. Immediately afterwards Billy Trew dropped a neat goal to put the home side 7-0 in front. Scotland roared back and, after a good passing movement, George Will broke away and outflanked several opponents to score a great try. At the end of a stubbornly contested first half, Wales led 7-3. Scotland scored another fine try early in the second half. From a movement in the centre of the field, Sandy Gunn broke through the defence and fed Jock Scott, who dashed forward and then passed to Milroy to give him a clear run to the line. Having a poor day with the boot, Fred Turner missed the conversion, 'and the Welsh men breathed freely as the ball passed wide of the uprights'. Now the Welsh forwards picked up the pace. After an irresistible rush and a scramble on the line, Ivor Morgan got a fingertip touch for a converted try. With ten minutes remaining, Fred Birt, the Newport centre, dropped another goal. Wales sealed the match when Trew went off on a run to the line, passing to Reggie Plummer, the Newport left wing, who cut through three Scottish defenders to score. Jack Bancroft converted to leave the home side winners 21-6. The win marked a turning point for Wales, who moved ahead of Scotland in the number of overall wins in the fixture for the first time. Scotland were to catch up again in the 1920s.

While Wales had never looked like losing the match, the final score had flattered them, especially in the days when drop-goals were worth four points. Scotland had made a good fight of it and scored two great tries. The decisive factor had been the cleverness of the Swansea halves, Owen and Trew, who were carried shoulder high in triumph to the pavilion at the end of the game. Always a threat, they had played at the top of their game while their opposite numbers, Gunn and Milroy, had not combined so effectively. Individually there had been some good performances on the Scottish side, especially Gus Angus in the centre who had been prominent in defence. As in the French match, Walter Sutherland had been starved of the ball and he had few chances to show his skills. The *Evening Dispatch* noted: 'As the game inclined more to the left wing, as in the French match, he never got a chance of showing his paces in attack.' Writing in the same paper, 'Honesty' pointed out that the Hawick man couldn't do anything without the ball:

It would as if Scotland had played at Swansea with three three-quarters instead of four. Sutherland is not mentioned... For sheer downright selfishness the Scottish centres are hard to beat, although when they do part with the ball they would rather send it on to Will than give the Borderer a chance. Gunn, of course, is to blame, too, for he seems unable or unwilling to pass it out to the right.

In his defensive play, Walter's fielding had been good, but some of his line kicking had been less satisfactory. 'Sutherland frequently gave one "the shivers" by the uncertainty of his kicking for touch,' said the *Evening News*. Overall, he had been 'nervy' and uncertain, not his best international.

Walter was left out of the Scottish team to play Ireland at Dublin at the end of February. 'It would surprise most people to learn that Sutherland has been dropped,' commented the *Evening News*, 'and great will be the chagrin in the Borderland.' In his next club match against Gala, he responded by scoring two tries, dropping a goal and kicking two conversions. 'Sutherland was in rattling good form,' said the *Evening News*. 'He had no fewer than fourteen points. He was simply great.' Walter's place in the Scottish team went to the South African student Steven Steyn, winning his second cap. Steyn could not prevent Scotland going down to another defeat, this time narrowly by 10-8. In a fast and open game, Scotland had been let down by poor handling among the backs, who squandered several chances. The defeat led to popular demand for the return of Walter Sutherland. It was now clear to everyone that he was a much better wing than Steyn. There was a flurry of letter writing to the newspapers about who should be in or out, but most writers agreed that Walter deserved his place. As 'F.H.' wrote in the *Evening Dispatch*: 'Sutherland will have to come back. He is undoubtedly the best wing three-quarter we have, and is just about perfection in that position as it is possible for a man to be.'

Once again, the selectors made several changes for the final game of the season against England at Inverleith. Walter was recalled to the right wing and there was a first cap for his Hawick club-mate William 'Billy' Burnet, who was chosen in the centre. A twenty-six-year-old teaching assistant at Denholm School, Burnet had first played for Hawick in October 1907. A solid and sturdy player, his selection was controversial. Some people doubted if he was truly international class. In a sense, Burnet owed his place to Walter Sutherland. The committee had finally woken up to the fact that Walter was a winger of rare attacking potential, but in previous matches he had been poorly served and his skills had been largely wasted. It was hoped that Burnet could get more out of Sutherland and bring out his latent talents. 'It is questionable whether Burnet would have gone in on his own merits,' commented the *Evening News*, 'but his association with Sutherland is a commendable effort to remedy a pronounced defect of former teams.' The *Glasgow Herald* adopted a similar line: 'Popular clamour has been silenced by the selection of the Hawick three-quarter but, while granting that Sutherland should never have been dropped, one is of the opinion that Burnet falls short of international standard.'

In their preview articles, most writers thought that Scotland had little chance of winning the match. 'Nobody thought that Scotland had a dog's chance,' said one. England was blessed with speedy backs and a huge pack of forwards. As a result they were the hot favourites. They had already beaten Ireland and Wales and were on course for their first Triple Crown in twenty years and to recapture their former pre-eminence in the international game. *The Scotsman* gloomily concluded: 'Everybody, Scotsmen as well as Englishmen, recognises that the visitors' chances of success are much more rosy than those of the Scots. It is difficult, as a matter of fact, to see how the Scots can escape defeat. If Scotland does, it will be a surprise indeed; if Scotland wins, it will be little short of a sensation.' Similarly, the *Evening Dispatch* wrote: 'Truth to tell it will be one of the biggest football surprises of modern times should Scotland succeed.'

On a beautiful spring afternoon, a crowd of around 25,000 people gathered at Inverleith to see if the Scots could produce an upset. 'All ages from the schoolboy sporting his colours to the octogenarian leaning heavily on his stick were represented,' reported *The Scotsman*. 'Of ladies there was an unusually large gathering, and the occasional shrill voice above the din told of the enthusiasm with which they entered into the game.' As the Scottish team took the field, an excited voice shouted out 'Play Up Hawick!', which caused lots of laughter and cheering around the ropes. As it turned out, the Border contingent soon had something to shout about. Reporting the early stages, *The Scotsman* said: 'Sutherland delighted the hearts of his Border friends by cleverly fielding an overhead ball, sprinting clear of the English forwards, and transferring play by a capital kick to the centre flag.' The first fifteen minutes took place almost entirely in the English half with the home forwards taking the game to the visitors. The match was 'no kid-glove affair' and the vigorous footwork of the Scots brought out courageous defence from the English. Midway through the first half the English forward John King suffered an accidental injury to his ribs and had to leave the field. Replacements were not allowed at this time so England had to battle on with a man short. Both sides enjoyed some good passages and came close on several occasions. As planned, Walter Sutherland was more in the game than on previous outings, enjoying better support from his centres. His running was penetrative and one effort was stopped right on the English goal line. At half-time, there was no scoring. The Scots were well in the game, more than anyone had dared to hope. The forwards were hungry and eager, and the backs had used their speed cleverly to check the best of the English attacks.

The second half had a sensational opening. With play inside the English twenty-five, Eric Milroy picked up a kick ahead and passed onto to J.L. Boyd, who in turn fed Billy Burnet. Then, as *The Scotsman* reported: 'From one Hawick man the ball went to the other, and Sutherland, showing his opponents a clean pair of heels, dashed in at the corner amid the wild shouting and cheering of his excited countrymen.' Many years later, the move was still fresh in the mind of Jock Wemyss, who was looking on from the stands. 'I remember too Scotland's first try scored by that great wing Walter Sutherland of Hawick, who took a pass from his club-mate W. Burnet, and scudded down the touchline with only inches in which to move, and when it seemed all England barred his way to the corner.'

1 Walter Sutherland's parents and grandparents were brought up in Wilton Dean village on the outskirts of Hawick. (Author's collection)

Right: 2 Walter was born at 10 Myreslaw Green, Hawick in a small flat above the Co-operative Store. (Author's collection)

Below: 3 and 4 Walter's eldest brother Jimmy was Cornet at Hawick Common Riding in 1901. The group photograph shows Jimmy with his Lass Lily Lawson and the principals of the previous two years. (Scottish Borders Museum and Gallery Service, Hawick Collection)

5 The Imperial Hotel (now Bar and Lounge) in the centre of Hawick was the Sutherland family business for twenty-five years and also Walter's home. (Author's collection)

6 Hawick had a strong military presence. The King's Own Scottish Borderers return from church parade in 1910. The Imperial Hotel is top centre. (Jake Coltman)

Above: 8 and 9 Walter's club, Hawick, played their home games at Mansfield Park, shown here around 1900. Note the blurred figures caused by the slow shutter speed of the camera. (Scottish Borders Museum and Gallery Service, Hawick Collection)

Right: 10 Bill Kyle was one of the leading players of the Edwardian era, winning 21 caps for Scotland between 1902 and 1910, an astonishing number for the time. (Hawick RFC)

Opposite below: 7 This view of a Hawick Common Riding from before 1914 shows Oliver Place, the street in the middle of the photograph. The Imperial Hotel is the large building in the left-centre. Across the road is Walter's school, Teviot Grove Academy, just visible to the left of the horse-drawn carriage. (Author's collection)

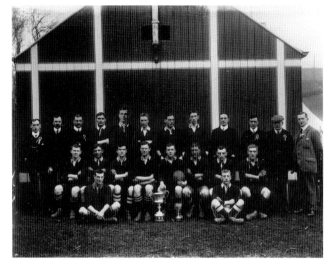

11 In his first season of senior rugby, Walter was a member of the Hawick team that won the unofficial Scottish club championship. He is shown here cross-legged front right. The captain is Sandy Burns. (Scottish Borders Museum and Gallery Service, Hawick Collection)

FOOTBALL—HAWICK V. WATSONIANS.

A striking snap-shot — W. R. Sutherland (Hawick) in the act of cross-kicking.
W. Burnet is shown alongside Sutherland, with two Watsonians also in attendance.

[Photo by Peter McNa]

12 Walter about to unleash a cross-kick against Watsonians at Myreside in March 1912. Billy Burnet is the other Hawick player. (*Hawick News*)

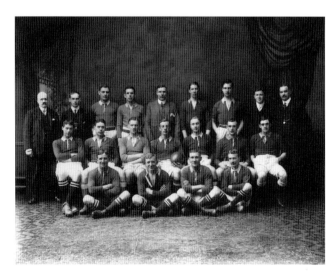

13 Walter was captain of Hawick in season 1911/12, shown here in the centre holding the ball. (Scottish Borders Museum and Gallery Service, Hawick Collection)

14 Hawick won the Border League in season 1913/14, the last before the First World War. Walter is seated next to the club president, Dr Hamilton. The captain is Billy Burnet. (Scottish Borders Museum and Gallery Service, Hawick Collection)

15 and 16 Between 1899 and 1925 Scotland's home internationals were played at Inverleith in the north of Edinburgh. *Above:* Action from Scotland *v.* England in 1912, showing the main grandstand. *Below:* Walter Sutherland charges down a kick against Wales in 1913. Note the bankings of spectators and the characteristic press box. (Scottish Rugby Union)

17 – 20 There was no television before the First World War, but occasionally rugby matches were filmed for the local picture house. These ghostly images are taken from a short film of the Gala *v.* Hawick match at Netherdale in March 1913, which was shown at Scott's Pavilion in both towns. Clockwise from top left: the crowd in the grandstand; Walter runs towards the camera; Walter in the centre of play; and tackling an opponent. (Scottish Screen Archive)

21 The Scottish team that played Wales at Cardiff in February 1910. Walter, looking nervous, is standing on the extreme right. His Hawick colleague Bill Kyle sits next to the captain, George Frew. (Scottish Rugby Union)

1. A line out.
3. A corner of the crowd.

4. Wiping the mud from a Scotchman's eyes.

2. The mud-covered players at half-time.
5. A try to Wales.

WALES BEAT SCOTLAND AT CARDIFF BY 14 POINTS TO NIL.

22 Scenes from Wales v. Scotland at Cardiff in February 1910, Walter's first international. Note the Welsh wag in the crowd with the banner. (Trustees of the National Library of Scotland)

23 Walter's second cap was against England at Inverleith in March 1910. He is standing in the back row, extreme right. The Scottish captain was George Cunningham. (Scottish Rugby Union)

1. A band of boy pipers play the Scotch team on to the field.
2. Crossing the touch line.
3. Play at the half-way line.
4. England converting their first try.

ENGLAND REGAINS THE BRITISH ISLES RUGBY CHAMPIONSHIP.—SCOTLAND BEATEN AT EDINBURGH.

By beating Scotland by 14 points to 5 at Inverleith last Saturday before a record crowd for Edinburgh, England regained the Calcutta Cup and Championship.

24 Action from Scotland v. England at Inverleith in March 1910. (Trustees of the National Library of Scotland)

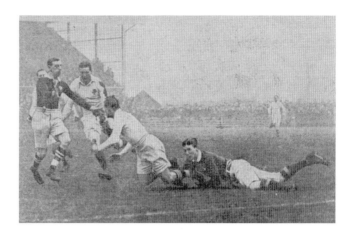

25 and 26 Action from England *v.* Scotland at Twickenham in March 1911. *Above:* Walter Sutherland awaits developments after a good tackle by Ronald Simson. *Below:* Waiting for a pass from Jimmy Henderson. (Trustees of the National Library of Scotland)

27 Resplendent in their white change strip, the Scottish team that played France at Inverleith in January 1912. Walter is sitting next to the captain, John MacCallum. (Scottish Rugby Union)

Above: 28 The Scottish team that played Wales at Swansea in February 1912. Walter is seated second from the right. Note the straw to protect the ground from frost. (Scottish Rugby Union)

Left: 29 The *Evening Dispatch* presents the Scottish team to take on England at Inverleith in March 1912. Walter is top right. (Trustees of the National Library of Scotland)

30 An early photograph showing Walter making a dashing run for the English Line.

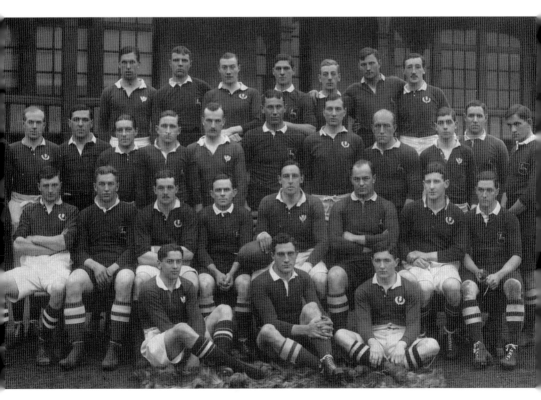

31 The two teams mingle together before the Scotland versus South Africa match in November 1912. Walter is third from the right in the back row. (Scottish Rugby Union)

32 Walter's final international was against Wales at Cardiff in February 1914. He is seated on the left of the captain, David Bain. Walter has a heavily strapped right knee from a previous injury. Note the ornate pavilion in the background. (Scottish Rugby Union)

33 This Hawick seven, containing four internationalists, won the Melrose Sevens tournament in April 1910. From left to right, back row: George Johnstone, Bill Kyle, Tom Wilson and Peter Hope. Front row: Walter Sutherland, George Laing, Billy Burnet and Carl Ogilvy. (Scottish Borders Museum and Gallery Service, Hawick Collection)

34 The winners of the Hawick Sevens in April 1911. From left to right, back row: George Brown, Bill Burnet, Bill Kyle, Carol Ogilvy and George Laing. Front row: Walter Sutherland and Tom Wilson. (Scottish Borders Museum and Gallery Service, Hawick Collection)

35 Walter was a key member of the Hawick seven that won all five Border sevens tournaments in 1912. From left to right, back row: George Laing, Robert Lindsay-Watson, Archie Drummond, Bill Kyle, George Johnstone. Front row: Danny Shannon, Billy Burnet, Walter Sutherland and Tom Wilson. (Scottish Borders Museum and Gallery Service, Hawick Collection)

Finish of the Amateur 100 Yards Sprint, won in brilliant fashion by W. R. Sutherland, who is shown breasting the tape with his arms extended. H. J. Christie, who was second, is beside Sutherland, and the third prize-winner, Archie Anderson, is shown on the extreme right of the picture.

36 In June 1913 Walter scored a notable win over his old rival H.J. Christie in the 100 yards sprint at the Hawick Common Riding. Christie is next to Walter in the striped top. (*Hawick News*)

Left: 37 The Teviotdale Harriers relay team that won the Wyoming Cup at the Hawick Common Riding in June 1910. From left to right, back row: Walter Sutherland and Adam Grieve. Front row: J.S. Turnbull and Rob Burton. (Teviotdale Harriers)

Above right: 38 Walter, looking quite dapper, pictured with his friends at the Hawick Common Riding in June 1914. On the left is William Ker, a fellow football player who joined up with Walter in September 1914. He was killed in action three years later. (Scottish Borders Museum and Gallery Service, Hawick Collection)

Above left: 39 Walter photographed in 1918 having just become an Army officer. (Author's collection)

Above right: 40 This portrait of Walter was taken in 1918 and was used in Sewell's *Rugby Football Internationals Roll of Honour*. (Author's collection)

41-44 Rugby casualties of the First World War. Clockwise from top left: George Will (Cambridge University and Scotland), killed in action March 1917; Eric Milroy (Watsonians and Scotland), killed in action July 1916; Jimmy Pearson (Watsonians and Scotland), killed in action May 1915; and Ronnie Poulton (Oxford University, Harlequins and England), killed in action May 1915. (Author's collection)

45 Bella and Alex Sutherland, Walter's parents (centre), and their next door neighbours Mr and Mrs G.L. Macdonald at Walter's grave. (Mrs Kitty Oliver)

Above left: 46 Walter is remembered on the Sutherland family headstone in Wilton Cemetery, Hawick. (Author's collection)

Above right: 47 Walter Sutherland's grave in Houchin British Cemetery, France. (Mrs Kitty Oliver)

It was a great try, which John MacCallum, the Scottish captain, was unable to convert. Scotland continued to press, throwing the visitors into desperate defence. Boyd and Will narrowly missed drop-goals and one Scottish forward wasted a great chance by ignoring Sutherland, who was standing in the clear. But England were not finished yet and they hit back with twenty minutes remaining. From a loose kick, Henry Brougham, the Harlequins wing, gathered and dashed away. Brilliantly tackled by George Will, the ball went to the chasing English forwards, one of whom hacked over the line. An unlucky bounce beat Gus Angus, and Dave Holland, a forward from Devonport, dived on the ball to score an unconverted try. With the scores now tied at 3-3, 'run and counter-run ensued'. Sutherland and Boyd came close for Scotland, and two English efforts were only stopped with great tackles near the line. After a good passing movement among the Scottish three-quarters, play moved to the English goal line. Sutherland and MacCallum tried to burrow their way over before the ball fell to Charlie Usher, the United Services forward winning his first cap, who threw himself across the line for the decisive try. MacCallum converted from an awkward angle to put Scotland in front. Amid breathless excitement, England tried hard to save the match but could not break the Scottish defence. At the final whistle, Scotland had won a famous victory 8-3. Laconic as ever, *Rowan's Rugby Guide* claimed that the result was as 'cheering as it was unexpected'. 'What was to have been a glorious Flodden Field,' chirped the *Evening Dispatch*, 'turned out to be a veritable Bannockburn.'

Scotland's win was based on a magnificent display by the forwards, who had played with 'a bit of Devil' about them. In fairness, England had been weakened when they lost one of their players early in the match. 'The Scottish forwards gave one of the finest all-round displays ever seen in an international,' commented the *Evening News*. Likewise, *The Scotsman* was full of praise for the Scottish eight. 'The Scottish forwards were masters of the situation, their speed, resolute tackling, capital footwork and eagerness enabling them to get the better of the opposition, and to spoil many of the passing movements initiated by the English three-quarters.' John Scott from Edinburgh Accies had been in great form, leading to claims that he was the best forward in the British Isles. The Scottish half-backs, J.L. Boyd and Eric Milroy, had played intelligently and their tackling had been invaluable. In the centre, Billy Burnet had been nervous and 'good and bad by turns', sometimes trying to do too much on his own and hanging onto the ball, but linking well with Sutherland, especially in the creation of the first Scottish try. 'Combination at last!' crowed the *Evening News*. The understanding between the two Hawick players had broken down occasionally but, on the whole, it had made a world of difference. 'Burnet gave Sutherland the best service he had had this season,' said the *Evening News*, 'and Sutherland was in excellent form.' Both of the Scottish wings, Sutherland and Will, had been very prominent in the game, using their speed to great effect, although at times Will's lack of stature had been exposed by the heavier English backs. For Walter Sutherland, the match had been a memorable occasion. As he later confided in his notebook: 'Game against England was the most exciting ever played in.' He had scored a great try and given his best performance on the international stage to date. *Scottish Referee* described him as 'the finest three-quarter on the field'. The *Glasgow Herald* commented: 'Sutherland played a great game and showed resource, pace, and resolution. His tackling was sound and he used his pace well in defence.' The *Evening Dispatch* reported that Walter 'was the best and most dangerous three-quarter on the field'. One English critic, 'TEW', wrote: 'Sutherland, I fancy, calls for special mention… he has never played a finer game than this.' There is no doubt that the England match in 1912 was the best victory of Walter's international career, allowing him to forget some of the old disappointments and look to the future with confidence and optimism.

As he recognised in his notebook, season 1912/13 was Walter's best. At twenty-two years old, he was nearing the height of his athletic powers. He was playing with more confidence and experience while the transition from callow youth into manhood meant that he had developed greater physical strength and presence. Walter played in all five international matches in the season, the only Scottish three-quarter to do so, during which he produced some dazzling and courageous rugby, notably against England at Twickenham in March 1913. Unfortunately, Scotland's results remained inconsistent with only two wins out of five. Walter also suffered a stroke of bad luck at the hands of the selection committee. During the championship games in 1913, he was moved to the left wing to accommodate a player called Bill Stewart, a Tasmanian, who went on to score seven tries from the right wing, four in one match and three in another. Nevertheless, there was much for the young Hawick player to savour and enjoy.

November 1912 was the time of the Springbok. Since the advent of professional rugby games against overseas visitors have become commonplace, with sides jetting in from all over the globe to play one-off Test matches. By contrast, in the era before the First World War, international tours were a great rarity. When Scotland played South Africa at Inverleith in November 1912, it was only the third time in history that they had played a side from the Southern Hemisphere. The next match, against the 'Waratahs' of New South Wales, would not take place for another fifteen years. In 1912 the South Africans played twenty-seven games in the British Isles and France on a tour that lasted over four months. The Western Province forward Billy Millar, who was also a heavyweight boxer and long-distance walking champion, captained the side. The South Africans arrived in Scotland on a mission of revenge. Six years earlier, on their original tour of Britain, they had gone down to a surprise 6-0 defeat against Scotland at Hampden Park in Glasgow. The Hampden match had produced one of Scottish rugby's historic moments. Playing at half-back, Pat Munro had fielded a high kick to the right where the flying winger Ken MacLeod, running at full speed, caught the wet slippery ball without letting it bounce and outpaced the defence to score at the corner. The try was so good that some of the South African players were said to have applauded it.

The Hampden defeat had scarred South African rugby and they had a score to settle when they returned to Scotland in 1912. The visitors were something of a family affair with two sets of brothers in the side, the Morkels and the Luyts. At full-back, Gerhard Morkel was a forceful tackler, 'all wire and whipcord', who could drop kick with either foot. His brother Jackie was a penetrative centre who specialised in the sharp cut-through. Two other members of the extended Morkel clan, Dougie, who weighed in at over 15 stone, and W.H. 'Boy' Morkel, were among the forwards. Dougie Morkel was a noted place-kicker and, during the Scotland game, he took one mighty effort from inside his own half that flew out of the ground and ended up on Ferry Road. Playing alongside the Morkels were the Luyt brothers: John, who played at forward; Freddie, at stand-off; and Richard, at centre. This was only the second time in history that three brothers have played together in the same international side, the first being the Finlay brothers for Scotland in 1875. Injury had forced Billy Millar to withdraw from the Scottish match and Fred 'Uncle' Dobin, a veteran scrum-half who had played against Scotland in 1906, took over the captaincy.

One of the great issues of Victorian and Edwardian Britain was the belief that the British race was in a state of physical decline. Harsh living and working conditions had stunted natural growth and created an unhealthy nation. Many Britons were paying the price for a lack of fresh air, proper diets and plenty of exercise. During the Boer War, scores of men from British towns and cities were rejected for military service because they were physically unsuitable and too weak. Touring colonial rugby teams such as the New Zealanders and the South Africans seemed to confirm the worst fears of the pessimists, sweeping through the mother country and brushing aside the best of British manhood with consummate ease. In 1912 one of the great strengths of the touring South Africans was their physical presence. They were tough, big-boned men who were also athletic ball players. As *The Scotsman* observed: 'The South Africans impressed from the moment they stepped on the field. Bulky and imposing of figure, they

Teams—SCOTLAND *v.* SOUTH AFRICA, 23rd November 1912

SCOTLAND	SOUTH AFRICA
(Scotland play in Blue Jerseys)	*(South Africa play in Green Jerseys)*
FULL BACK W. M. Dickson (Oxford University)	FULL BACK G. Morkel
THREE W. R. Sutherland (Hawick)	THREE J. A Stegmann
QUARTERS A. W. Gunn (Royal High School)	QUARTERS R. R. Luyt
A. W. Angus (Watsonians)	J. Morkel
J. Pearson (Watsonians)	E. M'Hardy
HALF E. Milroy (Watsonians)	HALF F. P. Luyt
BACKS *(Scrum Half)*	BACKS
J. L. Boyd (United Services)	F. J. Dobbin, *Captain*
(Stand-off Half)	
FORWARDS F. H. Turner, *Captain* (London Scottish)	FORWARDS D. F. T. Morkel
J. Dobson (Glasgow Academicals)	A. S. Knight
J. M. B. Scott (Edinburgh Academicals)	W. H. Morkel
D. M. Bain (Edinburgh Academicals)	T. Van Vuuren
D. D. Howie (Kirkcaldy)	J. A. Francis
W. D. C. L. Purves (London Scottish)	G. Thompson
P. C. Blair (Fettesian-Lorettonian)	J. Luyt
L. Robertson (London Scottish)	S. Ledger

Touch Judge—J. D. Dallas	*Referee*—F. C. Potter-Irwin	Max Honnet—*Touch Judge*
(President S.F.U.)	(English Rugby Union)	(South Africa)

The Ball for this match is made and supplied by Messrs Mackenzie & Sons, 148 Lothian Road, Edinburgh

The official programme gives the teams for Scotland v. South Africa in 1912. It was a family affair for the visitors with the three Luyt brothers and the extended Morkel clan. (Scottish Rugby Union)

had also the elasticity and litheness so suggestive of well-trained athletes.' Eleven of the fourteen forwards on the tour measured over 6 foot in height and eight of them were over 14 stone. By contrast, the average weight of the Scottish forwards was around 12 stone per man. One of the forwards who played against Scotland, T.F. van Vuuren, was a veritable giant at 6ft 4ins. The powerful combination of speedy backs and huge forwards made the South Africans an attractive and feared team, although they did not excite the popular imagination like their predecessors in 1906. Their form on tour had been strangely inconsistent and they had already lost two matches by the time they reached Scotland. Casting a critical eye, the *Evening News* observed: 'They can play a winning game brilliantly… but they can also play very badly, or at least far below the form of a great or even a very good national team.' *The Scotsman* commented: 'The South African team are difficult to estimate. Frequently they seem to be wound tight and to be therefore full of power and energy; on other occasions they appear slack and unwound, and their play is accordingly forceless and flaccid.'

Scotland approached the South Africa match in typically lackadaisical style. There were no trial matches so the selection committee went largely for the side that had beaten England in the spring. It was hoped that the Scottish forwards could reproduce their form of the previous match, take their opponents on up front and 'bustle and worry' the visiting backs off their game. The half-back combination of Boyd and Milroy was sound, but the three-quarter line was rather makeshift, several players having been ruled out because of injury. As *The Scotsman* commented in its preview article: 'A consideration of the three-quarters must, however, reduce the feelings of optimism inspired by the forwards and halves.' The two big concerns were that the Scottish three-quarters were too light and would be pushed aside by the burly South Africans, and also that several of them were playing out of position. Jimmy Pearson, normally a centre, was moved onto the right wing while the strong running Sandy Gunn, whose previous caps had been at stand-off, was moved into the centre. Walter Sutherland retained his place on the right wing for his eighth international appearance. By now Walter was settling into the side and great things were expected of him. As the *Evening News* commented: 'W.R. Sutherland cannot get too much of the ball, and he has cleverness as well as pace to commend him.' The match at Inverleith was probably not Walter's first encounter with South African rugby. On their original tour of the British Isles in 1906 South Africa had played a match against the South of Scotland at Mansfield Park. Local schools were given the afternoon off and it is more than likely that Walter went to the game, looking on as a star-struck fifteen-year-old.

Playing the sixteenth match of their tour, the South Africans were pleased to find a reasonably firm pitch, unlike the mud patch at Hampden in 1906. The crowd of around 20,000 people included a large number who travelled from the Borders on two 'heavy specials'. In Hawick the crush of bodies trying to get on the train had been so great that people joining further up the line had to sit in the guard's van. The crowd at Inverleith also included around 200 South African supporters, who had gathered from various British universities. The students had a whale of a time, singing their old school songs and making a lot more noise than the dour Scots. Despite opening nerves the South Africans were in control of the game from first to last. The Scots played with determination but the result was never much in doubt. Using tactics that would become one of their hallmarks in future, the mighty South African forwards softened up the opposition in the first half, bringing the speedy backs more into play in the second. The only score of the first half came after thirty-five minutes when Jackie Morkel, the South African centre, cross-kicked. The Scottish full-back Dickson took his eye off the ball and 'Boetie' McHardy, the athletic Springbok wing, gathered and fell over for a try. In the second half the South African backs opened out and their mesmerising passing movements were too much for the Scots. Jan Stegmann, a big, exceptionally strong runner on the right wing, scored two tries, and 'Boy' Morkel sealed the game with a late score. At the end several of the South African players were chaired off the field on the shoulders

This sketch from The Illustrated Sporting & Dramatic News *shows Walter in action against South Africa in 1912. (Trustees of the National Library of Scotland)*

of their ecstatic supporters, some with 'tears of joy streaming from their eyes' as captain Billy Millar later remembered, while the Scots left in a subdued mood. Winning the match had meant a lot to the South Africans. The news was telegraphed back home, where it was received with great enthusiasm. Later in the tour, the South Africans went on to defeat Ireland, Wales and England to become the first side to beat all of the four home countries on a single tour.

There was no doubt that the physical attributes of the South Africans had been match-winning factors. As the *Evening Dispatch* concluded: 'Scotland will have to rear a bigger and sturdier class of men, as well as speedier, before she can hope to triumph over such a stalwart and splendidly trained side as the Colonials fielded.' The Scottish team had not been lacking in the traditional qualities of 'grit and pluck', but they had come up against a side that was heavier, stronger and better organised. The South Africans were not only big but also they were superior athletes to the Scots, including forwards who possessed mobility and the ability to handle and combine, a foretaste of a new style of total rugby. Looking on, *The Scotsman* reporter was favourably impressed: 'The South African forwards picked up regularly and advanced like backs. They were exceedingly dependable with their hands, and always found someone to pass to.'

One of the few bright spots of a dismal afternoon for Scotland had been the play of Walter Sutherland. He was the only Scottish back to show up well and to have the speed and resources to match the dangerous South Africans. As *The Scotsman* commented: 'Sutherland must be exempted from the general condemnation; he alone had the necessary speed to cope with the South African attack or to make any impression upon their defence, and the Hawick winger was a distinct success.' Describing the Scottish three-quarters, *Scottish Referee* commented: 'There was really only one of the lot of international standard, and this was the Hawick representative, Sutherland.' In defence, Walter had pulled off some great tackles on much bigger opponents, in particular on Boetie McHardy, the sturdy, long-legged winger from the Orange Free State. 'It was exhilarating to see Sutherland dive into him time after time with dogged determination and lay him on the sod,' reported the *Hawick Express*. 'Sutherland's behaviour at critical times was superb, and his tackling grand.' Walter had also been prominent in attack, enjoying some fine runs and coming close to scoring on several occasions but lacking support from his colleagues. 'Sutherland was the only one of the Scottish threes worth a rap,' said the *Daily News*. 'With a decent partner he might have made a lot more trouble for the 'Boks.' Similarly, the *Evening Dispatch* claimed:

Sutherland was the best of the Scottish threes. How pluckily he tried to get through on two occasions, and how poorly he was supported each time. And the 'Teri' put in some fine tackling too, and not always on his own side of the field. Beaten though the Scots were, 'Watty's' runs were the best of the day as far as individual effort went.

Despite his good showing against the South Africans, Walter was shunted onto the left wing for Scotland's next three internationals. This was to make way for a new cap on the right, Bill Stewart, who had been born in Inverness but who had been brought up in Tasmania before moving to London to work as a doctor, playing his club rugby for London Hospitals. The Scots made the long journey to Paris for their opening fixture against France, which took place on New Year's Day 1913. Colombes Stadium was rendered unplayable because of heavy rain and flooding so the match was switched at the last moment to the Parc des Princes. On a bright, cool afternoon with no wind, the visitors were led onto the field by a piper 'playing a lively air,' knowing in the back of their minds that the previous visit to Paris had resulted in a humiliating defeat.

For a short period it looked like history was about to repeat itself. France opened the scoring after eighteen minutes when one of the forwards, Jean Sobadio, took an unexpected short throw to a lineout and hurled himself over for a try, 'amid tremendous cheering'. Keeping their collective nerve, Scotland hit back and Bill Stewart scored two tries in quick succession, one converted by Turner to put the visitors 8-3 ahead at the break. In the second period Scotland continued to attack vigorously, spending most of the time in French half. Roland Gordon, a polished newcomer in the centre, scored twice and Stewart ended the match with his third try. Turner landed two conversions and, at the final whistle, Scotland had won 21-3. The teams were more evenly matched than the final score suggested and it was only in the last five minutes that the Scots had managed to pull away. There had been little between the two forward packs and it was clear that French forward play had made great progress. The main difference had been in the backs where the visitors had been faster, and combined and finished better. Writing in the *Daily Telegraph*, Major Philip Trevor, one of rugby's great journalists, commented: 'The passing of the French backs was too stereotyped to threaten try-getting. Seldom did a Frenchman try to swerve or cut through.' The Scottish backs, in contrast, had all played well, their best performance for some time. 'The half-backs were quick and clean,' noted Trevor, 'and the play in the centre of the three-quarter line was excellently adopted to the needs of the two fast runners on the wing.' Stewart's hat-trick of tries had overshadowed Walter Sutherland's contribution, but the Hawick player had made some good runs and just missed scoring a try by touching down only a few inches from the line.

In fact, the French match in 1913 was better known for what happened at the end of the game rather than what took place during it. This became known as the 'riot match' or the match of *la bagarre*. During the game, some sections of the French crowd took exception to the strict refereeing of Mr John Baxter of England. Previously referees had been very lenient towards France, having sympathy with the newcomers to international rugby, but Mr Baxter took a very tough line against the French, repeatedly penalising them for foul or illegal play. The crowd grew increasingly incensed and, at the final whistle, one irate Frenchman, an army officer, attempted to get at Mr Baxter. The French police immediately arrested the man, but then released him again as the crowd threatened to turn ugly, and in turn chaired the man shoulder high off the field. The *Evening Dispatch* disdainfully observed: 'They did not, as they would have done in England, side with him to the extent of giving him simply a hearty British cheer… What they did was to lift the man up, and with many "Bravos" carry him shoulder high for some distance.' During the pitch invasion, several Scottish players were jostled, probably accidentally in the press of bodies, and some reports state that a few items were thrown at the referee that instead hit some of the players. Afterwards Mr Baxter was smuggled safely into a car disguised in a policeman's uniform. By evening, everyone had calmed down. The incident had done no real harm and at the post-match banquet Mr Baxter told everyone to forget all about it. But there was no such luck. The British media, who have never required a second invitation to knock the French, got hold of the story and blew it out of proportion. *The Scotsman* reported that the visitors had been roughly handled by 'thousands of frenzied Frenchmen'. It was all the fault of typical Gallic impetuosity, argued the same newspaper, unable to resist a little bit of national stereotyping. 'French crowds when roused are apt to do in their haste what they may deeply regret at their leisure.' The outcome of the affair was that the SFU took a stern approach and refused to play the fixture in 1914. The First World War intervened and the two sides did not meet again until Paris in 1920.

Following the final trial match on 16 January 1913, when Walter played on the left wing of the 'Scotland' side, there was enormous controversy at the announcement of the team to play Wales at Inverleith at the beginning of February. The left-wing berth was left vacant, temporarily filled by 'A.N. Other'. The selection committee had left the door open for George Will of Cambridge University, who was recovering from an ankle injury. The shabby treatment of Walter Sutherland, who was left out in the cold not knowing if he would play or not, outraged Border opinion. As the *Evening Dispatch* observed:

Not since the days, in the late 1890s, when the claims of Matthew Elliot and David Patterson to a place together in the national teams were persistently and successfully resisted by the SFU, has there been so much indignation raised in Hawick as has this week been provoked by the omission of W.R. Sutherland from the Scottish side to play Wales.

Writing in the *Southern Reporter*, W. Sorley Brown, who came from a famous rugby-playing dynasty in the Borders and was not the type of man to rock the boat, commented furiously: 'We can regard the Union's action as nothing short of contemptible. It is a dirty piece of work, chiefly the result of envy and prejudice.' The Edinburgh press also had some sympathy for the Hawick wing. As the *Evening Dispatch* put it: 'Every fair-minded person must admit he has been hardly dealt with.' 'The Slighting of Sutherland' seemed to confirm the widely held belief in the Borders that the SFU was biased against players who came from outside the Former Pupil clubs, the universities or the professions. The *Hawick Express* did not mince its words: 'The truth is Borderers are not wanted.' Bill Stewart did not have Walter's experience. Despite his three tries against France, Stewart was felt to be little more than a strong runner who would be exposed against Wales. Fortunately, events got the selectors off the hook. George Will's injury did not heal quickly enough and with a few days to go before the match Walter Sutherland was back in the side.

Scotland were confidently expected to win the Welsh match. 'The Scotsmen had been favoured with almost universal laudation,' commented the *Glasgow Herald*, 'The Welshmen had been taught to regard their mission as a forlorn hope.' The visitors came north with a very inexperienced team and only one player, the great Billy Trew, had played in Scotland before. There were snowfalls the day before and on the morning of the game, but the weather cleared by lunchtime to leave a bright afternoon with a strong, cold wind, 'which caused the ball to perform some curious gyrations, and chilled the players almost to numbness.' Despite the snow, the pitch was reasonably firm, although it cut up in places during the game. By 1913, the biennial 'Welsh Invasion' had already started to grip the douce Scottish capital. Groups of Welsh supporters had made their way to Edinburgh, clogging up the pubs and bars of Rose Street and proudly sporting their 'favours' of leeks and daffodils. Long before kick-off, the majority had gathered in front of the Inverleith press box, 'where they spent the time singing Welsh songs, music hall ditties and engaging in repartee, the burden of which was prophetic of victory for Wales.' 'The visitors regaled the crowd with plenty of singing,' noted the *Hawick News*, 'and the selections given were rendered with wonderful melodiousness.' Meanwhile, the Scottish contingent kept quiet, 'reserving their energies for the game'.

As it turned out, there was little for anybody to sing about. The match was a hopelessly dull encounter, mainly consisting of a tedious forward battle. 'It must be admitted that the game was a dreadfully dreary affair,' wrote the yawning reporter from the *Glasgow Herald*. 'A series of scrums, into which the halves had the greatest difficulty in introducing the ball, broken at intervals by a kick to touch, a fly-kick, or the referee's whistle announcing one of the frequent infringements.' To most people's surprise, Wales won the match fairly easily. The Scots were in 'pitiful form' and the visiting forwards were completely on top. 'The Welsh forwards so dominated the situation in front,' wrote the *Glasgow Herald*, 'that the wonder is that the visitors did not win by twenty points... We have never seen a Scottish pack so completely outplayed.' Despite having so much of the ball, the Welsh backs played conservatively, opting for safety first and rarely attempting any enterprising moves. Clem Lewis, the Welsh stand-off, scored the opening try after eight minutes, easily cutting through slack home defence. Most of the game in the second half took place in the Scottish half of the field. In the closing minutes, Lewis dropped at goal, the ball went wide and a wicked bounce beat two defenders to let Tuan Jones, the Pontypool centre, gather and score. Lewis converted to give Wales a surprise 8-0 victory.

The match had been an utterly dismal affair, one of the poorest in living memory. 'Saturday's international was extravagantly dear for those who had tickets at five shillings,' wrote the *Evening Dispatch*, 'and even those who had paid but one must have felt that they had been "taken in".' The crowd on the terraces found more fun watching the melting snow slide off the roof of the stand and down the necks of the spectators underneath. 'There was not a thrilling movement during the whole eighty minutes,' bewailed *The Scotsman*. Stuck out on the wing, Walter Sutherland hardly touched the ball and spent most of the time trying to beat the cold. Looking on from the warmth of the press box, the reporter from the *Glasgow Herald* observed: 'Sutherland's chief task appeared to be to keep his digits warm.' The *Hawick News* was furious that their man had been ignored once again. 'Borderers would have liked to have seen Sutherland with one of Stewart's chances,' said the irate reporter. 'There was not the slightest endeavour made to send the ball Sutherland's way, and the latter's work mainly consisted in compelling Trew to part with the ball.' Weighing up the match, *Scottish Referee* commented on Walter's performance:

In a team of comparative failures, W.R. Sutherland was one of the exceptions, although he was not a brilliant success, he could not be classed among the delinquents. Rarely has Sutherland failed to do his duty in international football, and the regret was general that he was so poorly assisted in Saturday's game. The only distinguishing effort he made was engineered by himself, but that was enough to prove conclusively that he is one of Scotland's greatest assets in rugby football. Four Sutherlands, and Scotland would have won the match against Wales, despite the failure of the forwards.

Walter's first encounter with the green shirts of Ireland was the reverse of the Welsh match: 'a delightfully open encounter' that was full of incident 'and sparkled with interesting movements'. In the original selection, Walter was moved back to the right wing and George Will recalled on the left, but Will dropped out so Walter switched across and Bill Stewart came in on the right. Unluckily for Walter, the match turned out to be a personal triumph for Stewart, who scored four tries. In perfect weather before a crowd estimated at around 18,000 people, including a large group of Irish students at Edinburgh University, who waved green banners and sang 'patriotic airs', the Scottish forwards took command of the game, playing with energy, determination and an unity of purpose. This was in spite of playing for more than an hour a man short. In the first half, the Scottish full-back Walter Dickson dislocated his shoulder and had to leave the field, John Scott moving into the back division. By contrast, the Irish forwards were slow and apathetic, and carrying a few 'laggards'. Playing for once behind a winning pack, Bowie and Milroy, the Watsonians half-backs, were in a 'happy mood', combining well and always a threat. However, there was no doubt that the star of the show had been Bill Stewart. Thanks to astute play by his centre partner Roland Gordon, who cleverly drew the defence and gave his wing room to move, Stewart used his speed and power to great effect, handling well and running with 'fire and spirit'. Stewart scored four of seven Scottish tries to leave the home side handsome winners 29-14.

Walter probably had mixed feelings about the Irish match: delight that he had played in an open and attractive game and also at Scotland's victory, but also disappointment at Bill Stewart's good fortune. As the *Hawick Express* confessed: 'Inwardly we were jealous, and wished that Sutherland had had his chances. There was nothing done by Stewart that could not have been done by Sutherland.' Walter came close to scoring in the opening minutes, but for most of the match play went to the right, which meant that he had little opportunity to show his paces in attack. By now, Walter was beginning to develop a reputation as one of the forgotten men of international rugby. His plight was similar to another great winger of the time, Cyril Lowe of England, a hugely talented player who was known as 'One-Pass Lowe' because he so rarely touched the ball. The comic satirist P.G. Wodehouse was so moved by Lowe's plight that he wrote a poem about him called *The Great Day*. Walter would have understood its sentiments very well:

> There he stood, poor little chappie,
> Looking lonely and unhappy.
> While the other players frolicked with the ball.
> For he knew he could not mingle
> In the fun with Coates and Dingle.
> He could simply go on tackling – that was all.

Reporting the Irish match, the *Evening News* commented:

Like C.N. Lowe, of England, W.R. Sutherland seems destined to be left out in the cold. His isolation was not so glaring as against Wales, but the game generally went the other way, and the 'Teri' suffered in consequence. What he got to do he did well, and he got in some rousing kicks. He was particularly good in defence.

Walter had shadowed his man, C.V. MacIvor of Dublin University, very well and snuffed out his threat. His defence, according to *The Scotsman*, was 'capital'.

Scotland's final match of the championship was against England at Twickenham on 15 March 1913. At the eleventh hour Bill Stewart withdrew from the side, so Walter Sutherland moved to his preferred position on the right wing and John Sweet, a dentist who played for Glasgow High School FP, came in on the left for his first cap. Walter played outside a new centre partner, Eric Loudoun-Shand, a tall and gangly 'freshman' at Oxford University, who was said to be something of a rugby prodigy. The annual clash for the Calcutta Cup was the highlight of the rugby calendar. 'It is the only game of the year that matters,' said *The Times*. In 1913 the game aroused greater interest than normal. England had already recorded their first-ever win at Cardiff Arms Park and had also beaten Ireland in Dublin, and were now heading for the mythical Triple Crown, their first clean-sweep in the championship for over twenty years. The home side were firm favourites to beat Scotland, especially in the vital forward battle. 'Although it may savour of a lack of patriotism,' said *The Scotsman*, 'it is difficult to escape the feeling that the Scottish forwards will be beaten in the tight scrums.' The Scottish three-quarters were fast and dangerous, 'but it is extremely doubtful if the forwards will provide sufficient chances for them to exhibit their ability in this direction.' As R.J. Phillips put it in his history of Scottish rugby, the Scottish forwards 'had more brain than power'.

England also possessed an extremely talented back division that had great scoring abilities, especially on the left-hand side of the field with the combination of Ronnie Poulton and Vincent Coates. Many writers have claimed that Poulton was the greatest centre ever to play rugby, although his reputation was certainly not hampered by his having attended the highly prestigious Rugby School and Balliol College, Oxford, and by playing his club rugby for

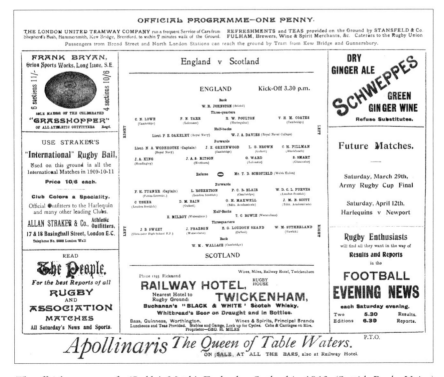

The official programme for 'Suddy's Match', England v. Scotland in 1913. (Scottish Rugby Union)

Frank Gillett's sketches in The Illustrated Sporting & Dramatic News *depict the action from the England versus Scotland match in March 1913. On the right is a portrait of Walter. (Trustees of the National Library of Scotland)*

the socially exclusive Harlequins. There is no doubt that Poulton was capable of great football. A gifted individual who once scored five tries in the Varsity match against Cambridge University, he was exceptionally light-footed, a player who twinkled rather than ran, capable of doing anything including the unexpected flash of genius that could turn matches. As one opponent said: 'How can one stop him, when his head goes one way, his arms another, and his legs keep straight on?' Poulton was not just a great footballer, but 'a man apart'. He was handsome, popular and had a purity of character, a special combination of qualities that made people want to be in his company and to follow his lead. Outside of Poulton on the left wing, and opposite Walter Sutherland, there was another danger man in Vincent Coates, a medical graduate from Cambridge University who played for Bath. Coates, who was born in Edinburgh, had been the 'find of the season' for England: a big, powerful and direct runner with a devastating hand-off who had to be tackled hard and low. 'A likely youth of serviceable build,' reported the *Evening News*, 'a robust and resolute runner, who would brook no check or interference in his flight.'

Played in front of the Prince of Wales and an almost capacity crowd, including many Scots who had made the long journey south, the England game in 1913 turned out to be Walter Sutherland's greatest international display, although ironically this was in defence rather than attack. On a heavy, damp pitch and in a strong wind, the English forwards took almost total control of the match, winning a steady supply of ball for their backs and denying the Scots any worthwhile possession. The feature of the match, according to *The Scotsman*, was 'the determined attack of the Englishmen, and the management and fearless tackling of the equally speedy though less aggressive Scottish three-quarters.' For Scotland, it was the Irish game in reverse. The opposition won almost everything, forcing the Scots to endure wave after wave of English attacks. 'Scotland, on the general run of play,' reported *The Scotsman*, 'might easily have been defeated not by three points, but by three times three.'

Despite having so much quality ball, the final outcome of the match was a meagre 3-0 win for England. The decisive try was scored in the first half by the Blackheath forward 'Bruno' Brown, a Rhodes scholar at Oxford who had been born in Australia. The much-vaunted English three-quarters had shown 'plenty of energy and dash, and resolution', but they had played unevenly and with little real skill, especially in their combined work and their finishing. They seemed, said one report, 'to get bewildered when on the brink of scoring.' The worst offender was Poulton, who had a poor game by his exalted standards, often taking the wrong option and dropping several passes when on the point of scoring. 'He was in one of his most feckless moods,' reported the *Glasgow Herald*, 'and as a wag wittily said, "was the best defender Scotland had".' On the wing, Vincent Coates had impressed with his physical runs, but he was 'far from clever' and was often hemmed in.

In addition, England came up against an outstanding defensive display by the Scottish three-quarters, especially from the wings John Sweet and Walter Sutherland. As the *Evening News* put it:

The Scottish backs put up a defence that will be recalled with enthusiasm many years hence... The particular heroes were Sutherland and Sweet, whose mobility really was extraordinary. Both are small, but each has any amount of pluck. It was not pluck, however, which carried them through – it was pace... Both seemed in delight, on Saturday, in cutting across to help the other, and both were acute in sensing danger... With such a pair of ubiquitous 'dancing dervishes' to deal with, the poor Englishmen could not develop their passing movements quickly enough to succeed.

Before the match, Walter had expressed his wish that he would get plenty to do, knowing that he had been largely a spectator in some previous games.

On this occasion, said the *Evening Dispatch* 'he got a rare dose of work on Saturday'. What made Walter's defence all the more remarkable was that, for over half the game, he effectively had to do the work of two men. Towards the end of the first half his centre partner Eric Loudoun-Shand badly wrenched his knee. There were no replacements so Walter moved into the centre and Loudoun-Shand went to the wing, a mere passenger, 'dead lame' and barely able to walk. 'With forty minutes to go,' said the *Evening News*, 'one despaired of three diminutive Scottish three-quarters keeping out four sound men with an unlimited supply of ball.'

But Walter and his teammates were more than equal to the task. In a memorable display of defence and resolute tackling, Walter used his speed and positional sense to single-handedly snuff out the joint threat of Poulton and Coates. 'With the heart of a lion,' said one reporter, 'he was able to do two men's work.' Poulton could make little headway against the Hawick player, who knocked him over time after time. Walter also had the powerful Coates 'well in hand'. As *The Scotsman* put it: 'Sutherland took it upon himself the burden of marking both Poulton and Coates, and he was so successful that he had the winger at the close of the game almost hypnotised into impotence.' Once or twice, Coates managed to escape Walter's grasp, but cleverly the Scot managed to knock him off his stride so that he was an easy target for Willie Wallace, the new Scottish full-back. It should be remembered that at this time forwards did not do much defending. The modern concept of the mobile and intelligent 'wing forward' wrecking havoc among the opposition backs was still in its infancy and did not really become the norm until the 1920s. Instead, back play was mostly lone combat, one against one. To successfully take on and contain two players, especially ones as dangerous as Poulton and Coates, had been an outstanding piece of tactical play and commitment. Walter was also the Scottish player who looked most likely to score. Largely starved of the ball, he had one great effort in the first half. Taking the ball on the English twenty-five-yard line, he danced around Coates and made a dash for the corner. The English full-back cut across and caught him right at the corner flag. According to some reports, Walter managed to get the ball down, but the referee hesitated and awarded a scrum to deny Walter his third try in a row against England. Walter also had one memorably gymnastic moment in defence when, running backwards, he caught a kick and having no time to turn hoofed the ball over the top of his head. After the match, it was reported that Walter was temporarily punch-drunk as a result of his heroic efforts during the afternoon.

Despite Scotland's defeat this was the game of Walter's life, as both the English and Scottish newspapers recognised. The *Evening Dispatch* commented: 'Long after Poulton's ineffective efforts, Vincent Coates's unsuccessful attempts at bullocking through, and C.N. Lowe's neat and tricky play are forgotten, we will recall the heroic tackling of W.R. Sutherland.' *The Scotsman* said that: 'The Hawick player was the outstanding man on the Scottish side, his speed being great, his tackling sure and fearless.' *Scottish Referee* commented: 'The Hawick representative was in a class by himself and he has rarely, if ever, played such a game for Scotland.' The critics from south of the border were also warm in their praise. *The Times* commented: 'Had Scotland been as well served at centre as they were on the wings they might well pulled the game out of the fire.' Similarly, the *Daily News* reported:

The best of the Scottish backs was Sutherland, a frail-looking player, but speedy as the wind and with the courage of a lion. Battered almost into insensibility once by the rugged impetuosity of Coates, he stuck like a hero to his job of going for the Somerset man. It was an unequal duel but Sutherland never gave in… it is rather strange that hitherto the Scottish authorities have been rather indifferently disposed to this fine player.

Admiration of Walter's play also came from closer to home. A week after the match at Twickenham, the *Hawick News* reported that a man in Galashiels had received a postcard from a friend in London who had been at the game:

Dear Yid, – I see that Gala and Hawick meet on Saturday. If Sutherland plays I hope that the Galashiels people will give him a rousing reception after his performance last Saturday. I never saw anything like it. A bit Hawick Callant laying out Oxford and Cambridge blues, etc. It nearly brought tears to my eyes. Give him three times three if he plays.

Another of Walter's admirers, 'Teribus', was moved to express appreciation in verse. As the rugby season drew to a close, the poem *Suddy the Hero of the Borders* appeared in the *Evening Dispatch*.

> *My song is of a hero,*
> *You know the man I mean,*
> *The finest wing three-quarter*
> *That ever wore the green.*
> *There are men who play for Scotland*
> *While Scotland wonders why,*
> *But his right to don the Thistle*
> *Not a Scotsman will deny!*
>
> *Suddy, Suddy Sutherland,*
> *The boy with the silver hair;*

English, Welsh, and Irishmen
Shall know when Suddy's there!

He can kick and run and tackle,
And a deer is not so fleet,
He can stop the Irish forwards,
Going down among their feet.
You will find him there and ready
Where there's daring work to do,
And the pluck that made the raiders
Is the pluck that pulls him through.

Suddy, Suddy Sutherland,
The boy with the silver hair,
He is game beyond all question,
He is grit beyond compare!

He is not so stout as many,
He is small and light of limb;
But who in pace and cleverness
Can hold a torch to him?
The swiftest of his foemen
Turns pale and takes a toss,
When like an arrow from a bowman
Comes the Borderer across!

Suddy, Suddy Sutherland,
Long, long may he appear,
To let the triple nations know
Old Hawick still is here!

Walter's display against England was the stuff of rugby legend. As Jock Wemyss wrote in the 1950s, it was 'a story told by old men to young boys in Hawick to this day.'

1914 began promisingly for Walter. He had recovered from the injury that had dogged the earlier part of the season and, in late December 1913, he had been in 'capital form' at the Scottish trial at Inverleith. Playing for the Home Scots on a miserable day of sleet and snow, he was the outstanding three-quarter on the field, putting in several spirited runs and scoring the final try 'in grand style' with a mesmerising dance through the defence. With no match against France in 1914 because of the crowd trouble the previous year, Walter's next, and final, international match was against Wales at Cardiff, where his career had begun four years earlier. The Scots approached the Welsh match with mixed feelings. They had not won on Welsh soil since 1892, a dreadful sequence of results that led many to believe that the Welsh were invincible at home. As *The Scotsman* commented: 'The monotony of defeat induced the notion that Wales could not be beaten at home, and some of our teams beat themselves in the train going south!' But by 1914 it was evident that times were beginning to change. Wales had recently lost a number of outstanding players. 'The Nicholls and the Morgans, and the Gabes and the Trews, and the Owens and the rest of the heroes have dropped out of the game, and their successors do not seem to belong to the same class.' Recent results, including three defeats against England, suggested that the Welsh were vulnerable. 'The old jaunty optimism is less apparent,' noted *The Scotsman*. Moreover, circumstances had forced a change of style in the Welsh game. Many of the talented three-quarters had gone and there was increasing reliance on a heavy and abrasive forward pack, which would soon become known as 'The Terrible Eight' because of their uncompromising style (despite being led by a clergyman, the Revd Alban Davies). As *The Scotsman* observed: 'Science is less in vogue, brawn is re-emerging at the expense of brain'.

Meanwhile, Scotland had gone to Wales with a new and experimental side. The build-up to the game shows the hopelessly chaotic nature of international selection at this time and the lack of serious preparation for big matches. The selectors had originally chosen a side with five new caps. Among the new forwards was Andrew 'Jock' Wemyss from Gala, who shared a room with Walter Sutherland and who would later became one of rugby's most distinguished writers and broadcasters. Walter was given his first start at centre, a position that he had occasionally played for Hawick and also for the South of Scotland. Some argued that Walter lacked enough experience in this position and should have been chosen on the wing, but injuries to other players had forced the selectors' hand and he had performed admirably as a makeshift centre against England the previous year. As 'C.D.S.' commented in *Scottish Referee*: 'Dire predictions regarding Sutherland's inclusion as a centre I pay no attention to. Sutherland is a man who can adapt himself to any position.' Besides, with Bill Stewart and George Will on the wings, Scotland had no shortage of pace out wide and Walter was too good to leave out of the team. He was partnered in the centre by a new cap, Ronald Scobbie, an Anglo-Scot from a military background who had played well in the trials, although Walter is unlikely to have known very much about him. The original selections at half-back were the Watsonians duo,

Tom Bowie and Eric 'Puss' Milroy, who were rated by the Scottish press as highly as any Welsh pairing, 'a club pair who work like machinery'. A few days before the match Milroy had to withdraw from the team because of a family bereavement and, in his absence, Bowie also stood down, either voluntarily or as a result of pressure from the selectors. In their place came two new caps. At stand-off, Allen Sloan from Edinburgh Accies was fast, smart and enterprising, although he lacked Bowie's knack for opening up the game. He was partnered by another new face, Andrew Hamilton, a solid but rather unspectacular scrum-half from the English club Headingley, who had shone in the trials.

As usual, the Scottish team travelled to Wales by train, leaving Edinburgh on the Thursday afternoon, picking up the Border players on the way, and spending the night in London before catching the 8.45 a.m. train from Paddington to Cardiff on the Friday morning. After lunch, the players went to Cardiff Arms Park for a look at the ground and to have a 'practice scamper', the nearest thing that the team came to a squad session or pre-match preparation. Despite the changes in the team, the Scottish rugby press was remarkably upbeat about Scotland's prospects. Although untested, the side had potential and could cause Wales some trouble. As *The Scotsman* dryly observed: 'Somehow one has developed the notion that their enterprise partakes less of the nature of a forlorn hope than usual.' The team had a fast, talented back-line that was built for attack, although the forwards were lightweight and it would be fatal for them to get dragged into a tight game. *The Scotsman* concluded:

If the Scottish forwards are mastered and overrun, it will be a 'blue look-out' for Scotland, for candidly, on paper, one is not impressed by the ability of the three-quarters to stand up against big, bashing, victorious forwards. Let us hope that they will not be called upon to engage in much of that kind of work!

The gentlemen of the press would have been less optimistic if they had known that Scotland's selection problems were not finished. Overnight, one of the forwards, John McDougall of Greenock Wanderers, fell ill and had to withdraw. The players were kept in the dark until the team-talk in the hotel just an hour or so before kick-off when, to everyone's surprise, one of the replacements, Roy Gailie of Glasgow Academicals, appeared in his playing kit. But even then the team was still not settled. On the way to the ground, the selectors had second thoughts and Gailie was told to stand down in place of another reserve, Archie Symington of Cambridge University. In other words, the Scottish team was not finally decided until the players were warming up in the pavilion, minutes before they went on the field. All of this meant that the Scots would play Wales with eight new caps, most of whom had never played together before and who barely knew each other. Walter Sutherland was the only member of the team who had played in an international match at Cardiff.

Cardiff Arms Park had been given a facelift since Walter's last visit in 1910. A new grandstand had been built down the south side of the field and the enclosure had been terraced. The weather was dull and cold, but the pitch was firmer than usual. The match began promisingly for Scotland. In the opening minutes, the ball flashed along the line to Bill Stewart, who fulfilled the pre-match prediction that he 'will raise a flutter if he is allowed room' by beating two defenders on a long run to score under the posts. 'Podger' Laing, one of the new forwards, landed the simple conversion to give the visitors a 5-0 lead. Scotland were in charge and might have gone further ahead if Laing had not missed an easy penalty kick soon afterwards. Gradually, as their nerves began to settle, Wales got back into the game. The Welsh forwards had several strong rushes, which were only checked by gritty defence from the Scots, among whom Walter was very prominent, saving one certain try with a courageous fall at the feet of three forwards. This turned out to be a very rough match, 'no kid-glove battle', as *The Scotsman* described it. In the thick of the action, Laing 'had to suffer a severe gruelling' from a Welsh forward, which prompted the referee, Mr Drennon of Ireland, to lecture the offending player, an event which was almost unheard of in international football. Laing quickly recovered and for the remainder of the match, 'no Welshman whom he subsequently tackled believed that his vitality had been impaired'. David Bain, the Scottish captain, sustained a severe injury above his right eye, which required hospital treatment after the game.

Walter had also been in the wars and his injury was to prove crucial to the outcome of the match. Towards the end of the first half, he badly injured his ankle while trying to stop the Welsh wing Ivor Davies. Replacements were not allowed in those days and Walter had the injury strapped and stayed on the field, but he was reduced to a mere passenger, unable to run or put pressure on his ankle. Later in the game, he was forced to change positions with George Will, but it might have been better if he had been taken off. Wales led narrowly at the interval 7-5 from a drop-goal and a penalty to a goal, but the writing was on the wall. In the second half Wales targeted the Scottish weakness and, after six minutes, the Welsh wing Davies broke through to score a try. Worse was to follow when a loose kick by the crippled Sutherland was charged down by the Welsh centre Jack Wetter, who gathered and raced away to score a converted try. Another drop-goal and a late converted try meant that Wales ran out convincing winners 24-5, Scotland's seventh successive defeat to the men in scarlet.

The final score had flattered Wales although Scotland, hampered by injuries, had played with a lack of purpose and cohesion.

For Walter, the Welsh game had been an unhappy one, although the experiment of playing him at centre had been reasonably successful. Prior to his injury, he had done some good work, especially in defence, but he had kicked too much and was caught out of position once or twice, giving his opponents time and space to exploit. On the plus side, clever handling on his part had led to Scotland's try. Several writers agreed that Walter's injury had been the turning point in the match. As 'C.D.S.' commented in *Scottish Referee*:

He continued to play, or rather he continued on the field but he was absolutely useless and favourable openings that came to him after Will and he had changed places were rendered valueless by his inability either to kick or run. The Welshmen were not slow to seize their opportunity and, playing to the crippled defence, were credited with at least two scores, which they never would have obtained had Sutherland remained sound. Twice at least Sutherland had a clear run in and had he been able he could not but help scoring, but unfortunately he could not raise a gallop.

After the match, Walter was barely able to walk. Catching the train home, he had to be wheeled along the station platform on a luggage trolley by his colleague Jock Wemyss. Walter's season had already been badly disrupted because of injury. In the team photograph, his knee was heavily bandaged. His latest injury was serious enough to rule him out of the rest of the season, although he did take part in some of the sevens in April and athletics meetings in the summer. Nobody knew it at the time, but the Welsh game in 1914 would be the last meaningful game of rugby that Walter would ever play.

six

PRINCE OF SEVENS

Seven-a-side rugby was tailor-made for Walter's love of speed and the open spaces. He was fortunate enough to grow up in the heartland of sevens and to play for a club whose record in the short game was second to none. It is a well-known story that sevens rugby began in 1883 in the abbey town of Melrose. The local club was desperate for funds and hit upon the idea of holding a sports day, including a football tournament played between teams of seven men each. The new game was an instant success and other clubs in the Borders quickly followed the Melrose example. Gala introduced a tournament in 1884, followed by Hawick in 1885, Jed-Forest in 1894 and Langholm in 1908. Autumn tournaments at Selkirk, Kelso and Earlston were introduced after the First World War. This chapter examines Walter's career in sevens rugby. Like many Border players, sevens played a big part in his rugby life. He had his first taste of senior rugby as a seventeen-year-old when he played for the Hawick 'B' seven at the Langholm Sevens in May 1908. The following year, in April 1909, he made his first appearance for the senior Hawick seven, winning the tournament at Gala. This was the first of many successes for Walter and he went on to have a great record in the sevens. Between 1909 and 1914, he played in twenty-seven tournaments, reaching the final twenty-one times and winning seventeen first prizes. It was with good reason that the *Hawick News* described him as 'the prince of the seven-a-sides'.

By Walter's era, the annual sevens circuit was firmly established in the Borders and all of the tournaments attracted large crowds. Thanks to the railway system, supporters could travel around quickly and cheaply, returning safely home in the evening provided they didn't get stuck in the local pub. The North British Railway Company ran specials to the sevens and these were always very popular. In April 1912, the company sold 1,850 tickets in Hawick alone for the trip to the Melrose Sevens. Others made their way to the sevens by horse-drawn vehicle, bicycle or, if they were wealthy enough, by the new-fangled 'motors'.

Some hardy souls walked to neighbouring towns, perhaps spending the night under a hedge. The annual sevens day was a great local occasion, creating a holiday-like atmosphere. In 1914, it was estimated that around 8,000 people swarmed into Melrose to see the sevens, swelling the population of the little town around eight times in a single afternoon. At Gala Sevens in 1912, around 4,000 people crammed into the newly opened Netherdale, allowing the club to pay off a sizeable chunk of its debt for the new ground in a single afternoon. Sometimes, grounds were barely able to cope with the press of numbers. During the Melrose final in 1909, the game was constantly interrupted as excited spectators spilled onto the field after each score. Earlier in the day, there had been trouble when some sections of the crowd tried to get out of the ground after one of the ties, heading for a quick drink between the rounds. The exit gates were unable to deal with the crush and some people took matters into their own hands, as the *Hawick News* reported:

The crowd was inclined to get a little bit out of hand and a gatekeeper was injured in a 'strushie'. After the Hawick-Watsonians tie, there was tremendous exodus from the field and barricades were torn down to let people out.

There were also more earthy matters to attend to. Tournaments lasted for several hours at a time and some grounds had little or no toilet accommodation. Gala's new ground at Netherdale came in for particular criticism. In April 1913, under the heading 'Lavatory Accommodation at the Sports', the *Hawick News* took up the crusade for decent facilities:

Our attention has been directed to the absence of such generally at Border football fields, more particularly as far as ladies are concerned. These are in the way of patronising seven-a-side contests to a considerable extent, and are surely entitled to some consideration. The conditions were particularly unfortunate at Galashiels, the field being so far from the town.

Marquees and tents were erected at the sevens for the sale of food and drink. The heady cocktail of fresh air, strong drink and excitement meant that there was always the threat of the crowd getting out of control. Way back in 1889, the final at Melrose was interrupted on several occasions because of fighting among the spectators. To counter this threat, some tournaments had temperance tents selling only soft drinks and hot tea. Describing the scene at Hawick Sevens in April 1914, the *Hawick News* reported:

The British Women's Temperance Association provided tea and temperance refreshments at very moderate prices in a large marquee, the efforts of the ladies to cater for the immense crowd proving of a most satisfactory description and being regarded as a great boon.

On the field, the early tournaments were often haphazard events. Replacement players were not permitted and a side that lost a man through injury had to battle on regardless. In the Melrose final in 1896, the home side faced Hawick with only six players, one of their side having been injured in the semi-final. Melrose lost another man in the final, at which point the players left the field, handing the cup to Hawick. In the Hawick final in 1914, Royal High School FP kindly offered their opponents Edinburgh University the use of a substitute for an injured player. Bizarrely, the University declined, preferring to play on with six men and predictably going down to a heavy defeat.

One of the big problems for organisers was to ensure that tournaments finished before it got dark. Preceding the rugby, there was usually a programme of other events, such as athletics, drop and place-kicking competitions and dribbling races. Often, these dragged on interminably until late afternoon, which meant that the later stages of the rugby were played in semi-darkness. At Melrose in 1914, ties were cut from fifteen to twelve minutes, but even then the final was played in near darkness. 'The final was spoiled from the point of view of many owing to the poor light,' grumbled the *Hawick News*, 'and there is no doubt about it that this happens too often at Melrose.'

The prizes awarded to the winning teams were varied and rather eccentric, such as travelling bags, clocks, reading lamps or tea trays. In the days before health promotion campaigns, silver cigarette cases were also popular. The Scottish rugby authorities were uncomfortable at prizes of this kind being given to amateurs. It was suspected that the players were taking the prizes and selling them on to make a little money on the side, which was seen as shadow professionalism. In 1907, the Scottish Football Union ordered that only medals or badges would be awarded to the winners of the sevens. At this time, Melrose was the only tournament to have a tangible trophy, the famous 'Ladies' Cup', a beautiful silver goblet that had been presented by the 'Ladies of Melrose' to the winners of the first tournament in 1883.

Modern tournaments usually have sixteen or twenty teams, but in the Edwardian era it was more common to have eight, ten or twelve teams at most. These were mainly local Border sides, but teams from Edinburgh also took part as well as Clydesdale from the west. In some cases there were often 'A' and 'B' sides from the home club, or perhaps a junior side, but their purpose was to make up the numbers and they were not taken very seriously. Reporting on the Langholm Sevens in 1913, the *Hawick News* complained that a Hawick 'B' seven were not worthy of their invitation:

The Hawick 'B' lot, one or two of the players at least, seemed to regard the fact of their being there at all to compete as more of a joke than anything else, and they got no further than they deserved.

Sevens tournaments might have been smaller and easier to win than their modern equivalents, but this should not obscure Hawick's remarkable record in the era before the First World War. A few bald statistics tell the story of the club's domination of the sevens circuit. Between 1900 and 1914, Hawick won at Gala ten times, Melrose eight, Hawick seven and Langholm five (from 1908). Jed-Forest was the only tournament that Hawick found difficult to win, managing only one title in 1912, the year that the club also completed a Grand Slam, winning all five sevens in a single season.

The annual sevens circuit took place in April and early May, the fifteen-a-side season having finished at the end of March. The circuit was always played in the same order: Gala, Melrose, Hawick, Jed-Forest and Langholm, a pattern that survived until the 1990s. Gala Sevens, the opening tournament in the annual circuit, was something of a happy hunting ground for Hawick. Between 1893 and 1913, Hawick appeared in every final with the exception of 1905. Walter Sutherland had a good record at Gala. He played in five tournaments and made it to the final every time, winning four in a row between 1909 and 1912. Walter's first appearance in the senior Hawick seven was at Gala on 2 April 1909. In an exciting final played in drizzling rain, he produced some 'beautiful work' to create the opening for a vital score, Hawick beating Gala 8-5. In the following three years there were some fairly easy wins for Hawick, the team not conceding a point in 1910 and 1911. The great run came to an end in 1913 when Hawick fell to their old rivals Gala in the final (0-10). With spectators 'on the tip-toe of excitement', the home forwards tore into Hawick, not allowing them to settle. Billy Burnet had a disappointing afternoon, but 'Bottler' Wilson and Walter Sutherland tried bravely to turn the tide behind beaten forwards. 'Sutherland proved as clever as yore,' said the *Hawick News*, 'but he was given too much to do in the final round.' Unfortunately, some Gala skulduggery cost Hawick an important score. Morison, the Gala centre, broke free but Walter would have caught him if he had not been deliberately tripped from behind. At the final whistle, 'the joy of the crowd knew no bounds'.

As the oldest sevens tournament in the world, Melrose was the Blue Riband of the circuit, the one that everyone wanted to win. Hawick had a great record at Melrose, winning seven times in a row between 1892 and 1898 and also in 1900 and 1901. Gradually, Melrose became a very hard tournament to win. It was taken much more seriously than the other events and from 1896 it attracted determined competition from Edinburgh, often coinciding with an Edinburgh holiday weekend. Watsonians won the cup three times in a row between 1905 and 1907, but there was huge relief in Hawick when the Greens recaptured the cup in 1908. When the team returned to Hawick station in the evening they were greeted with the Saxhorn Band and a crowd of cheering townspeople, who chaired some of the players and the veteran trainer Peter Hope through the streets.

Hawick's win in 1908 marked the beginning of another period of dominance at Melrose Sevens that lasted until the outbreak of the First World War. Hawick won the prestigious cup six times in a row and also reached the final in 1914. Walter Sutherland was a key man in this run of success. He made his first appearance at Melrose Sevens on 10 April 1909. In an eight-team tournament, played in magnificent spring weather, he 'captivated everyone with his clever play', both in attack and defence. The final between the old rivals Hawick and Gala was described as a 'cracker', fast and keen although marred by being played in poor light. Walter gave Hawick the lead with a penalty goal, but Gala drew back with a try. The winning score came from a burst from the halfway line by Tom Wilson, who was tackled but managed to get the ball to his captain Tom Neil for the clincher. At the end, the famous Ladies' Cup was presented to Bill Kyle to enthusiastic cries of 'Speech, Willie' and 'Come away with a verse of *Teribus*'. Like most grounds at the time, The Greenyards did not have proper changing facilities so jubilant Hawick supporters chaired the players back to their hotel, Tom Neil clenching the cup in his tired hands.

Melrose Sevens was, and still is, renowned for its good fortune with the weather. While the other sevens often took place in miserable conditions during the last throes of the winter, Melrose was regularly bathed in warm spring sunshine. As the *Hawick Express* commented in 1912: 'Melrose's luck in regard to the weather is proverbial.' In 1910, however, it was a poor day and the takings at the gate were down from £150 to £99. In an unattractive tournament with mostly tight and rather boring games, Hawick retained their title, scoring only 16 points in three ties and not conceding a single point. The weather and the quality of play improved the next year. Hawick lived up to their billing as the tournament favourites, putting on a fine display of sevens prowess and skill. Lindsay-Watson and Sutherland were in great form, Walter performing 'like the artist he is'. He scored a great try in the semi-final against Gala, taking the ball from Kyle's lineout catch and leaving his opponents standing with a sprint from his own twenty-five.

In an exciting final, Hawick overcame a plucky Heriot's FP (18-6), with Carl Ogilvy scoring two important tries. Afterwards, it was agreed that the Hawick seven were as good a side as any of their predecessors. Lindsay-Watson and Sutherland supplied the speed and finish, the half-backs Ogilvy and Burnet had guile and were excellent linkmen and the forward trio of Kyle, Brown and Wilson were strong and mobile. 'The form shown by Hawick being such as to send their own supporters into excesses of delight,' said the *Hawick News*, 'and even drag from unwilling Gala and Melrose followers expressions of appreciation.'

Promoting itself as 'Five Hours of Continuous Amusement', the Melrose tournament in 1913 turned out to be a great success. There had been some doubt if it would go ahead because in the morning the Borders was swept by a severe snowstorm, but miraculously the snow cleared by midday. Telegrams were sent to the competing clubs asking them to make their way over and the sevens went ahead in fine, crisp conditions, the surrounding hills covered in a blanket of white. Twelve teams took part, including four teams from Edinburg, and the juniors from Walkerburn, who were the 'surprise packet' in reaching the semi-finals. The 'tit-bit' of the afternoon was the second round tie between Hawick and Edinburgh University. Both sides had very strong sevens, the University having several international players in Andrew Ross of Scotland and Sam Campbell of Ireland as well as C.L. Marburg and Jan Stegmann, two South African students, the latter of whom had toured with the Springboks in 1912. The University were expected to give Hawick a stiff challenge, as the *Hawick News* reported:

The appearance of the redoubtable South African J.A. Stegmann, among the 'Varsity heavy-weights encouraged those Borderers who were renegade enough to hope that the 'Greens' would encounter more than their match. Hawick got it hard enough in all conscience, but their players knew they were up against 'hot stuff' and went at it accordingly.

In a 'ding-dong' encounter, Hawick opened the scoring with a kick-and-chase by Billy Burnet. The university hit back with a score by Marburg and, despite great efforts by both sides there was no further scoring and the tie went into extra time. Amid intense excitement, Bill Kyle, showing all his years of experience, broke from a lineout, handed off an opponent and scored in dashing fashion. It was a great victory for Hawick (8-5). Stegmann, the dangerous South African three-quarter, had his moments, but he was inexperienced in sevens and had been well policed by Walter Sutherland. In the semi-final, Walter scored the only try against Kelso 'in his best style'. Hawick had no trouble overcoming a weary Stewart's FP in the final (14-0). Fresh and full of running, Walter scored twice, the first from following up a sliced drop-goal attempt and the second a simple effort from a long throw-in at midfield. Billy Burnet, the captain, took the cup for Hawick and was chaired shoulder-high through the Melrose streets to the strains of *Hawick's Queen o' a' the Borders*.

Hawick also reached the Melrose final in 1914. Walter was back after ten weeks off through injury. 'The internationalist's display under the circumstances was quite a remarkable one,' said the *Hawick News*. 'The popularity of 'Suddie' was brought out in no uncertain fashion by the warm welcome he received from the crowd.' In the semi-final against Edinburgh University he scored a fine try, dancing through the defence in his old style. However, it was clear that he was a bit rusty after his long lay-off, lacking his usual sharpness and some of his speed. In the final against Watsonians, he was beaten for pace by his international colleague Jimmy Pearson. The city men were the better side and deserved their win (8-0), bringing to an end Hawick's great run at the premier sevens tournament.

The week after Melrose, the sevens bandwagon rolled into Hawick. After the heady feast at The Greenyards, Hawick Sevens sometimes seemed like plain fare, although locally it was taken very seriously. Predictably, Hawick performed well at their own event, winning it in 1909, 1911 and 1912, and reaching the final in 1910 and 1913. Walter Sutherland's first appearance at Hawick Sevens took place on 17 April 1909. In an eight-team tournament, his side easily made it to the final, where they faced Clydesdale. Hawick had a score to settle against The Dale. The previous year, the two sides had also met in the Hawick final. The home side had courteously agreed to shorten the game because Clydesdale had to catch the last train back to Glasgow. Hawick were expecting an easy win, but they were surprised when the visitors took an early lead. Time quickly ran out, leaving Clydesdale unlikely winners and Hawick with egg on their faces. In 1909 Clydesdale played the Queen's Park and Scotland football international Harry Paul on the wing, but he could not prevent Hawick running away with it 18-0. Shortly towards the end, Walter scored a great try, breaking clear to seal his side's win. In 1910, the Hawick Sevens were the source of much controversy. Watsonians withdrew at the last minute, forcing the organisers to throw together a scratch team to make up the numbers. Hawick's semi-final against Heriot's FP was a very rough match with the forwards almost coming to blows because of some 'over-energetic' play by the visitors. To make matters worse, it was a miserable afternoon with rain hammering down relentlessly. Long before the finish, the pitch became unplayable, 'in some parts being like a miniature lake', so the final between Hawick and Melrose was postponed until the following Tuesday. Even then, the problems weren't over. Bill Kyle, the veteran Hawick forward, was unable to play, but Melrose refused to allow a substitute in his place. Hawick therefore played the final with six men against seven, predictably going down to a 15-0 defeat. It was a happier story for Hawick the following year, although the weather remained squally and unsettled. The home side cruised through to the final where they gained revenge over Melrose (15-5). Walter Sutherland was the player of the tournament, as the *Hawick News* reported:

Sutherland stood out pre-eminently as the finest individual player engaged, and his two brilliant tries against Melrose were the outstanding features of the afternoon. The way in which Sutherland swerved past Ross and Bunyan aroused the spectators to an extraordinary pitch of enthusiasm; and when in the second period, the clever Hawick internationalist beat the whole Melrose back division, the intoxication of success seized hold of the crowd... Sutherland showed himself to be a prince of seven-a-sides and Hawick are fortunate indeed to have such an artist of a player in their side.

Hawick won again in 1912, but met their match the following year. As usual, the weather was not on its best behaviour. Military-style tents had been provided for the teams to change in, but the gentlemen of the press were left outside in the rain and cold. As one irate hack from the *Evening News* later complained: 'A snell wind blowing and rain lashing down on one's copy and converting it into pulp is not a pleasant experience.' Then he produced the ultimate insult: 'They do things better at Netherdale.' A cup of hot tea from the ladies of the BWTA managed to thaw him out a little. Hawick were the favourites to win the sevens and eased through to the final without conceding a point. Their opponents were a composite seven put together by the redoubtable James Henry Digby Watson. An Englishman born in Southsea, 'Bungy' Watson had come to Edinburgh to study medicine, playing rugby for the University and later at centre for Edinburgh Accies. A great all-rounder and 'a real good chap', Watson excelled at any sport that he tried, although as a rugby player he was very individualistic and sometimes erratic. As well as being a student boxing champion and representing Scotland at the long jump, he was a travelling reserve for the Scotland rugby team before winning 3 caps at centre for England in 1914. Watson's seven was very strong, drawing some of the best talent from Edinburgh. It contained five existing or future international players, including Jimmy Pearson, the Watsonians flying machine, Tennant Sloan, the experienced Scottish half-back and Sam Campbell, the Irish international forward. The rugby programme had not started until nearly 4 p.m. so the final was played in semi-darkness, which caused all sorts of difficulties. Despite being a scratch side, Watson's proved a very hot handful and Hawick were forced back in defence. The visitors took the lead with a try by Sloan, but Hawick hit back with a great run by Lindsay-Watson, sprinting from his own twenty-five and beating four men to score. All-square at half-time, in the second period Watson kicked a penalty and scored a late try and conversion to give his side the gold medals. Bill Kyle was knocked out trying to prevent the winning try and had to leave the field with concussion. The best team won and Watson had got through a power of work. For once the weather was kinder for the Hawick Sevens in April 1914. In the semi-final against Royal High School FP, Walter, who was just back from injury, scored 'one of his old-time famous tries, which worked the crowd up to a fine frenzy of enthusiasm'. Unfortunately, it wasn't enough and Hawick fell to the School, the eventual winners, in extra time.

Hawick didn't have it all their own way in the sevens. Jed-Forest was something of a bogey ground for the Greens. The Jed-Forest tournament had begun in 1894 and Hawick had won the first five titles in a row, but there had been no further successes since 1898. Nobody could explain it, except that the Hawick players had developed some kind of mental block at Riverside. Walter's first appearance at the Jed-Forest Sevens was in April 1909. On a soft, sloppy ground with a greasy ball, the backs were disappointing and Hawick made a semi-final exit to Melrose. 'Watson and Sutherland were under a cloud for the day,' groaned the *Hawick News*. There was no improvement the following year with an exciting semi-final defeat to Gala. In 1911, Hawick went out once again in the semi-final, this time to Edinburgh University, which turned out to be a bit of a grudge match. Hawick had already won at Gala, Melrose and their own tournament, and seemed to be heading for a sevens clean sweep. The university players had other ideas and, before the Jed-Forest tournament, they made no secret of their strong desire to stop Hawick's progress. This included a spot of gamesmanship by drafting in three international players from their near-neighbours Watsonians: Louis Speirs, Jimmy Pearson and Gus Angus, who was described as 'slippery as an eel and as elusive as a will o' the wisp'. The 'Two-Club Seven' could now boast five international players (plus one future cap), the three Watsonians internationals joining up with Freddie Osler and Andrew Ross, both of whom had just been capped. For Hawick, Bill Kyle had been forced out, having broken two of his fingers the previous week. Without Kyle's leadership to settle the side, the Hawick forwards were 'flurried and over-anxious', struggling to hold their own against much heavier opponents. Played in heavy rain, there was no score at half-time, largely thanks to great defensive work by the Hawick backs. In the second half, Hawick eventually cracked and Freddie Osler scored the only try from a lineout, although 'Bottler' Wilson claimed that he had got a hand on the ball first. The University managed to win 3-0, which brought about a very mixed reaction from the crowd. Enjoying the moment and some unashamed *schadenfreude*, many Border spectators were delighted that their Hawick cousins had been beaten at last. As the *Hawick News* reported:

There was witnessed at Jedburgh what may be described as an exhibition of unholy joy in so-called patriotic Borderers rejoicing in unmeasured terms at the defeat of a Border seven by a cosmopolitan lot.

The Hawick supporters, of course, saw things very differently and were furious that their side had gone down to a bunch of city slickers:

It remains to be said that a few of the Hawick supporters require still to learn to take a beating in a sportsmanlike spirit. To leave the field in a rage as some did because their favourites were ousted was not a good spirit to show.

Walter made his last appearance at the Jed-Forest Sevens in April 1913, where Hawick, the reigning champions, made an ignominious first-round exit to Kelso.

Introduced in 1908, Langholm Sevens brought the curtain down on the Scottish rugby season. Hawick always struggled at Jed-Forest, but they had few problems at Langholm, often winning quite easily. Between 1909 and 1914, Walter played for the senior Hawick team in six Langholm tournaments and won five of them, only missing out in a first round exit in 1910. With the season at an end, the standard of play at Langholm was not as high as at some of the other tournaments. In 1911, the sevens were described as being of 'poor quality' while in 1913 they were 'somewhat humdrum... [with] nothing specially noteworthy shown'. Langholm was a difficult place to get to from the rest of the Borders. The attendance was usually smaller than the other tournaments, although there were always a few die-hards who made great efforts to attend. In 1913 some hardy supporters cycled all the way from Hawick, but had to cadge a lift back home on the train as they were too exhausted or tipsy by the end. Walter Sutherland always played well at Langholm. In a tight semi-final in 1909, he scored the crucial try in extra time against Gala. Likewise, in the pouring rain in 1911, he was described as 'easily the most notable player on display', scoring the clinchers against Gala in the semi-final and Langholm in the final. 1913 was another wet year, although Hawick had 'a comparatively easy afternoon of it', beating Jed-Forest in the final. 'Sutherland displayed his usual adroitness in bewildering opponents,' noted the *Hawick News*, 'though he did not score as freely as at previous sports.' Walter's very final appearance in the green jersey of Hawick took place at the Langholm Sevens on 1 May 1914. By the club's high standards it had not been a very successful year, only reaching one final at Melrose. At Langholm it all went gloriously right. Played in favourable weather, which brought out a big crowd, Hawick had a good all-round seven, much better than previous weeks. Walter Sutherland was back on the wing, having missed Jed-Forest through injury, while Frank Beatson, 'Bottler' Wilson and the new boy John Charters made up a fast and clever back division. The forward trio of George Johnstone, Bill Anderson and John Corrie were irresistible. The big test came in the semi-final against Gala. In a 'stirring encounter', the tie was into extra time when Walter showed a neat piece of skill, kicking the ball away from the hands of a Gala player and racing away to score the winning try. Walter's ankle, which had troubled him all season, required some attention after his long run, but he was back to help his side defeat Kelso in the final. 'Hawick quite excelled themselves,' said the *Hawick News*, 'and had they done anything like as well in the previous sports they would not have caused people to wonder if their skill had left them.'

Hawick's greatest achievement in the sevens was in 1912 when the club completed a Grand Slam, winning all five tournaments in a single season. This was the first time that anybody had done this, although way back in the 1890s Hawick had twice managed to win all four tournaments (Langholm sevens was not introduced until 1908). The success in 1912 was built upon consistent selection, the side using only eight players in the five tournaments. In the back division, the international trio of Sutherland, Lindsay-Watson and Burnet provided the speed and finish. At half-back, there was guile and cleverness in the shape of 'Bottler' Wilson, the veteran sevens artist, and Danny Shannon, a nuggety little athlete who would soon turn professional. The forward unit of Bill Kyle, now in his thirties but as keen as ever, and the two Georges, Johnstone and Laing, played in all five tournaments together. The forwards were strong and mobile, fiercely competitive, good in the tight and tireless in open play.

The 1912 circuit opened, as usual, with Gala Sevens, which took place on a sunny but windy afternoon at the new field at Netherdale. The attendance was slightly down because the country was in the grip of a national coal strike and the North British Railway Company refused to run a special train from Hawick. In a ten-team tournament, Hawick cruised past Melrose and Gala before taking on the powerful Edinburgh University in the final. The match was described as a 'splendid tussle', producing four good tries and great excitement. After early pressure by the students, Walter Sutherland burst away from well inside his own half and skilful footwork allowed him to beat two defenders to score the opening try. The University hit back with two unconverted tries, but slowly ran out of steam. Hawick clinched it with a great effort by 'Bottler' Wilson. The veteran broke away and, when tackled, he just managed to throw the ball over his head to Walter, who crossed behind the posts. Walter kicked the match-winning conversion to give his side the final 8-6 win. 'Hawick, as was natural, had the better notions of the requirements of the game,' said the *Evening News*, 'but the students were eager and robust, and made a great fight of it.'

Melrose Sevens in 1912 belonged to the indomitable duo of Walter Sutherland and Robert Lindsay-Watson. On a balmy afternoon and in front of a large crowd, including 1,850 off the train from Hawick, the two flyers were at the top of their game. 'The names of Lindsay-Watson and Sutherland were on everybody's lips,' commented the *Hawick News*, 'and nothing grander has been accomplished on the Greenyards in the past.' An inconsistent player at times, Lindsay-Watson turned on the style, scoring a great try in the second round against Stewart's FP, taking the ball behind his own line, dodging and weaving out of defence, and running the length of the field to score. In the final against Gala, he produced a great chase of the Gala flyer W.L. Hunter, giving him several yards start before knocking him down. 'There was no question as to the effectiveness of his tackle,' said the *Hawick News* breathlessly, 'Hunter being firmly grasped and brought to Mother Earth.' Meanwhile, Lindsay-Watson's partner Walter Sutherland was 'cleverness personified', doing things that nobody else would even imagine. In the semi-final against Melrose, he collected the ball a few yards from his own line, streaked past the defence and away for a great score. 'With the proverbial inch or so from the touchline to work upon,' marvelled the *Hawick News*, 'he left the Melrose backs behind grandly after covering three-quarters of the length of the field.' Similarly, on the way to a memorable try in the final, 'nothing finer was witnessed than the manner in which he bamboozled the Gala backs time and again'. Combined with the outstanding play of their forwards and half-backs, Hawick ran out easy winners, defeating Gala 12-5 in the final.

Walter missed the Hawick Sevens because of an ankle injury. Billy Burnet, the international centre, took his place and helped the side to an easy win over Gala in the final (13-0). At Jed-Forest, Lindsay-Watson dropped out, having injured himself on his motorcycle, and Walter returned to the wing. In 1909 and 1911, Hawick had won four out of five tournaments, but each year had failed in the semi-final at Jed-Forest. Could they go one better and finally slay their bogey at Riverside? On another beautiful spring day, Hawick were made to fight all the way, narrowly squeezing past Edinburgh University, Heriot's FP and Melrose to reach the final against the 'surprise element' Selkirk. The stalwart forward Bill Kyle was in great form, trying his very best to win an elusive Jed-Forest medal at last. As the *Hawick News* observed:

'Kyle's working for his medal!' was a common remark around the ropes... seldom has this forward put in a harder or more effective afternoon's performance than on this occasion.

Over the tournament, Kyle scored three of Hawick's seven tries, the other four going to Walter Sutherland. This included a 'Sutherland Special' in the semi-final against Melrose when he beat several players then raced down the touchline at a great pace to score. Sutherland and Kyle scored in the final against a determined and rather unlucky Selkirk to secure Hawick's first win at Jed-Forest for fourteen years.

The following weekend, Hawick secured the Grand Slam at Langholm. In front of a larger crowd than normal, the Greens had no difficulty in reaching the final. Gala, their opponents, took an early 5-0 lead, playing with spirit and confidence. Kyle pulled back three points with a typical forceful run, but with three minutes left for play Gala were clinging to their narrow two-point lead. In a tight match, it seemed that the Grand Slam was lost, but then came a magical moment from Walter Sutherland. Taking the ball in midfield, he flew past the despairing efforts of the defence and scored at the posts. Danny Shannon added another late try to seal the tournament and the sevens Grand Slam for Hawick. At the final whistle, one supporter got so carried away that he ran onto the field and pinched the ball as a souvenir. When challenged, he supposedly replied: 'It's easy seen that Langholm disnae win many sevens. Ahm takin' this tae Hawick tae be addeet tae a kistfu' o' ba's.' It was a great achievement for Hawick to win all five tournaments, a feat that has been repeated on only two occasions since then. A genuine team effort with each man playing his part, Sutherland, Kyle and Wilson had been outstanding. As the *Evening Dispatch* noted:

For their successes, Hawick must again thank Sutherland, for his wonderful running, heady and gritty play, Kyle, who is still an easy first as a forward for his sound judgement, and Wilson, for his knowledge of 'sevens'.

As a key member of the 1912 team, Walter Sutherland had underlined his prowess at the sevens game. His speed, athleticism, tactical awareness and enthusiasm were perfectly suited to the demands of sevens and had brought him many successes, including five winners' medals at Melrose and the 1912 Grand Slam. He was one of the most popular players on the circuit, winning many admirers wherever he played. Truly, he was one of the great exponents of the short game.

seven

THE CINDER TRACK

Anyone who studies sport before the First World War cannot fail to be struck by the number of multi-talented all-rounders and double internationals, people who reached the highest level in more than one sport. The greatest of them all was C.B. Fry, who was born in Surrey in 1872. Fry's achievements were truly stupendous. He captained England at cricket, played in a FA Cup final and won a cap for England at football, represented Blackheath and the Barbarians at rugby, held the world long-jump record and won twelve blues at Oxford University. He also found the time to write a novel and had a successful career as a journalist, scholar and politician. Scotland also had its own share of gifted performers. Kenneth Macleod was one the greatest three-quarters of his day and scored a brilliant try against the Springboks in 1906. He retired from rugby at only twenty years old, but went on to captain Lancashire at cricket, and later became a very good golfer and an international curler. Another example of this multi-talented breed was Robert Lindsay-Watson, the Hawick three-quarter, who played rugby for Scotland and threw the hammer for Great Britain at the Olympic Games in London in 1908 (where he reached the final, but was unplaced). For good measure, he was also a fine golfer and a dab hand with the billiards cue. Successful all-rounders of this kind are now very rare. Modern professional sport demands years of dedication to reach the top and it is unlikely that anybody would have the time, the energy or the ability to excel at more than one activity. The difference was that, in Victorian and Edwardian times, sport was not taken as seriously as it is today. Training regimes were much less rigorous and special dietary and psychological preparations were unknown. As Brian Dobbs has pointed out, success in sport was based principally on natural ability rather than practised skills. At this time, it was still possible to get by on raw talent.

Walter Sutherland was another of the elite performers who won international honours in more than one sport. He made 13 appearances for the Scottish rugby team and he also won 2 caps for athletics, representing Scotland in the 220 yards in 1911 and 1913. He was Scottish Champion over 220 yards in 1913, and between 1911 and 1914 he was unbeatable on the Borders' amateur circuit, winning both the 100 and 220 yards titles for four years in a row. At this time, British athletics still used the imperial system of measurement rather than the 'Continental' metric system. This chapter examines Walter's career in athletics, where he enjoyed further success to go along with his rugby achievements.

Running is the simplest of all sports and people have run against each other since time immemorial. In the Borders, there was an ancient tradition of athletics at the annual Common Ridings or at special 'Border Games', such as Jedburgh and Innerleithen. The driving force behind these events was a lively culture of betting and gambling. The athletes were treated in much the same way as horses, being carefully assessed for their current form and given handicaps if they were performing too well. Running was a very cheap sport to take up, requiring little more than a half-decent pair of shoes. It gave working-class men a chance for enrichment although, unlike boxing or football, it was difficult to make a full-time living out of it.

Walter Sutherland had running in the blood. In the 1870s and 1880s his father Alex had been a successful professional runner (or 'Ped') on the Borders and Edinburgh circuits. Professional running was a very popular sport that attracted a passionate and very knowledgeable following. In Scotland, the high point of the professional year was the annual New Year's Day meeting at the Powderhall stadium in Edinburgh, which had opened in 1869 and which doubled as a venue for dog-racing. Crowds of up to 17,000 people turned up to watch the athletes and thousands of pounds changed hands on the outcomes of the races.

By Walter Sutherland's time athletics, like rugby, was divided along professional and amateur lines. Previously, all athletes had been professional in the sense that they ran for money, either in the shape of prizes or as part of a betting consortium. As the history of the Scottish Amateur Athletics Association put it:

These games were the only outlet for the budding aspirations of a young athlete and, whatever his first ambitions as to athletic glory might be, they were likely to be subordinate to the sordid considerations of £.s.d.

Amateur athletics had slowly spread from a small number of independent schools and universities, culminating in the formation of the Scottish Amateur Athletics Association (SAAA) in 1883. The SAAA had a similar ethos to that of the Scottish Football Union, which ran rugby in Scotland with a rod of iron. The general idea was that amateurism encouraged the development of a good

character, high moral standards and gentlemanly behaviour, and that the genuine athlete took part for pleasure rather than for profit. Success should be an
end in itself rather than a way of making money. Athletes should be free from
the pressures of the bookmakers and the need to win at all costs. Amateurism
also had the effect of entrenching class divisions by keeping the affluent middle classes separate from the uncouth workers. Lacking independent means to
support their leisure activities, many working-class people simply did not have
the means to take part in sport unless they took money to pay for it. In Scotland
there were close links between rugby and amateur athletics. Many rugby players, such as Walter Sutherland, ran in the summer to maintain their fitness levels,
a select few reaching the higher levels of competition. Some of the annual
seven-a-side tournaments in the Borders had athletics and races as well as a
rugby tournament.

Walter Sutherland was a member of his local athletics club, the Teviotdale
Harriers, which had been founded in January 1889, principally for cross-country
running but also for some track and field in the summer. Similar clubs were
formed in other Border towns but, despite their existence, the sub-culture of
professionalism flourished in the Borders and other working-class areas
of Scotland and the north of England. Professional runners excelled thanks to
their secretive and highly dedicated training regimes. In general, they recorded
better times than the amateurs and set much higher standards of performance,
although some of their methods were dubious and cheating was widespread.
In his autobiography *Running Recollections*, which was published in 1902, the
Jamaican-Scot Alf Downer admitted that professional runners were always ready
to jump the gun. 'No one, who is "on the job," ever dreams of waiting for the
report of the pistol, or whatever the signal may be, but is generally running
some five yards (this is no exaggeration) when the signal is given.' One of sport's
great characters, Downer had been an outstanding amateur sprinter, but was
permanently suspended in 1896 for accepting appearance money. Undaunted,
he turned professional and, for a time, he enjoyed a lucrative lifestyle, assuming
the title 'The Champion Sprinter of the World'.

In contrast to rugby, where any hint of professionalism was ruthlessly suppressed, the professional and amateur arms of athletics had an ambiguous
relationship with each other and there were many grey areas. Amateur athletes
were awarded prizes when they won races, such as household items, canteens
of cutlery, table lamps, Gladstone bags or cigar lighters. There was nothing to
stop athletes selling their prizes and pocketing the money. In the Borders, rugby
players ran in the professional races and took the prizes with impunity. In June
1908 Danny Shannon, the Hawick quarter-back, ran under the pseudonym 'S.

Hoy' at the Hawick Common Riding games, winning the 120 yards handicap. The race was reported in the local newspapers, some of which included a photograph of Shannon, but he continued to play rugby for Hawick, seemingly without censure. In contrast to the SFU, the SAAA were often ready to compromise with the professionals, happy to turn a blind eye when it suited them. Some professional football clubs, such as Glasgow Celtic and Rangers, were members of the SAAA, despite the fact that they paid their players. Athletics meetings were held at professional football grounds, such as Hampden Park in Glasgow, which could accommodate large crowds and therefore provide much-needed income for the amateur coffers.

Living in Hawick, Walter was fortunate enough to have the annual Common Riding games on his doorstep. These games were a mixture of amateur and professional events, usually one on the Friday and the other on the Saturday. As well as athletics, the games had bicycle races, tug-of-war and other more bizarre events, such as costume races, pillow fighting and climbing the greasy pole. (In 1909, nobody could reach the top of the pole and the flitch of ham hanging at the top was donated to the local poorhouse.) The Common Riding races operated under a handicapping system, giving certain runners a few yards' start depending on their age and form. This meant that the races were less easy to call. Technically, betting was illegal and signs were displayed that read 'No Gambling Allowed', but it went on regardless. The Common Riding games were far from parochial events and they attracted widespread interest and participation. Walter Sutherland took part in many of the Hawick events, often against stiff opposition. In 1910, he won the 100 yards open handicap off 6½ yards, but the following year he was unexpectedly beaten in the same event by a runner called W. Rule of Edinburgh Harriers, who was given a 5-yard advantage. In 1913 Walter was at the top of his form, winning the 100 yards in fine style over the talented H.J. Christie from West of Scotland. 'The Hawick international footballer ran magnificently,' reported the *Hawick Express*, 'and breasted the tape the most popular of winners, by a couple of yards in ten seconds dead.'

One of the highlights of the Hawick Common Riding games was the annual clash for the Wyoming Cup, a one-mile relay race that was open to all amateur harriers clubs in Great Britain and Ireland. The race was for a handsome silver trophy that had been presented by Hawick exiles living in Wyoming in the United States of America. The race was run over different lengths, starting with a 440 yards circuit, two legs of 220 yards and then a finish of 880 yards. Between 1909 and 1913, the race developed into a ding-dong affair between the local club Teviotdale Harriers and their arch-rivals West of Scotland, who were based in Glasgow. First blood went to the West team, who won a very close race in

1909. Walter Sutherland was not in the Teviotdale team until the following year, when the home side won the cup back again. The Harriers squad was of a very high quality and included several outstanding athletes. Adam Grieve, who was known as 'Yid', excelled as a cross-country runner and in the mile, where he won the Border Championship for six years in a row. The team also included Rob Burton, a Berwickshire man, who was an international middle-distance runner, once holding the Scottish record for the 880 yards. In the 1910 race, Teviotdale Harriers led all the way with Burton bringing the team home in grand style. In 1911, however, the West of Scotland gained revenge, as the *Hawick Express* reported:

It was known that the West of Scotland quartette [sic] *would make a big bid to regain the trophy from Teviotdale Harriers, and they did it well, with a particularly hot four in Unkles, Duncan, Christie and Rodger.*

The following year, the four-team race created 'immense interest' among an eager crowd of spectators, all hoping to see a home win. Teviotdale put out another strong squad with Jim Ballantyne on the opening lap, Tom Bell and Walter Sutherland on the sprint sections and Rob Burton on the anchor leg. At the halfway point, West of Scotland were slightly ahead of Teviotdale. Disaster almost struck at the changeover, as the *Hawick News* reported: 'When Sutherland got the handkerchief from Bell he was knocked off his running at the commencement by having to jump over a dog that had got in the way.' Walter regained his composure and set off in hot pursuit of the West runner H.J. Christie, passing him in the back straight. However, Walter had gone off too fast and should have timed his run better as Christie soon regained the lead. At the final changeover Walter handed on to Rob Burton, whose long, confident stride got him in front in the last lap, eventually clinching an easy win for Teviotdale. 'The local victory was naturally very popular,' said the *Hawick News*, 'and was greeted with much enthusiasm.' With two wins each, the final showdown between Teviotdale and West came in 1913. The rules stated that the first team to win the cup three times would be allowed to keep it and local pride was at stake. Unfortunately, the three-team race was something of a disappointment. The Teviotdale athlete Tom Bell ran poorly in the first leg, leaving West with a lead of over forty yards at the first change. Archie Anderson, Walter Sutherland and Rob Burton tried their best to catch up, but they had too much to do and the visitors were easy winners.

A step up from the Common Riding meetings was the annual Border Championships, organised under the auspices of the Scottish Border Amateur

Athletics Association (SBAAA), which had been founded in 1896 under the guidance of David Duncan, the energetic secretary of the national body. The inaugural Border Championships were staged at Galashiels in 1899 but, soon afterwards, various events were farmed out to the local clubs. Between 1911 and 1914, Walter Sutherland was one of the stars of the Border circuit, winning both the 100 yards and 220 yards four times. One of his best days was on 27 July 1912 when he won the two titles on the same afternoon. On this occasion, the Border Championship races were part of Gala Harriers' Sports Day, which took place at the local rugby ground at Netherdale. The afternoon opened in typical Edwardian style with a children's fancy dress procession and the crowning of the 'Gala Queen', who was described by the *Southern Reporter* as 'a shrine of beauty in her gorgeous attire'. Many of the spectators did not enter into the spirit of things and were more interested in the refreshment tent than watching the races. 'The crowd was not at all enthusiastic,' remarked the *Southern Reporter*, 'while it could not be said that the better class of people in the town graced the proceedings with their attendance.' Walter had little trouble in winning both his races, although he was pushed all the way by his namesake, the Gala Harriers runner A.E. Sutherland, as the *Southern Reporter* observed:

The day was a red-letter one, especially for W.R. Sutherland, the famous Scottish internationalist. He won the 100 yards Border Championship as he liked in 10.25 seconds, A.E. Sutherland, youngest son of Gala's former chief constable, being second. The famous 'Watty' was also first in the 220 yards Border Championship, winning by about a yard-and-a-half from 'A.E.' who ran a good race.

Later in the day, Walter ran in the 100 yards open handicap, but could only finish in third position. Sometimes, Walter allowed his enthusiasm to get the better of him. At the same sports in 1912, he was a member of the Teviotdale Harriers squad for the one-mile invitation relay race. Earlier in the day, he had run four times in the 100 yards and once in the 220 yards, and was feeling the effects by the time the relay race came round, which was eventually won by Edinburgh Northern. As the *Evening News* reported: 'Teviotdale put too much dependence on W.R. Sutherland, and he was in no fit condition to respond... in justice to his club, Sutherland should have contented himself with the championship... His previous exertions were already telling on the Rugbean.'

For amateur athletes, the most important day of the year was the annual Scottish Championships, which were held in June under the auspices of the SAAA. First staged in 1883, the event took place either at the Powderhall stadium in Edinburgh or at one of the big football grounds in Glasgow. Walter's first taste of the Scottish Championships came on 24 June 1911 at Hampden Park. On a miserable afternoon of incessant rain, which reduced the crowd to only a few hundred hardy souls, Walter ran in both sprints, but with mixed success. Seven competitors entered for the 100 yards flat race, which was run on the hallowed Hampden turf rather than the cinder track that encircled the pitch. In a tight and exciting race, the runners were in a line until the Anglo-Scot Bill Stewart broke clear and beat the defending champion R.C. Duncan of West of Scotland by a foot, stopping the clock at 10.25 seconds. A medical student, Stewart represented the London Hospital's Athletic Club and was a good rugby player, the same man who was capped in 1913 and who had taken Walter's place on the Scottish right wing. Walter tried hard in the 100 yards, but finished well down the field. 'Some interest attached to the appearance of W.R. Sutherland, the rugby three-quarter,' reported the *Evening News*, 'but he was not in it at the finish.' However, there was better news in the 220 yards. Walter put up a 'splendid effort' and finished strongly, but R.C. Duncan dominated the race, pushing the Hawick man into second place. As the *Glasgow Herald* reported: 'In the 220 yards, he [Duncan] ran beautifully and had a clear advantage of three yards over W.R. Sutherland, the Hawick rugby football player, whose championship debut gives promise of greater things in the near future.'

Walter's next attempt at winning a Scottish title took place on 28 June 1913 at Celtic Park in Glasgow. He seems to have taken the competition more seriously this time and underwent a special training programme to ensure that he was at his best. As the *Hawick News* reported in June 1913: 'Sutherland has been carefully trained for some weeks by James Jardine and is in the pink of condition.' For an amateur runner like Walter, training opportunities were limited because of a lack of time. In general, training consisted of a series of short sprint sessions and longer runs and walks dressed in heavy clothing, the idea being to work up a good sweat. Like rugby players, athletes also did work in the gymnasium such as ball-punching, dumb-bells and skipping. However, too much training was considered a bad thing. Special dietary preparation was largely unknown and athletes were more-or-less encouraged to eat what they fancied. Alf Downer, the great Scottish runner of the 1890s, recommended that the young athlete should eat meat three times a day, especially poultry, have toast rather than bread, and enjoy all sorts of milk and fruit puddings.

On a grey and unsettled day with a strong westerly wind and in front of a 'beggarly crowd', Walter was involved in a controversial finish to the final of the 100 yards. In the heats he was slow off his marks and, despite a great effort at recovery, he was well beaten by his old friend and rival R.C. Duncan. The final turned out to be the best race of the afternoon, an exciting three-way

Scottish Amateur Athletic Association.

THIRTY-FIRST ANNUAL

Championship

Meeting

AT

CELTIC PARK, Glasgow,

ON

Saturday, 28th June, 1913,

At 3.15 p.m.

Programme, Price TWOPENCE.

Walter won the 220 yards Scottish Championship at the SAAA meeting in Glasgow in June 1913. (Author's collection)

contest between Sutherland, Duncan and an athlete called H.M. Mackintosh of Cambridge University. The three runners were together at eighty yards but, in the closing stages Mackintosh managed to find a little extra and pulled away to cross in first position. 'The winner's reserve power told in his favour,' reported the *Glasgow Herald*, 'bringing him home a foot in front of Duncan with whom Sutherland just failed to tie.' That, at least, was the official version, but most people were convinced that Walter had beaten Duncan into second place. The *Evening News* was astonished at the judges' decision and commented:

Nobody seemed of a mind with the official verdict that Sutherland was beaten by Duncan for second place. The Hawick man led the field at a long distance and, at eighty yards or thereabouts, he was challenged by MacIntosh, who took a lead that he held to the tape, though Sutherland was going very fast at the finish, and was beaten by the narrowest margin. Duncan was six inches behind, and the decision as above was disputed, not only by the pressmen (who were level with the tape), but by officials of more experience than some of the judges.

The *Scotsman* agreed that Walter had been cheated out of his rightful place:

Sutherland was leader most of the way, he was headed by Mackintosh but never by Duncan, in fact there were inches between Sutherland and Duncan at the post. Yet the second place went to Duncan. Macintosh won, but he is little better than the 'Teri'. He did not get quite so quickly into his running, and he was not travelling quite so fast at the finish. He ran a more uniform race, that was all.

Fortunately, Walter could look for compensation in the 220 yards, which was his better event. With the reigning champion Bill Stewart opting to stay in London and not to defend his title, this turned into a two-horse race between Walter and an athlete called R.A. Lindsay of Blackheath Harriers. Run without heats and into a strong headwind, Walter produced a marvellous and deter-mined performance, beating Lindsay by half a yard to win the Scottish title. *The Scotsman* takes up the story:

The Border rugby internationalist, W.R. Sutherland, also proved himself a capital run-ner… [He] probably exceeded the expectations of his friends – outside, that is to say, of Hawick, where they 'see red' when a weed of criticism is levelled at the popular idol down that way. Sutherland ran a grand race. Lindsay and he were in a line nearing the tape, but the Borderer was going the faster in the last ten yards, and he surprised many people by his pace and grit.

It was a great achievement for Walter, although his winning time of 24.4 sec-onds was the slowest in the twenty-two-year history of the championships. The strong wind had certainly held the runners back.

As well as the regional and national championships, there were many other athletics meetings held in Scotland during the summer. The big football clubs in Glasgow held annual sports days, which were very popular events. In August 1912, the Celtic Football Club Sports at Parkhead were estimated to have attracted around 40,000 people, a much larger crowd than attended Scotland rugby internationals at Inverleith. Sports days included a variety of events, such as invitation and open races, obstacle races, bicycling and five-a-side football, often with a brass band playing away in the background. Unlike the Scottish Championships, the races employed a handicapping system. The organisers often went to great efforts to attract some of the biggest names in the athlet-ics world, bringing top-class 'Continental' and American runners to compete. In August 1912, the Celtic Sports featured some American 'cracks' on their way home after the Olympic Games in Stockholm. In the 220 yards invita-tion race, Walter lined up against a runner called Donald Lippincott from the United States Olympic team. There was great interest in the race, especially because Lippincott had won a silver medal in Stockholm and also had broken the Scottish all-comers record for the 220 yards the previous weekend at the Rangers Sports. Walter was given a handicap of eight yards, his old friend R.C. Duncan five yards while Lippincott, the hot favourite, started from 'scratch'. In a tight and exciting race, Walter managed to win by a yard from Duncan, beating Lippincott into third place, despite a 'praiseworthy' effort by the American to catch up and win. 'Sutherland's win in the invitation handicap, when he ran a great race, was very popular,' said the *Hawick News*.

Walter was less successful the following year at the Rangers Football Club Sports at Ibrox Park. The 220 yards invitation handicap race was billed as an Anglo-Scottish clash between Walter Sutherland, who had just become Scottish Champion, and an English runner called Willie Applegarth from the English club Polytechnique Harriers. A small man who ran with machine-like precision, Applegarth was the outstanding British sprinter of the pre-war era, especially in the 220 yards. He won two medals at the Stockholm Olympic Games, including gold in the 4 x 100m relay, and in 1914 he equalled the world record for the 220 yards (on the bend), a record that was to stand for eighteen years. In a controversial race Walter was pushed out of position and forced to run very wide, eventually finishing in fifth position while Applegarth, on the inside lane, had an easy run to take the title. 'The 220 yards invitation handicap at Ibrox Park proved a fiasco,' reported the *Evening News*. 'Much was expected of W.R. Sutherland, the Scottish Champion, who was in receipt of five yards from Applegarth, but he was run so wide on the turn by G. Nicol (6) and H.J. Christie (7) that he might as well have been in Hawick for all the chance he had.' In the relay race, Walter performed better and managed to give Applegarth a good contest but, despite their best efforts, the Scottish team could not prevent the English visitors coming out easy winners.

By this stage, Walter's prowess on the athletics track could take him into some strange situations. In June 1914, a special historical pageant was staged out-of-doors at the Volunteer Park in Hawick to celebrate the 400th anniversary of the capture of the town flag. The pageant included one episode called 'Old Hawick in 1513', which had a character named 'Steenie Speedie', a humble shoemaker, who was played by Walter Sutherland. Walter's acting abilities left something to be desired and he was given only one line to say: 'And yet ye slew the lot?' Later in the episode, the king's messengers arrive in the town and ask to be taken to a nearby castle. The locals have no horses, but there's one lad who can help, 'that would keep pace wi' the best charger o' your company.' Step forward the fleet-footed Steenie, who ran around the arena leading the king's men. The audience must have loved it.

As well as representing Scotland at rugby, Walter Sutherland also made two appearances in the Scottish athletics vest (which was blue with a lion rampant in yellow on the left breast). Before the First World War there were few opportunities for international athletics although, since 1895, Scotland and Ireland had held an annual international match, which was hosted alternately. The match had a mixed programme of track and field events, a point being awarded to the country of the winning athlete in each event. Following his good showing in the Scottish Championships in June 1911, Walter was selected to represent Scotland in the 220-yard sprint along with the champion R.C. Duncan. On 11 July 1911, Walter and the rest of the Scottish team arrived at Ballsbridge in Dublin to take on their Irish counterparts. The beautiful summer weather brought out the best in the Scottish team, who won the match by 7 points to 4. The 220-yards sprint turned out to be a repeat of the Scottish Championship race the previous month. In a race with four athletes Walter put up a great fight, but he could not match the finishing speed of Duncan, who won with several yards to spare, pushing Walter into second place. 'The usual scramble took place at the first turn in the 220 yards which was run left hand against the wind,' reported the *Glasgow Herald*, 'but R.C. Duncan repeated almost to an inch his championship win over W.R. Sutherland, who quite justified his selection.'

Two years later, on 19 July 1913, Walter made his second appearance for the Scottish athletics team, again in the 220-yards sprint. This turned out to be one of the highlights of his athletics career. The match was held at Celtic Park in Belfast, but the fine summer weather could not compensate for some poor organisation on the part of the happy-go-lucky Irish. There were some lengthy delays between the events, leaving the athletes hanging around aimlessly and wasting a lot of time. As the *Evening News* thundered in its report: 'The delightful weather and beautiful surroundings of the enclosure at the foot of the Belfast Mountains were not compensations for the reckless waste.' To make matters worse, there had been some aggravation in the quarter-mile race when one of the Scottish athletes had been knocked off the track, an incident that, according to the *Evening News*, 'left a bad taste in the mouth'.

By the time the 220 yards came round, the fifth event of the afternoon, the Scottish team desperately needed a shot in the arm, having lost most of the events so far. The Irish runner T.R.S. Shaw of Dublin University was hot favourite for the race, having already won the 100 yards in a time that equalled the Irish record. At the trackside, the bookies gave odds of 7-2 on Shaw, 'there being, let it be noted, no restriction upon the operations of the pencilling fraternity in Ireland'. However, Walter Sutherland had other ideas. Drawn on the inside lane next to Shaw, he ran the race of his life. The Irishman was just ahead going into the straight, but Walter kept his form. Digging deep within himself, he fought to the front, eventually crossing the line with a couple of yards to spare. It was a brilliant display by the Hawick man, full of determination and pluck. His winning time of 22.35 seconds was a personal best and one of the fastest times ever recorded by a Scotsman over the distance. As the *Evening News* reported:

It was a match between the two... Shaw was quickly on terms with his man and, at half distance, he looked a likelier winner than he had ever done in the sprint, but Sutherland came again and, though his spurt made him rock, and looked like upsetting him, he kept his footing and, running with determination, sent his compatriots into a frenzy of delight by beating Shaw by three yards. It was great running and more than justified Sutherland's position in the Scottish Championship. The delight of the Scottish party was the greater because Shaw had looked a 'certainty,' and Sutherland was warmly congratulated on all hands on a bit of running that none of the Scots who saw it are likely ever to forget.

Walter's success in the Scottish Championship and the Irish international was the pinnacle of his athletics career. He ran several races in the summer of 1914 and successfully defended his two Border titles, but he did not take part in the Scottish Championships or the international match because of a serious rugby injury that hampered his preparation and overall fitness levels. So how good an athlete was Walter Sutherland? In rugby and other team sports, comparisons between players are often subjective, but in athletics the runners are timed, which gives some sort of independent measure. Having said that, the Edwardians used hand-held stopwatches rather than modern electronic devices, and human error has to be taken into account.

Walter Sutherland was most successful in the stamina-sapping 220 yards, where his best time was 22.35 seconds, achieved in the Irish international in July 1913. This was an excellent performance, just one-tenth of a second short of Alf Downer's Scottish record of 22.25 seconds, which had been set in 1895. By comparison, in 1914 the world record for the 220 yards was 21.2 seconds, a long way ahead of Walter's best time. At the Stockholm Olympics in 1912, the 200 metres, a slightly shorter distance than the 220 yards, was won by Ralph Craig of the USA in 21.7 seconds (add 0.1 for the 220 yards), about half a second faster than Walter's personal best.

An interesting comparison can be made between Walter Sutherland and Eric Liddell, the famous Olympic gold medal winner of the 1920s who also played rugby on the wing for Scotland. At his peak, Walter could have given Eric Liddell a good race. Liddell's best time for the 220 yards (on the bend) was 22.2 seconds, slightly faster than Sutherland managed, although Liddell recorded consistently better times over the course of his career. The statistics show that Walter Sutherland was among the leading Scottish athletes of his day, although a little short when compared with the best British or world sprinters. He achieved much on the track and probably knew his limitations. He was principally a rugby player and running was a bit of a sideline, a good thing to do in the summer to keep in shape. Perhaps he might have done more if he had concentrated only on athletics. Nevertheless, eight Border titles, a national championship and 2 international caps represent a considerable achievement by anyone's standards.

eight

A GREATER GAME

B y the beginning of the twentieth century, most people in Britain were literate, thanks to improved educational provision in the previous fifty years. There was an insatiable appetite for the written word in the shape of books, newspapers and magazines. Hawick alone had three weekly papers, the *Advertiser*, *News* and *Express*, broadsides that were crammed with local and national news, stories, gossip and other tit-bits. At this time, press reports of rugby matches were unremittingly factual, providing blow-by-blow accounts of the action, designed to meet the needs of readers in the pre-television age. Some newspapers carried reviews and 'critical notes' on matches, which assessed individual and team performances. If all this sounds quite modern, there was an important difference: the players were never allowed to speak to the press. On no account could they write columns, voice an opinion or be quoted in the papers. Anyone who broke the rules faced immediate censure and the likelihood of a lengthy ban from rugby.

The result is that printed media can only ever provide a limited picture of Walter Sutherland. There are plenty of stories about what he did and what he achieved, but precious little about what he thought and felt about the world around him. None of Walter's personal papers are known to have survived which makes it difficult to uncover the 'inner man' or to know about his private thoughts and opinions. What sort of person was Walter Sutherland? After his death in October 1918, some of his friends submitted obituary articles to the papers. At this time, writers were much given to hyperbole and journalistic licence, emphasising all of the good things but turning a blind eye to any faults or misdemeanours. Despite this, the strong impression is that Walter Sutherland was a very personable young man. The most common description of his character was that he was one of nature's gentlemen, someone who was genuinely modest about his achievements. As the *Hawick News* put it: 'It is doubtful if anyone ever carried his great athletic honours more lightly than he did. Unassuming and gentlemanly in his demeanour in private life, he displayed the same qualities in the realm of sport.' Walter Hume, one of the stalwarts of the Hawick rugby club, wrote: 'At the height of his fame he was still the same bright, unassuming character, loyal to his home, his friends, and native town. His boyish disposition remained with him to the end.'

Walter's attitude to sport seems to have been based on solid Corinthian principles. He took games seriously, but accepted the prevailing wisdom that they were essentially trivial and were to be played for fun, even at the highest level. 'He early recognised that all outdoor sports were for recreation only,' wrote Walter Hume, 'and are not the serious business of life, and it was in that spirit and with that aim in view all his energies were directed.' It would be wrong to say that winning didn't matter to him, otherwise what was the point of keeping the score? But it was just as important to try one's best, to play the game in the right spirit, to take victory with humility and defeat with good grace. As Walter Hume wrote:

He had enjoyed success, and naturally loved victory; but he also knew how to acknowledge defeat, and no one was more generous to admit gifts in worthy opponents. Success made no unwelcome inroads on his character; empty self-esteem he had none; modesty reigned supreme.

Walter Sutherland was well known for his good sportsmanship, his respect for his opponents and his sense of fair play. 'Of him it could truly be said that there was not a cleaner player,' wrote the *Hawick News*. 'One of the cleanest and fairest of sportsmen,' said the *Border Telegraph*. The Glasgow-based *Scots Pictorial* observed: 'Temperamentally suited for the rough-and-tumble work of rugby football, he never lost his "wool", and in this, as in other things, he was a fine model to younger players.' Finally, here is Walter Hume again: 'His play was always bright, natural, honest and above-board. He scorned to do a mean action. He had no occasion to trick or stratagem; his play was, like his life, clean and wholesome. After the most stubborn or exciting contest no action of his ever left a sting behind. He made no enemies.'

We should not, of course, be too naive or misty-eyed about Walter Sutherland or any of the players of his generation. Rugby was a very hard, competitive sport and nobody got to the top without a streak of ruthlessness and single-mindedness, even in those halcyon Edwardian days. 'And what was the secret of his success?' wrote Adam Turnbull, another prominent member of the Hawick club. 'It was not altogether due to ability. Ability he had, but this was aided by a determination, by consistency in training, by a delightful temper, and unassuming manner.' Walter might have been modest and down to earth, but he would also have had a certain degree of self-confidence. He sang at rugby club dinners and other social functions, which suggests that he was uninhibited by shyness or self-doubt, not too much of a wallflower. He captained Hawick and the South of Scotland, and became a second lieutenant in the Army, positions that called for self-assurance and leadership qualities, the ability to inspire confidence, trust and loyalty in others. Overall, Walter seems to have been a genuinely popular person who won the respect and admiration of others, something indeed of a golden boy. Regarding his captaincy of the Greens, the *Hawick News* said: 'There has seldom been a more popular, considerate, or painstaking skipper.' Walter Hume wrote that he was 'beloved by troops of friends, who admired him as the truest type of sportsman.' Similarly, after his death, the *Evening News* commented: 'It is questionable if any other attained the hold on the affections of the general sporting community that fell to the "Teri", who had a winning personality all of his own.' Ultimately, all the evidence about Walter points to a fine example of Muscular Christianity, that vigorous combination of Christian living with a devotion to a healthy body. It is not known if Walter and his family were strong believers or particularly devout, but most people in those days were regular churchgoers, especially those who aspired to social respectability. It might be relevant that after his death a rosary was found among his personal belongings, although it is known that the Sutherland family were members of the Church of Scotland communion.

Did Walter have a steady girlfriend or 'lass', as he would have known her? He was a good catch for any girl: an international footballer who attracted lots of attention, some of which would rub off on anyone in his company. Intelligent and admired wherever he went, he was a respected member of the community who had a steady job with good prospects. In short, he was a very eligible bachelor who was likely to have turned heads. While researching this book I was contacted by an elderly woman in Hawick who told me that her late mother had once been engaged to be married to Walter Sutherland. Out of respect to her mother's memory, she asked not to give her mother's name and I will identify her only as Mary. On my visit, the woman very kindly gave me two medals that had once belonged to Walter, which he must have given to Mary as keepsakes or tokens of his affection. One was the gold medal from the SBAAA Championship in 1914, inscribed on the reverse '220 Yards Border Championship won by W.R. Sutherland'. The other medal, which seems to have been turned into a brooch, is inscribed with the initials 'WRS' and on the back is 'HK 1908'. The medal is most likely to have come from the Border Junior Sevens in April 1908, when Walter was the star of the tournament and first made his name.

One insight into Walter's character was his reaction to the outbreak of the First World War. Shortly after Britain had declared war on Germany on 4 August 1914, Lord Kitchener, the Secretary of State for War, issued his famous appeal to civilians for the creation of a 'New Army' of 100,000 men. Kitchener's appeal caught the popular imagination of young men all over the country and Walter Sutherland was no exception. The summer of 1914 was a brilliant one with long, hot days and clear, settled weather. On the final weekend of August, Walter and five of his friends took themselves up the Borthwick Water near Hawick for a short camping trip in the beautiful Border countryside. Walter was accompanied by his friends Alan Hopkirk, Andy Turnbull, Dan Cavers and the Ker brothers, Ronald and William. Turnbull, William Ker and Walter Sutherland were teammates in the Hawick First XV while Cavers was a well-known distance runner with the Teviotdale Harriers. During the weekend, the six friends discussed the war and came to the decision that they would leave their jobs immediately and join the Army together. The next day, they went to Haddington and tried to enlist in the Lothian and Border Horse Yeomanry. Initially, they were rejected because some of them had never ridden a horse before, but the following day they tried again and 'after some bother' they were all accepted.

The Lothian and Border Horse had been established in 1908, although it had links with earlier cavalry regiments that had been set up in the late eighteenth century to fight foreign invasion and suppress political radicalism. Based at Amisfield camp near Haddington, it was a territorial regiment with different squadrons covering the Lothian and Border counties. Before the First World War its members had trained and drilled at the weekends and also taken part in an annual summer camp. The regiment was popular and carried a certain social cachet about it. Members were expected to have their own horse or the means to hire one. The uniform was quite dashing and attractive, always a plus point with the girls. Unlike the plain old khaki of the other territorials, it had 'French Blue' strapping and hatbands. Members were often mistaken for officers, earning the regiment the nickname of the 'Princes Street Lancers'. Walter and his friends seem to have chosen the Lothian and Border Horse because they knew some Hawick men already serving in it. They might also have been attracted to the glamour of the cavalry rather than the humble footsloggers in the infantry, just as in the Second World War lots of people were drawn to the RAF.

Why were Walter and his friends so eager to join up? With the benefit of hindsight, these enthusiastic volunteers now seem hopelessly naive and credulous, allowing themselves to be led away to the slaughter with unquestioning loyalty and devotion. But in 1914 attitudes were very different. Notions of patriotism and honour were very influential, something that we now find very difficult to appreciate. In schools, churches and workplaces, organisations such as the Boys Brigade or the Boy Scouts as well as the popular press, people were exhorted to take pride in their country, to be loyal to Great Britain and the Empire, and to be resolute in its defence. Many young men were genuinely idealistic and willing to fight for King and country. Since boyhood they had been encouraged to hold the military in high esteem, not just as the guardians of the state but as a source of social and spiritual values, the embodiment of Christian warriors. Moreover, there was a powerful sense of duty and responsibility, and young men and women were under considerable social and moral pressure to do what was expected of them. This was a war of national self-defence. Germany was seen a threat to international security and it was seriously felt that the Germans were planning to invade Britain in the near future. Many felt that the Germans had been sabre-rattling for too long and it was time for the British to teach the unspeakable Hun a lesson, especially after the reports of German atrocities against French and Belgian civilians. Ignorant of the sordid realities of war, it was believed that civilisation was under threat and the war was a great crusade for liberalism, decency and democracy. Men also flocked to the colours because it was an opportunity for a new life or a quick way of escaping the old one. The army offered excitement, a change of routine, the chance to become a hero and to travel the world and see new places. Nobody, of course, knew what kind of war it would become.

It must also be said that rugby players were particularly susceptible to the pro-war atmosphere. By playing the game, they were more likely to support the war and be drawn to a military way of life. Rugby football and warfare had much in common: the emphasis on teamwork at the expense of the individual; personal sacrifice for a collective goal; the intense maleness and camaraderie of it all, often in situations of extreme stress and pressure. In the Edwardian era, the playing field was presented as an arena for feigned combat and war was sport continued by other means. Schoolboys and young men were encouraged to seek honour and glory in both, as if real combat could somehow be honest and heroic, an essentially decent affair. In the past, war had been seen as one of the Four Horsemen of the Apocalypse. In 1914, many people believed that it was little worse than a spot of football.

Across the country, the rugby community had responded very positively to the war. The 1914/15 season was immediately suspended and players and club members were strongly encouraged to join-up. At the Annual General Meeting of the Hawick Football Club in early September 1914, it was unanimously agreed that no serious football would be attempted during 'the present crisis' and that the election of a club captain would be held over. A special committee was chosen to look after the club's affairs during the war, which included Walter's father Alex. A donation from the club's funds was given to the National Relief Fund and the Belgian Relief Fund. The committee organised a few charity matches at Mansfield Park, the profits going to war funds and to promote local recruitment. On 10 October 1914, a hastily arranged match took place between teams representing the South of Scotland and the 4th King's Own Scottish Borderers (KOSB) Service Battalion, which was currently based at Galashiels. The South team contained a host of well-known Border players, including the Hawick favourites Walter Sutherland, Frank Beatson, 'Bottler' Wilson and George Johnstone, while their opponents were also made up of local boys. On a glorious afternoon, a large crowd saw a game that was 'wonderfully fast and interesting'. Walter Sutherland was in grand form, scoring the opening try and kicking a conversion to give the South an 8-3 win. The 'Terriers' had given the South a good game, showing themselves to be in 'the pink of condition, as might have been expected from their military training'. Their captain, J.M. Ballantyne of Hawick, had kept a close eye on Walter Sutherland, coming through this 'arduous task' with great credit. However, Walter's class had been very apparent, producing some fine runs and playing 'about as good as ever'.

Rugby players made good soldiers, and soldiers often made good rugby players. The Army liked sport because it was an ideal way of keeping the men fit and gave them an outlet for their frustrations. The Lothian and Border Horse had a useful rugby team, of which Private Sutherland was an important member. In February 1915, the regimental magazine *The Yeoman* reported that the side 'have done very well, our team including such experts as Sutherland'. In late 1914, the L&B Horse XV played a couple of games against the Loretto School XV, winning both matches after close struggles. There was also an exciting game against the 9th Royal Scots, who were known as the 'Dandy Ninth'. On New Year's Day 1915, the Lothian and Border Horse sent a side to Mansfield Park to play a scratch Hawick XV, possibly on Walter Sutherland's suggestion. In the worst possible conditions, the match ended with a 3-3 draw, but the small crowd were deprived the sight of their local favourite. As the *Hawick News* explained: 'W.R. Sutherland was unable to play for the Yeomanry owing to his having received a kick from a horse.'

The highlight for the Lothian and Border Horse on the rugby field came at a special military sevens tournament held at The Greenyards, Melrose on 17 April 1915. Eight teams took part from the KOSB, the Lothian and Border Horse, the Royal Scots and the Forth RGA. A smaller crowd than usual saw some mediocre fare, lacking any of the normal passions, as *The Scotsman* reported:

All over the football was below the usual for Border seven-a-side meetings and there was not the customary enthusiasm, which was only to be expected when there was none of the usual rivalry between town and town and club and club. The excitement attached to the usual Hawick-Gala tie at the seven contests on the Borders in normal times was conspicuous by its absence.

During the afternoon, recruiting officers wandered among the spectators, targeting any young man who was not in uniform. They did not have much success, although the tournament raised some money for 'one or more patriotic funds'. Walter Sutherland played for the Lothian & Border Horse 'A'; a seven made up of various Border and Edinburgh players, including his friend Andy Turnbull of Hawick. Predictably, Walter was the player of the tournament, head and shoulders above the rest and 'a great asset' to his side, helping them to win the tournament. As the *Southern Reporter* wrote about the first round tie: 'The very fact that Sutherland was appearing in this game helped an otherwise apathetic crowd of spectators to show some enthusiasm.' The game of the day was a tight semi-final between the Lothian & Border Horse and the 1/4th KOSB. Walter scored the decisive try with a fine individual effort and repeatedly got his side out of trouble with some good defence. In the final against the 2/5th Royal Scots, Walter scored one of his side's four tries with a typical breakaway from the halfway line. Mrs Scott Plummer of Huntleyburn, a formidable local worthy, presented the gold medals to the winning side, but the famous Ladies' Cup remained firmly locked away.

Endless hours of rugby, cross-country running, boxing and other sports could not disguise the growing sense of boredom and frustration that slowly permeated the Lothian & Borders Horse camp at Amisfield. Like tens of thousands of eager young men all over the country, Walter and his friends had joined up expecting to get a quick crack at the Hun. Instead they found themselves stuck at home, kicking their heels through the winter and spring of 1915, far removed from the real action in France. This does not mean that they were sitting around doing nothing. The Army abhorred inactivity and kept everybody busy with a rigorous training regime, designed to break an individual's will so that in time he would obey orders automatically, turning a raw recruit into a hardened fighting man. Many hours were spent on rifle drill and musketry, practising with the bayonet, scouting, signalling and semaphore work, lectures and physical training. The army was notorious for placing great emphasis on monotonous tasks, such as cleaning, scrubbing and polishing, and the men had little choice but to buckle down and get on with it. As a cavalry regiment, there were several hundred horses to be looked after, which in many respects received better treatment than the men. A typical day at Amisfield Camp began with reveille at 5.30 or 6 a.m. The horses always came first. They had to be watered, fed and groomed, and be ready for action at a moment's notice. One member of the regiment, John 'Chap' Landles, later recalled:

One of the things that was always imposed on you was that no matter what else needed doing, your horse was your first duty. It was impressed on you that your horse was your best friend. An infantryman's best friend was his rifle, but a cavalryman's was his horse because it got you out of trouble.

After breakfast there was a mounted parade, which was followed by various exercises, drills and scouting work. Around midday, the horses were returned to the stables and the men had their dinner. In the afternoon, they took part in another parade and more training. The day usually ended in the stables. For the time being, the regiment was charged with defensive duties on the coast. It was feared that East Lothian was a possible site for a German landing and the regiment was to shore up the seaboard defences and keep an eye out to sea, ever-watchful for the Teutonic invader.

Low morale was a very bad thing for the army. It could lead to mental depression and sluggishness, even (in extreme situations) to disobedience and revolt. The men wanted to be fighting Germans, not peeling potatoes or shovelling horse manure. The sense of disenchantment and growing cynicism comes through strongly in the pages of the regimental magazine *The Yeoman*, which appeared for three issues in 1915. Some of the men responded to their situation with black humour, such as 'W.K.H.' who submitted a poem entitled *1965: A Pessimist's Prophecy*, clearly expecting to spend the next fifty years stuck in camp:

Remnants of swords were hung beside each one,
Polished so long that half the steel was gone;
Rifles with barrels worn to nothing, too,
From years and years and years of pulling through.

To make matters worse, the camp at Amisfield was a bleak place, especially in the midst of a Scottish winter. The rush of volunteers at the beginning of the war had caught the authorities unprepared. All over the country, there were desperate shortages of equipment, uniforms, basic supplies and decent living accommodation. At Amisfield, men had to sit out the winter in flimsy wooden huts, stable blocks and tents, often without proper heating or facilities. Inevitably, the constant passage of boots, hooves and wagon wheels churned

up the ground and turned it into a muddy morass. As the official history of
the regiment states: 'The inevitable wet weather had meanwhile reduced the
horse-lines – and indeed the whole park – to an indescribable mass of mud.' Or
as 'W.K.H.' put it in *The Yeoman*:

> *I saw a village; bare asbestos huts*
> *In a morass deep-scored by flooded ruts*
> *Where roads of sleepers formed the only track*
> *Across unsounded sloughs of slimy black.*

In May 1915, the regiment was finally on the move, but only a few miles down
the coast to Hedderwick near Dunbar for yet more training and inspections. By
this time, many of the soldiers had reached breaking point and decided to take
matters into their own hands. As John 'Chap' Landles later recalled:

*There was no sign of us being sent on service. Some of them were brash, you know, 'Ah
want tae do the fighting'… The result was that there was quite a number that left and
went away to join other regiments. Deserted! Deserted from our regiment. One of them
was a very famous rugby player called Walter Sutherland.*

In early July 1915, Walter left the Lothian & Border Horse for good and slipped
away to Glasgow. On 7 July, he enlisted in the 14th Battalion the Argyll &
Sutherland Highlanders, giving a false name, 'John McCallum'. He might have
plucked this name out of thin air, although John MacCallum was the name of the
great Scottish rugby forward from Watsonians (Ironically, MacCallum, a minister's
son, was a conscientious objector). An interesting detail from his enlistment form
shows that he had two distinctive marks on his body: prominent scars on the
right shin and right shoulder, probably both the results of rugby injuries. He gave
his address as 585 New City Road, Glasgow, presumably because he stayed the
night there before enlisting, although it's not clear with whom. One guess is that
a man called Thomas Lunn, a spirit salesman with a Hawick-sounding name, was
a tenant in the block and Walter might have known him through the drink trade.
Walter seems to have chosen the 14th Battalion because his friend and teammate
from the Hawick First XV, George 'Geordie' Johnstone, was also a member of it.
The Argyll & Sutherland Highlanders had been formed in 1881 following an
amalgamation of two older regiments, the 91st (Argyllshire Highlanders) and the
93rd (Sutherland Highlanders), the latter having fought with great distinction in
the Crimean War. During the First World War, the regiment expanded to twenty-
seven battalions, the 14th (Service) Battalion having been raised in Stirling in

early 1915. A kilted regiment, the Argylls were the only regiment to wear a distinctive red and white dicing on their Glengarry bonnets.

Walter's desertion from the Lothian & Border Horse is a rather murky episode in his life and military career. His actions suggest that he was a little headstrong and impulsive and was not fully attuned to army life, still thinking of himself as a civilian in uniform, having the right to come and go as he pleased. The army treated desertion extremely seriously and deserters could expect severe punishment, in theory execution by firing squad at its most extreme. Inevitably, military justice caught up with Walter. By the end of March 1916, his secret was out and he had confessed to the authorities about his fraudulent enlistment. Fortunately, the army seems to have accepted his explanation and treated his case with some leniency, perhaps recognising that they had a fine soldier who was too good to waste. At the end of July 1916, a court martial was dispensed with and Walter was allowed to continue serving with the 14th Battalion. However, he forfeited all his service in the army up until March 1916, which meant that he lost any outstanding pay and pension entitlement.

In the meantime Walter, or rather Private McCallum, had to get on with life in the Argylls. Ironically, he should have bided his time and stayed put. The Lothian & Border Horse went abroad in September 1915, but the Argylls were destined to remain in Britain for another year, moving from training camps at Ernesettle, near Plymouth; Witley, near Guildford; and Blackdown, near Farnborough. Living in the south-east corner of England would have been a strange experience for many of the Scottish soldiers, some of whom came from tough working-class districts of Glasgow and Dundee. At a time when travel was much more limited than today and regional identities far stronger, southern England was virtually a foreign country. On both sides, people talked with robust accents and there would have been a great deal of mutual incomprehension between the Scots and their southern neighbours. To give them a taste of home, the Argylls held a special Highland Gathering at the United Services Sports Ground at Plymouth on 31 July 1915. The afternoon included a programme of Highland dancing, bagpipe music and athletic events, Private J. McCallum of 'A' Company taking part in the 100 yards and the relay race. Occasionally, the men were given time off and the bright lights of London were not very far away. This could lead to some surprising coincidences when local men bumped into each other in the unlikeliest of settings. One of Walter's training partners from Hawick, Jimmy Grierson, who served in a different regiment, later recalled:

I can mind of being in London once. I stopped to see a pal of mine and we went for a walk on the Sunday morning. I knew Wattie Sutherland was at a place near Aldershot,

14th (Service) Battalion
Argyll and Sutherland Highlanders

Highland Gathering

Under the patronage of
Major-General A. P. PENTON, C.V.O , C.B.,
Commanding Plymouth Garrison.

United Services Sports Ground,

On SATURDAY,
31st JULY, 1915
Commencing at 2 p.m.

In July 1915 Private John McCallum took part in a Highland Gathering sports day at Plymouth. (Author's collection)

but too far to go and see him. Just going into Hyde Park gates and who was coming out but Wattie! It was funny meeting him there, in London of all places. He was one of the great lads, a nice chap.

For the most part however, life in the camps was an unremitting round of training, fatigues and routine, much of it tedious and dreary, just as it had been at boring old Amisfield. Between June and September 1915, the Argylls were stationed at Ernesettle camp, which was infamous for its damp and drizzle blowing in from the English Channel. Conditions were often grim, as an anonymous poet recounted in the battalion magazine *The Dud* (to the traditional ballad *D'Ye Ken John Peel?*):

> *D'ye ken a' the joys o' Ernesettle Camp,*
> *Whaur the sojers drill in a tramp, tramp, tramp;*
> *Whaur its never really weet, though its whiles a thingie damp,*
> *When the rain comes doon in the mornin'.*

> *For the huts are weel contructit, if it werna for the way*
> *That the roof lets the rain in, by nicht and by day;*
> *And ye dream every nicht that ye're underneath the spray,*
> *And ye fin' that its true in the mornin'.*

Throughout these months of training, the real war still seemed very far away. There was an increasing sense of frustration and world-weariness about many of the men. Writing in *The Dud*, another anonymous poet contributed *Witley (Disillusioned)*:

> *Thocht I, tae France, I'll gang awa,*
> *And earn a D.C.M. or twa;*
> *And syne I'll can come hame and craw,*
> *When my famous deeds I mention.*
> *But though we've got gas-helmets queer,*
> *At hame we'll bide for many a year;*
> *And while I doobt we'll still be here*
> *When we draw wor Auld Age Pensions.*

At the beginning of June 1916 the Argylls were finally on the move, the moment that had long been expected and in some cases hoped for. On 4 June, the Argylls said goodbye to Blackdown camp and made for Southampton. Unfortunately, the weather in the English Channel was at its worst and their crossing was delayed for twenty-four hours. The men had little choice but to bed down on the floor of one of the dock sheds. In typical army fashion, they put a brave face on things and along with some other battalions held an impromptu concert, one individual giving a fine rendition of the soldiers' favourite *It's Nice to Get Up in the Morning*. The following evening, three battalions crammed onto the troopship Marguerite for a stormy overnight crossing to Le Havre, during which many of the men suffered from copious sea-sickness.

During the war, soldiers wrote letters home to their families and loved ones as often as they could. Many of them also recorded their experiences in diaries, although the authorities disapproved of this in case they fell into the wrong hands. E.H.D. Sewell mentions that Walter Sutherland wrote letters to his parents in Hawick, but unfortunately these have disappeared and were probably destroyed many years ago. The result is that we have to largely rely on secondary sources to find out what happened to Walter during his time on the Western Front. The Battalion War Diary of the 14th Argylls is still preserved in the regimental museum in Stirling Castle, which details the movements of the battalion in France. Also preserved in the museum is a diary written by one of the officers, George Hugh Freeland Bartholomew. A doctor's son from Edinburgh, Bartholomew had been a good rugby player at school and was planning to study Classics at Oxford University until the war intervened. He joined up at the beginning of the war and was killed in action in France in October 1917, aged twenty-one. Another useful source on the 14th Argylls is a collection of letters written by Private Bob Lawson to his sister Bessie, which are preserved in the Imperial War Museum in London. Lawson served in the 14th Battalion from June 1915 to his death in July 1918. It seems reasonable to assume that the experiences of George Bartholomew (albeit an officer's perspective) and Bob Lawson would have been broadly similar to those of Walter Sutherland. Coupled with the Battalion War Diary, their writings can be used to provide some of the background to Walter's life between June and December 1916, probably the closest that we can come to him. However, all that is known for certain about Walter at this time is that from 5 to 10 October he was in a field hospital having a septic boil removed from his face.

On their arrival in France, the 14th Argylls were packed into cattle trains and taken on an eighteen-hour journey to their base camp at a village called Ecquedecques, north west of Béthune, where they remained for the following week. The countryside around the camp was rich agricultural land broken up by tall poplar trees and red-roofed farms and villages. The local inhabitants had grown used to the influx of soldiers and were happy to take advantage. Bob Lawson wrote home: 'The kiddies here are simply great and their great cry was "souvenir, souvenir". An English army biscuit appeared to be the thing they wanted most.' George Bartholomew recorded:

The people on the whole rather insanitary and dirty… The attitude of the inhabitants to the soldiers is evidently varied; some frankly resent the intrusion of strangers and show it, but at the same time they don't mind squeezing as much money from them as possible… Others are very friendly, and will go out of their way and make sacrifices and even spend money to make the troops comfortable. On the whole, they like the Scotch troops far better than the English.

The nearby town of Lillers had been largely taken over by the British and could provide many home comforts. Soldiers could buy *Punch* and *The Strand* in the stationer's shop, Bird's Custard and Oxo Cubes in the grocer's and enjoy a pint of Bass or Worthington in the local *estaminets*, provided they had any money. Their camp also boasted the luxury of a large open-air bath, the men unabashed at squashing in together and trying to get themselves cleaned up.

Until now the war had seemed far away, something of a waking dream. For all its trials and privations, army life had been a bit of a lark. But now, in France, the reality of the situation began to take over. The base camp at Ecquedecques was close enough to the front for the sound of the guns to form an ominous rumble in the background, a steady drumming on the nerves. On 15 June, the Argylls were moved to a mining village called Annequin, just short of the front line. In time-honoured fashion, they slogged fifteen miles on the hard cobbled roads with full pack, at one point coming under artillery fire, the moment when the war finally came alive. The following night, the Argylls moved from their billets up into the front-line trenches, which were opposite a notorious German strongpoint called the Hohenzollern Redoubt. The first casualties occurred within twenty-four hours, one man being killed by a rifle grenade and eight others wounded by shrapnel and rifle fire.

For the next four months, the Argylls were based in the sector to the north and west of the town of Lens. This was a grim industrial district given over to mining and scarred with pits (known as fosses), dumps of mine waste (crassiers) and other workings. The previous year, it had been the scene of very heavy fighting at the battle of Loos, one of the worst battles of the war when tens of thousands of men, including many Scots, were killed for precious little territorial gain. In 1916, it was officially known as a 'quiet' sector as the battle of the Somme raged further south. This did not mean that it was a safe haven or a comfortable soft spot. During their tour of duty, the Argylls faced many hazards and suffered a steady flow of casualties, including several men who had to be withdrawn because of shell shock. On 24 July, the Battalion War Diary recorded, 'Sniping by enemy active – rifle fire by him again going strong.' Four days later the diary noted:

Enemy shelled our left from 14 to 17 hours. Whiz bangs and H.E. [high explosive] – doing considerable damage – our guns retaliated. We sent over some Stokes and rifle grenades. Enemy replied rifle grenades and aerial darts. Intermittent shelling on both sides till evening when gun fire on both sides became very hot at times.

Conditions in the trenches were also desperately poor in places, especially when the weather turned foul, turning the trenches to glutinous mud. George Bartholomew recorded that during their second spell in the front line in later June the Argylls were caught in a downpour:

Before we had been in a few hours a most severe thunderstorm came on, and turned the trenches into swamps of mud and flooded our dug-out; in fact, there was a regular stream pouring down the shaft.

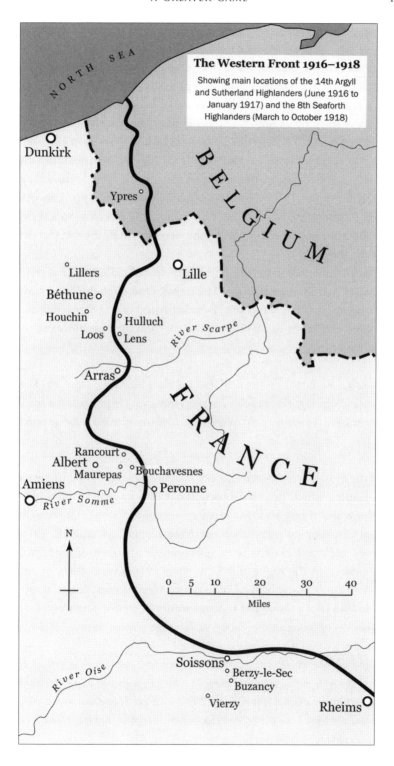

The Western Front 1916–1918

Showing main locations of the 14th Argyll
and Sutherland Highlanders (June 1916 to
January 1917) and the 8th Seaforth
Highlanders (March to October 1918)

To make matters worse, the Argylls could not find any fuel for their cooker and there was no hot food or drinks available. Stuck in the trenches, soldiers could not, of course, wander off to find somewhere warm and sheltered to dry themselves off. They had no choice except to stand through the rain and mud, stoically enduring their miserable lot. Another hazard of the trenches was that they were a breeding ground for rats and other vermin, attracted by the huge quantities of waste that the army generated. In July 1916, Bob Lawson wrote: 'Our worst enemies here are rats, which are legion. We are constantly after them with bayonets and stones, and if anything is left lying around they make shot of it.' In August 1916, George Bartholomew was sent some chocolate in a parcel from home. Eagerly looking forward to it, he placed it on a shelf above his bed, but the next morning it had gone, demolished by the rats that swarmed around the dug-out.

Life in the line was generally one of unrelieved tedium interspersed with moments of heart-stopping action. The trench system required constant maintenance because of enemy shelling, the weather and day-to-day activities. Much of the time was spent in making repairs or consolidating old work. As Bob Lawson wrote:

We do not get much time for sleep. All day and night there are a lot of jobs to do, such as filling sandbags, repairing trenches, carrying rations, etc. We just snatch a few minutes when we can and always have the company of numerous rats and crawling insects of all kinds.

One of the most hated jobs was keeping the barbed wire in front of the trenches in good order, which involved crawling out into no man's land under cover of darkness and trying to make repairs without any noise. The Argylls were expected to make regular patrols across to the enemy lines, either to listen in for intelligence, to check their wire for gaps, capture prisoners or simply to throw a few bombs. On the night of 9 September 1916 a small party managed to blow up a sniper's post which had caused the Argylls a great deal of trouble. The Battalion War Diary shows the hideous nature of trench warfare and the fatal consequences of being in the wrong place at the wrong time:

A bombing raid was made with a 20lb bomb against an enemy sniper's post… Enemy's sentry was too wide awake to permit our men getting near enough to put the bomb inside their post so it was thrown just outside… The German sentry was brave enough and after he had challenged our men… he came out towards them and must have been blown up in the explosion.

Only a minority of men were in the front line at any one time. The British system on the Western Front meant that battalions were constantly rotated, spending three or four days at the sharp end, a similar period in the support trenches and then a few days in reserve before going back into the line. This gave them the opportunity to psyche themselves up and wind themselves down. The Argylls spent their reserve billeted in a series of French villages, most of which had been severely battered by shellfire. George Bartholomew described one of them, a village called Vermelles, as 'a regular city of the dead – every house has been battered down time after time'. In some cases the men could enjoy the luxury of a change of clothes and communal baths, but there was always more training, instruction, cleaning and repair work to be done. Being behind the lines was no guarantee of safety and billets regularly came under fire. On 15 August, the Argylls were in the village of Les Brebis, which came under heavy shelling during the afternoon. The local *estaminet*, where the men had their coffee, omelettes and *pommes frites*, was blown apart and one officer was killed and several other men were wounded. As the Battalion War Diary reported: 'Shelling then continued, mostly 5.9s, around within 150 yards of church area, doing considerable damage and loss in mules etc.'

The Western Front was harsh and unforgiving, a kind of living nightmare, but very occasionally there were moments of great beauty and poignancy. George Bartholomew, who was a great lover of nature, recalled marching along a French road with his battalion on a sunny day at the end of June 1916:

Most impressive marching along this road on a warm summer's day. Fields lying on each side of the road, without any hedges to separate them; they are covered with fine long grasses, and among the grass are sprinkled beautiful red poppies; near the road beside the ditches they grow thicker, sometimes you find them in bunches; they like barbed wire and cluster around it. As you pass every now and then you come across a small grassy mound, sometimes a group of two or three; over this mound is placed a simple wooden cross with his name and the date he died on, or else the simple inscription 'Inconnu'. On the mound the long grasses grow and the red poppies are dotted in bunches. They are the most beautiful graves I have yet seen. In spite of the closeness of the front line a feeling of oppressive peace and nature strikes you here.

Within two and a half years, George Bartholomew, Bob Lawson and many of the men marching with them, including Walter Sutherland, would be gone forever, poppies for a lost generation.

nine

FLOWER OF THE FOREST

By the end of 1916, Walter Sutherland's battalion, the 14th Argyll & Sutherland Highlanders, had arrived on the Somme. The battalion had finished their tour of duty in the sector around Lens at the end of October. They spent the next few weeks behind the lines recovering from their exertions, getting back to full strength and doing more training and fieldwork. Fortunately there was some time to let off steam, the men taking part in several football and rugby matches, including one passionate affair against the West Yorkshire regiment. The Argylls also enjoyed several impromptu concerts, the men crammed together in a wooden hut to hear Sergeant Tynedale's spirited rendition of *How We Took the Double Crassier*. Around Christmas time there was a traditional festive dinner, although the food was only lukewarm with 'a couple of pints of awful French beer' and the surroundings less than cheerful, the men having to squat down on the sodden earth. On 26 December the Argylls left their camp at Maurepas and moved to the front line near the village of Bouchavesnes, not far from Péronne on the River Somme. By now, the great Allied offensive on the Somme had petered out, having advanced the front line only a few miles at a cost of tens of thousands of casualties. The weather had closed in and heavy rain had reduced the churned-up battlefield to a muddy morass. The Battalion War Diary recorded:

Part of the front line was impassable causing gaps which were constantly patrolled. C.T.s [communication trenches] were in such a condition with mud (in some places waist deep) that most traffic was over the top. During the whole spell of 5 days, rain fell nearly every day, which made any special work on the trenches absolutely impossible… the bringing of rations was very hard… the going was very slow and parties were constantly held up by someone sticking in the mud. Dug-outs were very scarce and any that there were were old and damp… little more than occupation of the trenches was possible.

The Argylls were relieved on 31 December 1916 but, on 4 January 1917, they were back in the front line, this time a little further north at a village called Rancourt. In a letter home, Bob Lawson described the scene that faced the Argylls:

We are now in the most God-forsaken looking place you could see... It looks as if all the mud in France had been collected and dumped here, and all to be seen are shell holes and mud. There is no trace of villagers at all, these having apparently been swept away, and it is now over four weeks since I have seen a civilian, let alone any females.

At one stage conditions became so bad that the Argylls had to wear trews rather than their kilts, a great comedown for a proud Scottish regiment. Enemy action was not the only problem that soldiers faced on the Western Front. The cumulative effect of the cold and wet, filthy living conditions, vermin and poor diet meant that the sickness rate was very high. The type of conditions that the Argylls encountered on the Somme meant that disease and illness were rampant and created a major problem for the army authorities. On 31 December 1916 the Battalion War Diary recorded that 'many men went sick with Trench feet'. The same day, George Bartholomew noted that over twenty men were sent to hospital because of sickness.

In early January 1917 Walter Sutherland fell desperately ill, having contracted dysentery while serving at the front. The disease was spread either by person-to-person contact or through contaminated water or food. It meant bloodied diarrhoea, stomach cramps and fever; a dreadfully humiliating disease and potentially a killer. Victims had to be sent home for a long period of recovery. Walter was stationed at the village of Combles on the Somme. Initially, he was taken to the war hospital at Rouen. He returned to Britain on 26 January 1917 aboard the hospital ship HMHS *St David* and was admitted to the University War Hospital at Southampton. Fortunately, by early March, he had recovered sufficiently to be discharged for ten days leave or 'furlough'. He was still unfit for service overseas, having lost a lot of weight. He was posted to the 3rd Reserve Battalion of the Argyll & Sutherland Highlanders, which was based at Dreghorn Camp in Edinburgh. By May 1917, he had been promoted to the rank of lance-corporal. His promotion suggests that his earlier misdemeanours had been forgotten and that his service had been more than satisfactory.

With more time on his hands and a chance to think about his future, Walter applied to an Officer Cadet Unit in the hope of obtaining a temporary commission in the regular army. This suggests that he enjoyed army life and that he was confident enough to see himself as a leader of men. Walter's preference was to become an infantry officer in the Argyll & Sutherland Highlanders or failing that 'any other Scottish Regiment', which showed that his heart was in the right place. He asked the minister of Wilton Parish, the Revd John Rudge Wilson, to supply him with a reference of good character. On his application form, Walter was not entirely honest and did not declare his previous service or his desertion from the Lothian & Border Horse. He had recovered sufficiently from his recent illness, weighing 10st 7lb at the medical examination and having good eyesight but requiring some dental treatment, probably to remove a few rotten teeth. Unfortunately, bad luck delayed the start of his officer training. In late September, he sustained severe contusion or bruising on his right thigh, which involved a month's stay in the military hospital in Edinburgh Castle.

On 9 November 1917, Walter was posted to the 19th Officer Cadet Battalion, based at Pirbright Camp near Woking in Surrey. The old professional army had recruited its officers almost exclusively from the public schools, grooming them at Sandhurst and at Woolwich. With the expansion of the army in 1914 and the fearful casualty rates during the war, university men and undergraduates were used to plug the gaps. By 1917, the army could not afford to be so choosy. A typical division required fifty fresh officers monthly just to keep up with 'natural wastage'. Consequently, the social composition of the officer corps began to change with more recruits from the lower-middle and working classes. Force of necessity meant that the army had to open the door to individuals who could display enough character, determination and good mental powers. Enthusiasm for sports also carried a lot of weight. In many cases, the working-class replacements proved just as capable as the public school officers who preceded them, often acquiring the same mannerisms and habits. The biggest problem for officers recruited from the Other Ranks was that it required a major shift in an individual's mindset. The life of a humble private was moulded around deference and obedience: the new officer had to quickly reverse these trends.

On 3 March 1918, Walter had completed his training and he was discharged to commission. Initially, he was posted to 51st Graduated Battalion of the Gordon Highlanders, who were based at Barnham Cross Camp near Thetford in Norfolk. On 27 March 1918, he was gazetted second lieutenant in the Seaforth Highlanders, staying for a short time at the regiment's depot at Fort George before joining the 8th Battalion in France. Like most soldiers, Walter would have taken great pride in his regiment and his battalion, learning about their traditions from the old sweats and the regulars, the few that remained. The Seaforth Highlanders had been formed in 1881 following the amalgamation of two older regiments, the 72nd Duke of Albany's Own Highlanders and the 78th Highlanders, the Ross-shire Buffs. Both of these dated back to the late eighteenth century and had served in various colonial wars and other conflicts. The Seaforths recruited from a huge area, all over the north of Scotland, the Moray Firth and the Orkney Islands. The cap badge of the regiment showed a stag's head with the Gaelic motto *Cuidich 'n Righ* ('Help to the King'). Being a Highland regiment, they were entitled to wear the kilt, in this case in the MacKenzie tartan. The 8th Battalion had been raised in September 1914 as part of Lord Kitchener's New Army. Alongside battalions from other regiments, they were part of the 15th (Scottish) Division, which had seen action at many of the major battles in the war, including Loos (1915), the Somme (1916) and Third Ypres (1917).

As an officer, Walter would have had a more privileged life than the other ranks, although he would have had little time to himself. A typical second lieutenant was spared the usual drudgery of manual labour and was provided with a batman to look after his personal needs, a reflection of the gentleman and servant relationship. Officers enjoyed better living conditions, even at the front, superior clothes and rations, and also higher pay. Their bravery had a greater chance of recognition and they were less likely to be punished for indiscipline. However, regimental officers lived close to their men and shared many of their privations and dangers. When in the line, their principal responsibility was for the defence and maintenance of the trenches. This involved a myriad of tasks, such as checking the extent and thickness of the barbed wire in front of the trench, looking after the stores of ammunition and food, ensuring that the field telephones worked properly and keeping the paperwork up to date, often the greatest bugbear of an officer's life. An officer was expected to uphold and instigate orders from his superiors, often having to reconcile them with the men under his command. In addition, officers were responsible for training, directing working parties and the onerous task of censoring the men's letters home. A good officer would take it upon himself to maintain a sense of *esprit de corps* and give his men plenty of encouragement. This might have involved a simple reward system, such as giving the men cigarettes. After his death, two cigarette cases were found among Walter's possessions and it now strikes us as unusual that an international athlete should also be a smoker (although he might not have smoked when he played rugby). The health risks of smoking were not known at this time and most soldiers in the trenches smoked as a way of reducing stress and fear. In July 1916, Bob Lawson of the 14th Argylls wrote: 'Cigarettes are the great want here. We never can have too many and it is wonderful how cool one keeps during a bombardment if he lights up to puff, puff, puff.' Smoking was a mark of comradeship and an officer could relieve the pain of a wounded or dying man by the simple act of giving him a cigarette.

Out of the line, regular sports and games were another way of maintaining morale and group solidarity as well as keeping large numbers of virile young men occupied and in good physical shape. Team games bonded soldiers together and were played at every level of the army. Boxing and athletics tournaments were popular and there were also more light-hearted exercises, such as wheel-barrow races and tug-of-war contests. Soldiers took great pride in representing their particular group and were always anxious to do their best and not let their comrades down. Officers were expected to organise these events and to play a full part and join in. For a top-class athlete like Walter Sutherland, these occasions were an ideal opportunity to show his talent and lead from the front. On 11 October 1918, the *Hawick News* gave the following report about Walter's prowess on the Army sports field, showing that after four years of war he had lost none of his athletic abilities:

Lieutenant W.R. Sutherland, Seaforth Highlanders, the well-known Hawick three-quarter and rugby internationalist, has been adding fresh laurels to his athletic career in the rest periods when he has not been chasing the Huns at the front. Those who know his great prowess as a rugby football player will be pleased to learn that he has also been playing soccer to some purpose behind the lines, and he was a member of the platoon team that carried off the handsome cup, and he received one more medal to add to his already handsome collection. He also won the 100 yards race in 11-2-5 secs. – not bad time keeping for conditions at the front, and for one who had just been taking a hand in something more serious and strenuous. In the relay race he was set the task of finishing from the 220 yards position. When he started off he was thirty yards behind his man, but quickly overhauled him, and breasted the tape first in what, one who knows him says, was perhaps the finest race Sutherland ever ran. But these were not the only events in which 'Wattie' excelled. Everyone knows that he is fleet of foot, and a brilliant football player; but most of his acquaintances will be surprised to hear that he also figured strongly in the boxing competition, and disposed of all his opponents. He went through the first two rounds splendidly, and also the semi-final, and came out victor without either a twisted nose or a black eye!

Histories of the First World War often gloss over 1918, preferring instead to concentrate on its notorious predecessors and in particular the great set piece battles at the Somme (1916) and Passchendaele (1917). In fact, 1918 was a momentous year that saw great swings of fortune, the fall of dynasties and collapse of nations, and ultimately the end of the worst war the world had ever seen. It is often forgotten that 1918 was the year when the Allies, and in particular the British, brought about the defeat of the German army on the Western Front, probably the toughest and most tactically astute army in the world. The casualty lists were enormous. The British, who at one point were threatened with a Dunkirk-style evacuation away from France, lost more men in 1918 than any other year of the war and indeed more than the whole of the Second World War. On 21 March 1918, the Germans launched their great offensive on the Western Front, which was designed to win the war before the United States could put its full force behind the Allied effort. Initially, the German offensive made spectacular gains, pushing the Allies backwards and threatening to capture Paris. Fierce fighting continued through the spring and early summer, but by June the offensive was running out of energy and the lines were beginning to stabilise once again, in part due to a lack of supplies and low morale among many German soldiers.

In mid-July, the Seaforths and the rest of the 15th Division were moved away from Arras to the regions of the Marne and Aisne rivers, around seventy-five miles to the south. Since late May, this region had been the scene of very heavy fighting. A huge German offensive had pushed the Allies back to the line of the River Marne, but on 18 July a surprise attack by a combined force of French, British and Americans had started to recapture much of the lost ground and force the Germans back. The 15th Division was called upon to relieve the 1st (American) Division, who were attacking the German line just south of the ancient city of Soissons, which had recently been captured by the Germans. In particular, the 15th Division was ordered to capture the German positions between the tiny villages of Berzy-le-Sec and Buzancy. On taking up position in the front line, it was found that the Americans, who had been attacking for several days, had not had enough time to bury their dead, leaving the Scots with the grisly job of gathering identity tags and papers and disposing of the bodies.

The first assault at Buzancy began at 5 a.m. on 23 July. However, this did not involve Walter Sutherland's battalion, the 8th Seaforths, which was kept in reserve a few miles away from the main battle. This was still a dangerous position, being well within the range of German artillery fire and aeroplanes. On 27 July, the Seaforths lost their commanding officer, Lieutenant-Colonel H.H. Kennedy, to shellfire. The initial assault at Buzancy had only limited success, advancing the line only a few hundred yards at best in return for huge casualties. The 7/8th Battalion of the King's Own Scottish Borderers suffered over 300 casualties, including four officers killed and ten wounded. Two days later, on the night of the 25 July, the Seaforths moved up to the front line and prepared for the second attack on Buzancy, which was scheduled to take place on 28 July.

During the war, the British Army had been on a steep learning curve. By mid-1918, the attrition battles of the previous two years were things of the past and the British had evolved more effective and sophisticated methods of over-coming enemy defences. The attack at Buzancy on 28 July was carefully planned and employed an effective combination of weaponry and communications sys-tems. During the morning there was an irregular series of artillery barrages, but zero hour was timed at 12.30 p.m., which was designed to catch the Germans off their guard. A 'lightning barrage' of two minutes' duration preceded the attack, expertly targeted against German strongpoints. The attacking infantry took with them specially trained teams of machine-gunners and trench-mortar operators to hold back any counterattacks and consolidate captured ground. Buzancy village contained many ruined buildings and deep vaults so groups of 'sappers' from the Royal Engineers were used to demolish any of these obstruc-tions quickly. The French Army loaned a couple of men with flame-throwers, a truly hideous weapon that shot jets of liquid fire and could be used to clear out cellars and other obstructions. Finally, aeroplane fighters were used to drive away the Germans and to observe and direct the battle from above.

For Walter Sutherland, the attack on Buzancy represented the quintessential experience of the First World War: that of going 'over the top' into No Man's Land in the face of the enemy's gunfire. In a sense, all his military training and the long months of boredom had led up to this point. We can barely imagine his feelings as the hours and minutes slowly ticked by, knowing that he faced the imminent prospect of his own death or serious injury. Standing a few yards away from Walter was a fellow officer, Lieutenant Alexander Thomson, who came from the Isle of Lewis. In the battle, he would win the Military Cross for gallantry. A few weeks later, he contributed an article to the *Stornoway Gazette* recounting his experiences, which would have been very similar to Walter Sutherland's:

The morning of 28 July found us holding a front position in one of the thick woods which overlooked Buzancy – thick treacherous woods, where we knew the stealthy enemy machine gunners lay and watched. Aeroplanes circled overhead, puffs of white smoke around them as the enemy's 'archies' burst, artillery well hidden among the trees occasion-ally boomed – all was quiet and peaceful. At 12 noon we crept stealthily and silently forward to our assembly positions, and waited grimly for the end of the period which was to elapse before the artillery and machine guns dropped their curtain of fire and enabled us to go forward to the assault. It seemed an eternity as I stood with watch in hand beside Captain Macmillan…

With ten minutes to go we were both silent – our minds far away with our loved ones… our Highland hills home scene passed in a panoramic flash before us, and from the bottom of our hearts we prayed that all would be well.

The barrage fell. It seemed as if the heavens had opened to a rolling thunder all along the line. Shells burst in their hundreds of thousands on the village and the chateau grounds. Machine guns rattled like the severest hailstorm, and the attack was launched. The boys advanced as if they were on the parade ground at Cromarty, the enemy machine guns took their toll, but never a waver – the broken gaps were quickly filled, the line went forward to the chateau walls and entered the 'unknown', behind which lurked – who can tell?

I never saw anything like the advance of the Seaforths that day. Through the thick woods surrounding the chateau they advanced, and nothing could stop them. On, on, ever forwards they went – every minute their ranks getting thinner as the Germans got our range, but the boys never faltered until they had carried the village and consolidated on the ridge behind it.

The objective of the 'bite-size' attack was to capture the village, the nearby cha-teau and its grounds, and also the plateau of high ground to the east. The initial assault went very well with all the objectives taken within the first hour, despite some stiff resistance. By mid-afternoon however, the Germans had started to counterattack. To the south-east of Buzancy, the French had failed to take their objectives, their attack foundering on a German strongpoint. This meant that the British right flank was dangerously exposed, eventually forcing a general with-drawal back to the original starting line by 6 p.m. The attack at Buzancy had put pressure on the German lines and taken many prisoners, but the British and French had sustained many losses. As the *Official History of the War* put it: 'The 15th Division, which had been in most of the heavy encounters of the war since Loos in September 1915, regarded the action on this day as the severest and "most gruelling" of them all.' Fortunately, Walter Sutherland was not among the casual-ties, although it must have been a close thing. According to E.H.D. Sewell, Walter wrote home to his father after the battle informing him 'that he was one of the four unwounded officers out of eighteen to emerge from the fighting line'. The battered remains of the 15th Division were relieved the following night under very difficult circumstances: the Germans firing gas-shells into the British lines, forcing the exhausted troops to wear respirator masks almost the whole night.

For the 15th Division, the third phase of the battle of Buzancy took place on 1 August. Working closely with the French, it was planned that the divi-sion was to take part in a great encircling movement to the south of Buzancy and to capture some neighbouring villages and strong points. Once again, the 8th Seaforths were not involved in the first attack, but were held back in reserve slightly behind the front line. Crossing over very exposed ground, the initial attack made little progress and was eventually driven back to its original starting point. However, by the next morning, events had taken an unexpected turn. The Germans had secretly withdrawn from the Buzancy area in order to straighten out their line. Realising what had happened, the British and French, including the 8th Seaforths, now took part in a general advance, pushing the line forward nearly three miles in a single day and encountering little opposition, apart from a few rearguard actions designed to delay the pursuit. The greatest hazard was that the retreating Germans had drenched the area with poison gas and some officers and men were temporarily affected by it. This kind of rapid advance across open ground was a near-miraculous experience in the First World War and many soldiers could hardly believe the order to move forward. The advance finally stopped near the villages of Amberif and Charcrise where the 8th Seaforths and the Gordon Highlanders were ordered to hold the front line. Torrents of rain fell during the evening as well as intermittent artillery fire, but neither of these could dampen British spirits after an extraordinary day. The 15th Division was relieved the following day, the Seaforths spending the night at the village of Dommieres before a thirteen-mile route march took them to relative safety at Vierzy.

The fight for Buzancy, of which Walter Sutherland was part, is not very well remembered, just another incident in a very long war. The attack helped to force the Germans back, but at a cost of many hundreds of casualties. Between 21 July and 7 August, the 15th Division lost over 3,500 officers and men, either killed, wounded or missing. The French Division, who relieved the Scots after the battle, were greatly impressed with the courage of their allies and awarded them several medals and honours as tokens of their respect. They also built a small monument at the point where they had found the body of the Scottish soldier who had advanced the furthest on the 28 July. The monument, which still stands, had a medallion with thistles and roses, and underneath there was the inscription: 'Here the noble thistle of Scotland will flourish forever among the roses of France.'

Following their exertions at Buzancy, the Seaforths and the rest of the 15th Division spent ten days licking their wounds. In mid-August, they were back in the trenches, this time to the south east of Arras near the River Scarpe. Fortunately, this was a quiet sector, the emphasis being on night-time patrols and keeping a close eye on enemy movements. On 23/24 August, the division was relieved by the Canadians and moved slightly further north to the area in front of the Loos Salient. For any old stagers left in the 15th Division, this would have sent a shudder up the collective spine. Three years earlier, in September 1915, the division had suffered horrific casualties at the Battle of Loos. By 1918 the line had advanced only a few yards from its earlier position, despite the loss of thousands of lives. The old front line had long since been battered out of existence. Instead of a continuous line of trenches, there was a series of observation posts and strong points, each covering the other and the barbed wire in between. An unusual feature of the battlefield was a series of tunnels cut into the solid rock, running from the reserve lines to the front posts. These tunnels not only provided a safe and convenient way for the movement of men and supplies but also sheltered accommodation, work areas, command posts and dressing stations, a veritable rabbit warren all lit by electric light or candles. Above ground, the 8th Seaforths were charged with looking after the line in front of the village of Hulloch. Walter Sutherland already knew the area, having been there in 1916 with the Argylls.

By the end of September it was clear that the Germans were beginning to buckle. Since the failure of the March Offensive they had been under tremendous pressure, both on the Western Front and also back home, where the Allied naval blockade was reducing the population to near-starvation levels. Increasingly, there were signs that the Germans were preparing to make a strategic withdrawal. On 1 October, the 15th Division came under particularly heavy artillery fire with all sorts of shells being pumped into the lines. This was an attempt by the Germans to empty their ammunition dumps before their guns were taken away. In the evening, the bombardment died away completely, leaving the area eerily quiet as if a great storm had passed. The following morning, the British pushed forward, in some cases so quickly that the Germans were caught still eating their breakfasts. By 3 October, the Seaforths had captured the villages of Hulloch and Wingles and were preparing to take the buildings of a nearby steelworks called the *metallurgique*, which presented a formidable obstacle. In two days the line had advanced over two miles, an incredible distance by the standards of the war, and there had been only light casualties. There was still much to be done, but the British were entitled to feel confident about their prospects.

In the First World War, nowhere was safe. Men and women were killed many miles behind the front line by training accidents, infections from rusty wire or by standing on unexploded ammunition or shells. The biggest killer in the war was artillery, which has been estimated to have caused well over half of all casualties. Its effects were truly murderous. A single burst sent hundreds of red-hot steel fragments through the air, mutilating, ripping and tearing any human flesh or bone that happened to be in the way. Artillery guns could fire shells from a long distance, which meant that, unlike previous wars, many soldiers in the First World War never saw the enemy that caused their deaths.

Walter Sutherland was killed in action on 4 October 1918, five weeks before the Armistice and seven before his 28th birthday. The circumstances of Walter's death were recorded by E.H.D. Sewell, probably drawing on information supplied by the Sutherland family and others who knew him. According to Sewell:

The manner of his death was that, such was his anxiety to be with his men after a period of rest, he hired a bicycle to cover the distance separating him from them. Passing through the village of Hulluch, a stray shell from the enemy reached his vicinity – 'a bow at a venture' – and he was killed, not leading his men as he would have desired, but, nevertheless, in just such a manner as he lived, doing his duty.

Walter's body was taken to a field hospital near the village of Houchin, but his life could not be saved. A telegram was sent from the War Office to Walter's mother and father at the Imperial Hotel, who would have spent the last four years dreading its arrival. The stark message said: 'Deeply regret inform you that 2/Lieut WR Sutherland Seaforth Highlanders was killed in action fourth October. The Army Council express sympathy.' There is no reason to doubt that Alex and Bella would have been anything less than devastated at the loss of their brilliant son.

Walter's personal possessions at the time of his death were inventoried before they were sent back home. They provide a small insight into his character and show that he was a typical soldier with a few photographs of his loved ones, some letters and papers and a handful of other items:

The telegram with the dreadful news of Walter's death in October 1918. (Author's collection)

Photos and visiting cards
Two cigarette cases
One stamp and note case
One advance book
Book of stamps
One rosary
One autograph album
One leather pocket wallet
Letters, papers, etc.
One whistle and lanyard
One regimental badge
One identity disc
Two coins
One general service certificate
One receipted account
Unreceipted accounts

The news of Walter's death came as a great setback to his many friends and admirers in Hawick, the Borders and the wider sporting world. 'It shook a' the Hawick folk,' as one of his friends later recalled. Walter's popularity was reflected in lengthy tributes and obituary articles in many newspapers and magazines. The sense of loss was genuine and profound. The *Kelso Chronicle* described him as 'one of the cleanest and fairest of sportsmen'. The up-market *Field* said he was 'the finest and most popular all-round athlete in the Scottish Border district… He never played a bad game and he had few equals as a try-getter from the twenty-five flag. His place in Scottish sport will be indeed difficult to fill.' Under the title 'A Fallen Hero', the *Sporting Chronicle* commented:

With Border folk… he was as great an idol as ever. Inverleith matches will come round again, but there will be no more 'Weel played Wattie!' from the southern crowd, in whose memories, however, will be cherished thoughts of the pale-faced, fair-haired lad who served his country on the footer and athletic grounds.

Similarly, under the headline 'Noted "Teri" Killed', the *Evening Dispatch* wrote:

Rugby football in Scotland has been shorn of still another of its outstanding personalities in Lieut. W.R. Sutherland: the Borders of its greatest and most popular player. A Hawick team without Sutherland will be to the 'Teri' something with a great big blank on it… Sutherland was chiefly outstanding as an individualist and, in the open play of the 'sevens', he was indeed a terror to opponents and a source of unbounded delight to his 'ain folk'. Possessed of speed far above the average and having a natural aptitude for the game, there were few who could out-rival him if but half a chance presented itself. How often have his single-handed efforts roused the enthusiasm of the Border crowd to the highest pitch? There was inevitably something electrifying about his play.

Closer to home, the *Hawick News* carried a lengthy 'Appreciation' by Adam Turnbull, the old Hawick player and international referee who knew Walter and his family and who had closely followed Walter's career. Deeply moved by the youngster's death, Adam Turnbull wrote:

The writer shall never forget the first time he saw Sutherland playing. He was a school-boy then and, in this particular game, he simply ran through when it pleased him. From then he never looked back, in the sense of promotion, and when very young he played for his country and played often and well. Indeed, he is classed as one of the finest exponents of rugby football that ever played… He was adored and revered as a hero by all, and regarded as a true and just opponent… His loss is a severe wrench to us who have fol-lowed his career, and who knew him so well, and admired, adored – nay, verily loved him so deeply.

Writing in the *Border Standard*, 'G.H.T.' was moved to commemorate Walter in a poem entitled *A Gala Tribute: Lieutenant W.R. Sutherland ('Suddy'), Seaforth Highlanders, killed in France, 1918.* At this time, people often turned to poetry to express their feelings and provide an outlet for their grief. The poem now reads rather awkwardly with its grandiloquent language and classical allusions, but there is no doubt that the sentiments it expressed were honest and sincerely felt:

I see a shouting multitude mad and exultant,
In their keen impartial pride, throating their hero's praise –
With eager eyes and all the wildest frenzy of amaze.
They feel the glow and glory of his play, and with him pulse and pant.
No stout Olympian this, but slim and ariel, a soul
Sure-footed as the gods that sped on Sparta's shore –
The master athlete of the crowning hour, he bore
The Border ball afar, and kicked the fairest goal.

At last, but not in 'green' nor on the Border sward,
But on a dabbled field of blood, striving with hideous foes,

He plied that ancient courage that so often and so grandly rose,
Filling the vast arena with Scotland's proud regard;
Destined to die as fate decreed, he played the game,
And in the final gleam we see him 'pass' before he fell—
The orb of Victory on — and with a brave farewell,
Throw himself upon the crimson pyre of British fame.

Arguably, the most moving tributes came from Walter Hume, who had followed Walter from a promising schoolboy into a seasoned international player. Reflecting his deep sense of personal loss, which was shared by many, Hume concluded:

It is hard to realize that one who so recently had walked the streets of the old Border town, who was held in such affection by its youth, whose bright smile and cheery nature were like rays of sunshine, had gone and would never again adorn its peaceful life. In all he achieved, the reward he most appreciated and cherished was the affection of his friends and admirers. The memory of such a life, with so many just claims to remembrance, will always stand out as a permanent inspiration and a bright example to all who may follow the rugby game.

Second Lieutenant Walter Riddle Sutherland of the 8th Battalion Seaforth Highlanders is buried in Houchin British Cemetery. Houchin is a typical little French village, a few miles south of Béthune, close to the Belgian border. The cemetery was opened in March 1918 next to the site of a casualty clearing station. Hospital work became unsafe during the German spring offensive, but from September 1918 it became an important medical centre. Like millions of other bereaved families, Alex and Bella Sutherland were anxious to see the places where their son had fought and to pay their respects at his grave. A minor industry developed after the war taking parties of 'pilgrims' to the cemeteries and memorials scattered over the old battlefields. For all of the bereaved, it was an attempt to understand a little more, an act of catharsis, a chance to put the ghosts and uncertainties to rest. In the early 1920s, Alex and Bella made the long trip to northern France to visit Walter's grave. At the time of their visit, the cemetery at Houchin was in a state of transition. The Imperial War Graves Commission, who were charged to look after these sacred sites, were slowly replacing the old wooden crosses with permanent headstones made from white Portland stone. Walter's memorial, which was in place by the time of his parents' visit, bears the badge of the Seaforth Highlanders and the simple inscription:

SECOND LIEUTENANT
W.R. SUTHERLAND
SEAFORTH HIGHLANDERS
4TH OCTOBER 1918 AGE 27

Bereaved families had the option of adding a personal message, but they had to pay extra for it and Alex and Bella chose not to do this. Walter Sutherland was one of 670 Commonwealth burials in Houchin Cemetery. There were also thirty-nine German war graves and one Belgian. Later, two graves were added from the Second World War, all united in death.

Having laid a wreath of remembrance, Alex and Bella stood proudly at the grave to have their photograph taken by their travelling companions and neighbours from back home, Mr and Mrs G.L. Macdonald. Bella was dressed in sombre clothes and understandably she wore a haunted look. Her likeness to Walter in the photographs is unmistakable. Each time, Alex gazed away from the camera and down on his son's grave, perhaps trying to hide his emotions. Like hundreds of other military sites all over the world, Houchin military cemetery was given to the British government in perpetuity, which means that it will never be disturbed.

In one sense, Alex and Bella were fortunate. The terrible nature of the war meant that many bodies were never recovered or identified. Tens of thousands of soldiers had no known grave and were only commemorated on huge memorials to the 'Missing'. Not very far away from Houchin stands the Loos Memorial to the Missing, which records the names of over 20,000 officers and men who were lost in the vicinity. One of them was Private Danny Shannon of the Cameron Highlanders, Walter's old friend from the Grand Slam-winning seven of 1912. Danny took part in the battle of Loos in September 1915, where he was fatally wounded in the face. In the heat of battle, his body was lost, blown into pieces by shellfire or buried in the mud. All that remained was an inscription on a wall.

The scale of the losses in the First World War is truly staggering. Rugby football paid a heavy price for its enthusiastic response to the call for men. In 1919, the Hawick Rugby Club published a roll of honour of the players and members who had served in the war. It was calculated that out of 158 members, thirty-six were killed or died of wounds, a casualty rate of just over one in four. This took no account of the men who were wounded or maimed. Among the casualties were two international players, Walter Sutherland and Walter Forrest, the risk-taking full-back from Kelso. A member of the Territorial Army and a staunch church-goer, Major Forrest fought at Gallipoli and later won the

Military Cross for reconnaissance work, but was killed in the attack on Gaza in Palestine in April 1917. There were many other poignant losses among Walter Sutherland's team-mates. Willie Ogg, one of three rugby-playing brothers, had been a key member of the team that shared the club championship in 1908/09, Walter's first season for the Greens. 'A keen and clean player who was respected by friend and opponent alike,' reported the *Hawick News*, 'and there was no harder worker in the scrum than he.' A good cricket player, Gunner William Ogg fell in France in the terrible fighting in May 1918, leaving behind his wife and two children. Packing down with Willie Ogg in the championship side, there was Tom Wilson, the Cumberland county player who was sounded out for the British tour of New Zealand in 1908. A civil engineer by trade, Wilson was posted to East Africa because he was already familiar with tropical conditions, having worked in Singapore. He was awarded the Military Cross for bravery, but was killed in action in June 1917.

The war also claimed younger players of great promise. At half-back, the teenage John Charters was a good prospect, nippy from the base of the scrum and always ready to have a go. He enlisted shortly after the beginning of the war, going on to become a lance-corporal in the Gordon Highlanders. Charters fought at the dreadful battle of Passchendaele in August 1917, where he was fatally wounded. A mere twenty-two years old, his last act was to recite the 23rd Psalm with the company chaplain. John Corrie was the big man from Langholm who came to play for the Greens, winning several international trials and seemingly destined for the highest level. Corrie and two of his companions were killed instantly by a shell burst at the battle of Messines Ridge in June 1917. 'He was one of the finest men in my section,' wrote one of his superiors, 'and was liked by both officers and men.' Willie Ker had been one of the six friends who had joined up with Walter Sutherland. A promising three-quarter who worked in a local bank, Corporal Ker stayed in the Lothian & Border Horse and spent much of the war in the Balkans. He was killed in September 1917, aged twenty-three. 'Off and on the field,' commented the *Hawick Express*, 'his gentlemanly demeanour and pleasant disposition endeared him to hosts of friends.'

One of the most keenly felt losses for the Hawick club was that of Tom Wilson. 'The ranks of the famous "Greens" are being sadly thinned by this devastating war,' reported the *Hawick News* in September 1918, 'but of the many gallant lads who have played their last game none will be more missed than "The Bottler".' A popular personality and a born footballer, Tom Wilson had played for almost twelve years. He was pugnacious and versatile, 'a veritable handyman', who at one time or another filled every position in the team. A fine sevens player, his greatest strengths were his sense of humour and engaging personality, the cheeky chappy who was admired by players and spectators alike. A father of two, Tom enlisted in the Royal Engineers in 1916, seeing action in Italy and France. He was killed by shellfire in 1918, a few months before the end of the war. Two of his brothers were also lost in the war. 'Since the war began many intimations have been received in Hawick of well-known citizens having been killed in action,' recorded the *Hawick Express*, 'but few of these sad announcements have given rise to such widespread sorrow and regret as that which told of the death of Sapper Tom Wilson.'

Up and down the land, other rugby clubs suffered equally grievous losses. Hawick's old rivals Gala supplied 167 members to the colours, of whom thirty were killed, 'including a good number of their most prominent players'. Jed-Forest lost fifteen out of the eighty members who served, including the international player James Huggan, who fell in the opening weeks. In Edinburgh, 141 past and present players joined up from the Heriot's FP rugby and cricket club, of whom thirty-six never returned. International rugby also bore a heavy burden. From the eight rugby-playing countries, a staggering 112 international players were lost. Scotland had the highest total of all, losing thirty. Among these were several of Walter Sutherland's international colleagues. Eric 'Puss' Milroy, the multi-talented Watsonians scrum-half, won his first cap with Walter against Wales in February 1910. A polished performer, he made 12 international appearances, toured with the British team to South Africa in 1910 and captained Scotland against England in March 1914, the last international match before the war. Milroy was a lieutenant in the 8th Battalion The Black Watch and fought at the Battle of the Somme, losing his life at Delville Wood in July 1916, aged twenty-eight. His body was never recovered or identified. He was commemorated on the Thiepval Memorial to the Missing, which bears the names of over 72,000 soldiers whose remains were never found. An unassuming and generous man, Milroy was very popular and his death was keenly felt. As one obituary said: 'That boyish smile, with which he would emerge from the feet of the opposing forwards, was an open sesame to a wide circle of friendship… He was ever sunny, modest and gentle.'

Jimmy Pearson was another great Watsonians internationalist, small and elusive and a good all-rounder who partnered Walter Sutherland in the Scottish three-quarter line. A humorous and likeable man, Private James Pearson of the 9th Battalion The Royal Scots was killed in action at Hooge, Belgium in May 1915, aged twenty-six. His colonel wrote to Pearson's parents: 'He was as popular with the men of my battalion as he was at Myreside.' Then there was George Will, the trim little winger from Cambridge University who had pushed Walter for his place, famous for his spirited runs, ball held tightly in both hands, going at full speed with a distinctive effortless gait. Lieutenant Will was a member of the glamorous Royal Flying Corps, but was killed in a dogfight with enemy aircraft over Arras in March 1917, aged twenty-four.

Scotland was not the only country to suffer. France had played international games for only eight years, but lost twenty-three players. Similarly, England lost twenty-six internationalists, including Ronnie Poulton, the dashing and much-vaunted three-quarter who met his match in Walter Sutherland on that famous day at Twickenham in March 1913. Poulton had changed his name to Poulton-Palmer in March 1914 in order inherit a fortune from an elderly relative. One of the most popular players of his generation, Lieutenant Poulton-Palmer of the Royal Berkshire Regiment was killed by a sniper's bullet at Ploegsteert Wood, Belgium in May 1915, aged twenty-five. In a letter of condolence to his family, one of his fellow officers said: 'When I went around his old company, as they stood to, at dawn, almost every man was crying.'

Rugby football did not perish in the war. In the 2,500-year-old *Iliad*, Homer wrote 'Men in their generations are like leaves of the trees. The wind blows and one year's leaves are scattered on the ground; but the trees burst into bud and put on fresh ones when the spring comes round.' In early 1919, a few scratch games were played in the Borders and the sevens circuit resumed in the spring, Hawick winning the tournaments at Melrose and Jed-Forest. In September 1919, the Hawick club held its first Annual General Meeting for five years. The chairman, George McDonald, remembered how they had been looking forward to season 1914/15, but that 'a more strenuous game' had intervened. 'How well the wearers of the green jersey responded to the call,' remarked McDonald. 'It was difficult to imagine a Hawick team without its Sutherland or "The Bottler", and as long as the game of football was played, these names would ever be remembered.' But there was much to be optimistic about. A strong fixture list had been prepared and in early October the new pavilion was finally opened, four years after completion. The club also reaped the benefits of the far-sighted policy of encouraging junior rugby during the war. There was a rich crop of youngsters coming through, such as Doug Davies, a forward of great promise, and the versatile Roy Thomson, who was billed as the new 'Bottler' Wilson. In addition, a few old heads were still around and ready to lend a hand, such as Frank Beatson, Andy Turnbull and Teddy Morgan, fast develop-ing into 'a fine exponent of the forward game' and who was chosen to captain the side. 'On the whole,' said one newspaper, 'the prospects of the "Greens" are much rosier in every respect than could have been anticipated by the most sanguine follower of the club's fortunes.' However, the past was not easily for-gotten. Many still lamented for the glory days before the war, longing for the sight of that slim, fair-haired laddie on the wing who seemed to ghost through the opposition at will. 'Hawick are very much to the fore as usual,' reported the *Evening Dispatch* in October 1919, 'though at Mansfield the tendency is to hark back to the days of Walter Sutherland. That tendency is often unfair to the present players, as some would have that there can never be such great exponents of the game as those who have gone before.' In fact, the 1920s turned out to be a very successful decade for Hawick. The club won the Border League nine times in a row and in season 1926/27 won the unofficial club championship. International rugby resumed on New Year's Day 1920 when Scotland beat France in Paris 5-0. Seven of the Scottish team were pre-war caps.

Meanwhile, Walter Sutherland's family had to carry on with their lives. Alex Sutherland, Walter's father, left the rugby club committee in 1918, but he remained a member and supporter of the Greens for the rest of his days, poignantly representing his late son at a special gathering of the club's international players in 1922. The previous year, he had finally bought over the Imperial Hotel but, in April 1925, he left the business after twenty-five years in the trade. Alex and Bella moved into a commodious new semi-detached house called 'Ashton' at 27 Weensland Road, which they shared with several of their children. Bella Sutherland, who had borne many troubles in her life, died at home on 2 December 1928, aged seventy-two. Alex survived his wife for over five years, living until his late seventies. His obituary in the *Hawick Express* described him as 'a familiar figure in the community, his well-knit, erect figure gave little indication of his advanced age'. He remained in good health until a few weeks before his death on 20 February 1934.

With the obvious exception of Walter, all of the Sutherland children lived to a good age. Jimmy and Tom served in the First World War, but both survived. In the 1920s Jimmy moved away to Edinburgh, living at Hutchison Cottages not far away from Murrayfield Stadium. He returned to his old trade as a compositor on *The Scotsman* and also worked as a reception clerk with the Grand Lodge of Freemasons. Jimmy remained in demand with his fine tenor voice. At the Hawick Common Riding in 1934, he gave a spirited rendition of the local favourite *Hawick Among the Hills* when the Colour Bussing ceremony was relayed live by the fledgling British Broadcasting Corporation. Jimmy returned permanently to Hawick in the 1940s, running a small general store in the town's Wellogate Place and picking up on many of his old friendships. He died of cancer in the Royal Infirmary in Edinburgh in August 1944 and was cremated at Warriston crematorium. Tom Sutherland, who was also known as 'Suddy' like his famous brother, spent his life in Hawick. Before the First World War he had married a woman called Elizabeth 'Lizzy' Ballantyne, but they had no children.

He died in February 1953 and is buried in the Wellogate Cemetery in Hawick, next to his wife. Walter's sisters Mary and Bella remained close throughout their lives, devoting much of their time to looking after their elderly parents and their little brother Sandy, who required special care and attention (although at one point the family were wealthy enough to employ a housekeeper called Mrs Jack). Mary and her husband James Robertson, along with Tom Sutherland, ran the Mansfield Bar, which was on the road to Mansfield Park and did a roaring trade when the Greens played at home. Bella Sutherland remained a spinster, perhaps because of her family commitments. Quiet and reserved people who kept themselves to themselves, Mary and Bella were a well-known sight in the town, two small and thin women who went about together, usually accompanied by their brother Sandy. Sandy continued to think the world of Walter's fiancée Mary, never forgetting the woman who would have been his sister-in-law if fate had not intervened. When he saw her in the street, he would run across and try to give her a hug, even when she was married with children of her own. After Walter's death, Mary found love with another man and was married in 1921. By coincidence, one of her grandsons turned out to be a very good athlete who excelled in professional sprinting.

Walter's sister Mary Robertson died in February 1957, followed by Sandy in November 1962. The last of the Sutherland children, Bella, died the following year. With the exceptions of Jimmy, Tom and, of course, Walter, all members of the Sutherland family were buried in the family plot at Wilton Cemetery in Hawick. After Walter's death in October 1918, his parents erected a large headstone 'in loving memory' of two of their sons, Walter and also John, who had died in infancy in the 1890s. Through time, the names of Alex and Bella, Mary, Sandy and young Bella were added. The headstone is inscribed with details of Walter's death and his burial place at Houchin British Cemetery, and bears the cap badge of the Seaforth Highlanders, showing that the family was enormously proud of his service in the war and his willingness to give his life for others. Years of exposure to the Scottish weather have corroded the copper badge leaving streaks down the headstone, as if it was shedding a silent tear. After Bella's death, the family home at Ashton was sold and the family possessions discarded. However, a few items escaped. When I was researching this book, I was shown a red scrapbook containing a collection of newspaper obituaries about Walter, lovingly compiled by either his mother or one of his sisters. There were also a couple of Walter's war medals and ribbons, and a set of silver eggcups and spoons, which Walter had won at some race. Walter's international caps are in good hands, but his medals and papers and also the Sutherland family photographs seem to have been thrown away and are now lost, probably forever.

EXTRA TIME

And that is the story of Walter Sutherland, one of Scotland's greatest rugby players. How to sum up his life and achievements?

Walter did brilliantly to win 13 international caps, especially playing for one of the less fashionable clubs in Scotland. Early in his career he suffered from the erratic selection policies of the Scottish selectors and he had to fight hard to earn his place. As the *Scots Pictorial* magazine commented in 1918:

Those responsible for the destinies of rugby football in Scotland were slow to recognise the worth of Lieutenant Sutherland… Provincial players, as a rule, receive very little encouragement in Scotland, and Lieutenant Sutherland for a time was no exception. It was by sheer good play that he won his honours.

Some of the criticisms are very familiar today, in particular about the selection of Anglo-Scots and colonial players over home-produced talent. Walter was unlucky to play at a time when the Scottish team was going through one of its customary barren patches. The Scottish forwards often came off second best and some players in the back division were of limited quality, making it difficult for a winger to have much of an impact. In several games Walter was largely neglected and had little opportunity to show what he could do, having to live off scraps and a lack of ball. As the *Sporting Chronicle* observed in 1918: 'Had W.R. Sutherland been in a Scots team of the early years of this century, when reasonable chances were given to wing three-quarter backs of scoring, he would have earned many a try.' It says much about the nature of Scottish rugby at this time that Walter is best remembered for his outstanding displays in defence. He was courageous against the big South African tourists in 1912 and his performance against England in 1913, when he did the work of two men, has gone down in Scottish rugby folklore. He played his best international rugby against England, scoring tries in consecutive matches against them in

1911 and 1912, the latter taking Scotland to a memorable victory. It is a great pity that Walter did not have the means to take his place on the British tour of South Africa in 1910 where he might have blossomed on the harder grounds and behind better forwards.

At club level Walter was in a class of his own, the stage on which he truly shone. As the *Evening Dispatch* commented after his death: 'It is doing no injustice to his powers to suggest that the best was seen of him on the various fields of the Border clubs – Mansfield, Netherdale, the Greenyards, etc.' He was a great club player, an invaluable asset to his side. He was capable of doing anything that was asked of him: tackling, kicking, running, beating a man with speed or guile, and scoring astonishing tries from all over the field. No wonder the Hawick and Border crowds loved him. He was an excellent sevens player, ideally suited for the open spaces, winning eighteen gold medals. His great speed meant that he was also a very good sprinter, becoming a national champion and twice representing Scotland on the track.

Walter's sporting talents and achievements are clear, but they would mean little without his winning personality. All the evidence about Walter points to a genuinely pleasant man, someone full of life and vitality, always ready to have a go but modest and unassuming about what he could do. Adam Turnbull, a man who knew him well and watched his progress, wrote:

In spite of universal praise, as witnessed by the thunders of applause as he called forth on the football field or at the end of some finely run race, or the praise of his abilities that has been written about all over the British Isles, he valued such praise at its true merit and, keeping his head, was the same unassuming boy through it all.

This book is intended as a celebration of Walter's life, but inevitably his early death in the First World War casts a shadow over everything. Rightly or wrongly, we are now very cynical about the First World War. The millions of deaths and all of the terrible suffering seem to have been for nothing. The war was followed by an even greater conflict and smaller wars have raged ever since. But in 1914, concepts of honour, heroism, loyalty and patriotism were powerful and influential, far more so than they are today. They helped to motivate an individual like Walter Sutherland, who believed that his country was threatened and that it was his duty to defend it. Sadly, the First World War was not the war to end all wars, neither did it create a land fit for heroes, but this should not prevent us from admiring Walter Sutherland's courage and his willingness to lay down his life for others. As Adam Turnbull wrote in his obituary article, quoting the book of Isaiah: 'He has given his life for us who are left. He is one of the many noble heroes who in the first breath of danger stepped forward and said: "Here am I: take me."' The modern reaction to Walter's death is one of moral outrage, a sense that a brilliant young life had been needlessly thrown away. His family, friends and admirers would have been devastated at his loss, but they would also have been offended by the suggestion that his life was wasted or that his death was futile. In their opinion, Walter had selflessly given himself to protect the things he loved. His sacrifice had helped to win the war, to defeat German militarism and bring about a victory for democracy and decency. It is significant that, on the family headstone in Hawick, his parents chose to record his military service, including a replica of the Seaforth Highlanders cap badge, but not to mention his many sporting achievements. It's just that we know that Walter Sutherland was part of an ill-used generation upon whom fate played a cruel trick.

Walter Sutherland was a great sportsman who deserves to be better known. He was also, I would argue, a great man, cut down before he reached his full potential. As they said at the time, he came from the mould of which heroes are made. I trust that this book will be a fitting memorial to this magnificent son of Hawick.

Wattie Suddy.
Aye.
They don't make them like him anymore.

FURTHER READING

As I stated in the introduction, the starting point for this book was E.H.D. Sewell's *Rugby Football Internationals Roll of Honour* (Edinburgh and London, 1919), which contained information about Walter Sutherland that is not available elsewhere. The Edwardian era was the heyday of the local press and much of the information contained in this book was drawn from newspapers, many now crumbling away at the touch. Among others, I consulted the *Hawick Advertiser*, *Hawick Express*, *Hawick News*, *Southern Reporter*, *Edinburgh Evening News*, *Edinburgh Evening Dispatch*, *The Scotsman*, *Glasgow Herald* and *The Times*. A special mention must go to *Scottish Referee*, a twice-weekly sports paper produced in Glasgow, which became a casualty of the First World War.

Anyone interested in the history of rugby in Scotland will quickly discover Sandy Thorburn's books *The History of Scottish Rugby* (London, 1980) and *The Scottish Rugby Union Official History* (Edinburgh, 1985), both of which were invaluable. An older study is R.J. Phillips' *The Story of Scottish Rugby* (Edinburgh, 1925). At a local level, two books of great help were Walter Hume's (ed.) *Fifty Years' Football in Hawick 1873-1923* (Hawick, 1923) and Bill McLaren's (ed.) *100 Years of Hawick Rugby* (Hawick, 1973). Most of the senior rugby clubs in Scotland have their own history books and there are many histories of national sides and of rugby generally. A rare biographical study of a rugby player (who played just before Walter Sutherland) is David Parry-Jones' *Prince Gwyn: Gwyn Nicholls and the First Golden Era of Welsh Rugby* (Bridgend, 1999), which gave me the idea for this book. To place Edwardian rugby in a wider historical context, I would recommend Derek Birley's *Play the Game: Sport and British Society 1910-45* (Manchester, 1995), Brian Dobbs' *Edwardians at Play: Sport 1890-1914* (London, 1973) and Richard Holt's *Sport and the British: A Modern History* (Oxford, 1989). On athletics, see Kenneth Whitton and David Jamieson's *Fifty Years of Athletics: An Historical Record of the Scottish Amateur Athletics Association* (Edinburgh, 1933).

On the First World War, I was lucky enough to have *Hawick and the War: A Pictorial Record*, which was published in weekly supplements by the *Hawick News* in 1919. The book is a goldmine of local and family history as well as being moving and evocative. A useful modern account is Derek Robertson's *All These Fine Fellows: Hawick and District and the Great War 1914-18* (Newcastleton, n.d.). I was able to trace Walter's war service through the war diaries of the 14th Argyll & Sutherland Highlanders and the 8th Seaforth Highlanders, also from W. Sorley Brown's (ed.) *War Record of the 4th Battalion KOSB and Lothian & Border Horse* (Galashiels, 1920) and John Buchan and J. Stewart's *The Fifteenth Scottish Division 1914-1919* (Edinburgh, 1926).

APPENDICES

APPENDIX ONE

Walter Sutherland's International Appearances

5 February 1910	Wales	Cardiff Arms Park	Lost 0–14	
19 March 1910	England	Inverleith	Lost 5–14	
2 January 1911	France	Colombes	Lost 15–16	
18 March 1911	England	Twickenham	Lost 8–13	1 try
20 January 1912	France	Inverleith	Won 31–3	2 tries
3 February 1912	Wales	Swansea	Lost 6–21	
16 March 1912	England	Inverleith	Won 8–3	1 try
23 November 1912	South Africa	Inverleith	Lost 0–16	
1 January 1913	France	Parc des Princes	Won 21–3	
1 February 1913	Wales	Inverleith	Lost 0–8	
22 February 1913	Ireland	Inverleith	Won 29–14	
15 March 1913	England	Twickenham	Lost 0–3	
7 February 1914	Wales	Cardiff Arms Park	Lost 5–24	

Summary: 13 appearances, 4 wins and 7 defeats, 12 points from 4 tries.

APPENDIX TWO

Other Representative Games

Walter Sutherland's team shown first.

1909/10

27 November	South of Scotland *v.* London Scottish & District at Richmond	Won 8–6
11 December	South of Scotland *v.* North and Midlands at Mossilee	Drew 3–3
25 December	The Provinces *v.* Anglo-Scots at Inverleith	Won 22–3
8 January	The Rest *v.* The Cities at Inverleith	Lost 5–13

1910/11

| 16 November | South of Scotland *v.* Monmouthshire at Mansfield Park | Won 17-3 |
| 10 December | South of Scotland *v.* North of Scotland at Aberdeen | Lost 8-9 |

1911/12

| 9 December | South of Scotland *v.* North of Scotland at Mossilee | Lost 8-9 |
| 23 December | The Rest *v.* Anglo-Scots at Inverleith | Lost 3-21 |

1912/13

14 December	South of Scotland *v.* North of Scotland at St Andrews	Lost 0-6
21 December	Probables *v.* Possibles at Inverleith	Won 27-8
18 January	Scotland *v.* Rest of Scotland at Inverleith	Won 15-6

1913/14

1 November	South of Scotland *v.* Cumberland County at Warwick Road	Drew 3-3
13 December	South of Scotland *v.* North of Scotland at Netherdale	Won 14-11
27 December	Home Scots *v.* Anglo-Scots at Inverleith	Lost 9-13

APPENDIX THREE

Walter Sutherland's Appearances and Scoring for Hawick 1908-1914

	Played	Tries	Conversions	Penalty Goals	Drop-goals	Mark Goals	Points
1908/09	17	10	4	0	0	0	38
1909/10	17	13	10	2	0	0	65
1910/11	20	16	2	1	0	0	55
1911/12	22	21	7	0	1	0	81
1912/13	19	14	3	0	0	1	52
1913/14	11	8	1	0	0	0	26
	106	82	27	3	1	1	317

APPENDIX FOUR

Walter Sutherland's Appearances in Border Sevens Tournaments

	1908	1909	1910	1911	1912	1913
Gala	–	Winner	Winner	Winner	Winner	Runner–up
Melrose	–	Winner	Winner	Winner	Winner	Winner
Hawick	–	Winner	Runner–up	Winner	–	Runner–up
Jed–Forest	–	Semi	Semi	Semi	Winner	1st rnd
Langholm	Semi★	Winner	1st rnd	Winner	Winner	Winner

	1914	1915	Played	Finals	Won
Gala	–	–	5	5	4
Melrose	Runner–up	Winner★★	7	7	6
Hawick	Semi	–	5	4	2
Jed-Forest	–	–	5	1	1
Langholm	Winner	–	7	5	5
		Totals	29	22	18

★Playing for Hawick 'B'
★★Playing for the Lothian & Border Horse

APPENDIX FIVE

Major Athletic Meetings

Scotland *v.* Ireland International

Date	Venue	Distance	Walter's Position	Winning Time
15 July 1911	Dublin	220 yards	2nd	23.35 seconds
19 July 1913	Belfast	220 yards	1st	22.35 seconds

Scottish Championships (SAAA)

Date	Venue	Distance	Walter's Position	Winning Time
24 June 1911	Hampden Park	100 yards	Unplaced	10.25 seconds
24 June 1911	Hampden Park	220 yards	2nd	23.25 seconds
28 June 1913	Celtic Park	100 yards	3rd	10.2 seconds
28 June 1913	Celtic Park	220 yards	1st	24.4 seconds

Border Championships (SBAAA)

Date	Venue	Distance	Walter's Position	Winning Time
22 July 1911	Galashiels	100 yards	1st	10.25 seconds
26 August 1911	Peebles	220 yards	1st	23.15 seconds
27 July 1912	Galashiels	100 yards	1st	10.25 seconds
27 July 1912	Galashiels	220 yards	1st	24.45 seconds
6 June 1913	Hawick	220 yards	1st	27.15 seconds
12 July 1913	Galashiels	100 yards	1st	10.35 seconds
25 July 1914	Galashiels	100 yards	1st	10.25 seconds
25 July 1914	Galashiels	220 yards	1st	25 seconds

APPENDIX SIX

Battle Dawn

Almost ninety years after his death, the memory of Walter Sutherland continues to inspire.

In 2004 Alan Brydon, a talented musician from Hawick, was moved to compose a bagpipe tune *Battle Dawn*, which he first performed at Walter Sutherland's grave in Houchin Cemetery in France. Iain Scott of the group Scocha later added these lyrics:

> *At sunset you were a callant lad,*
> *At day as a man ye faced yer battle dawn.*
> *A see aw thae Portland stanes,*
> *Lined up like yer cauld white banes.*
> *How many mair have fa'an,*
> *And faced their battle dawn.*

Battle Dawn is a haunting memorial to Walter Sutherland and indeed all young men who have died in war. The song is available on the album *The Land We Love*. There is more information on the website www.scocha.co.uk.

INDEX

Other titles published by Tempus

Immortal Harlequin The Story of Adrian Stoop
IAN COOPER

Adrian Stoop's revolutionary leadership led Harlequins to become the greatest club side in England before the First World War and as national captain he made Twickenham synonymous with free-flowing, attacking rugby. He was seriously wounded fighting in the war but made a full recovery and was to be widely credited with inventing modern rugby. This book tells the story of a man who forged a nation's sporting identity.

0 7524 3180 3

Wizards and Bravehearts A History of the Scottish National Side
DAVID POTTER

The history of Scotland's national football team from 1872 is full of highs and lows, thrills and heartbreaks, passion and pride. Taking in thrilling World Cup campaigns and famous victories – notably over the Auld Enemy – the story has also featured many world-class players, such as Kenny Dalglish, Denis Law and Graeme Souness. This illustrated history records the ups and downs, the great characters and the classic games, and is essential reading for anyone with an interest in Scottish football.

0 7524 3183 8

The Mighty Quinn Jimmy Quinn, Celtic's First Goalscoring Hero
DAVID W. POTTER

Jimmy Quinn was the spearhead of Willie Maley's great Celtic side of the early twentieth century. Making over 300 appearances and scoring 216 goals for the club as they won six League titles in a row, Quinn also became the hero of Scotland when in 1910 he almost single-handedly defeated England to become the undisputed best player in Great Britain. Some of the very essence of Scottish football lies here in the story of Jimmy Quinn.

0 7524 3460 8

A Century of the All Blacks in Britain and Ireland
DAVE FOX, KEN BOGLE & MARK HOSKINS

In 1905 the New Zealand rugby side first toured Britain and Ireland, winning 31 out of 32 games and setting new standards in fitness, attitude and skill which British teams took many years to reach. This book tells the story of that tour, and of all the subsequent tours up to today. Thoroughly researched and illustrated with contemporary memorabilia, it is a superb reference book and an essential volume for anyone interested in the history of rugby.

0 7524 3355 5

If you are interested in purchasing other books published by Tempus, or in case you have difficulty finding any Tempus books in your local bookshop, you can also place orders directly through our website
www.tempus-publishing.com